SPIES, CODES, CAPERS, GADGETS, AND CLASSIFIED CASES REVEALED

CRISPIN BOYER &
SUZANNE ZIMBLER

NATIONAL GEOGRAPHIC
WASHINGTON, D.C.

TABLE OF CONTENTS

CHAPTER 1 SECRET AGENCIES

CHAPTER 2 SECRET HISTORY

ROSETTA STONE

CHAPTER 3 SECRET IDENTITIES

CHAPTER 4 SECRET PLANS

CHAPTER 5
SECRET GADGETS

CHAPTER 6
SECRET PLACES

FORT KNOX

CHAPTER 7
SECRET CODES

CHAPTER 8
SECRETS ALL AROUND YOU

The information inside this book is **TRIPLE TOP SECRET,** supremely classified, strictly confidential, and possibly downright dangerous if it winds up in the wrong hands. The contents herein are for **AUTHORIZED EYES ONLY.** Do not proceed beyond this point unless you have the **HIGHEST-LEVEL SECURITY CLEARANCES,** are a certified spy-in-training, and possess a superhuman level of curiosity.

Still here? Good. You obviously have what it takes to tackle *Top Secret*, the most comprehensive collection of classified facts outside Area 51. You're about to enter the shadowy world of dashing spies and masters of disguise, ninja assassins and the highly trained bodyguards of the U.S. Secret Service. You'll unearth the truth behind crashed-UFO conspiracies and what really goes on in those secret government bunkers deep beneath your feet. By the time you reach the final chapter, you'll know how to run your own spy network, sniff out a scammer, communicate in secret codes, find Easter eggs in your games and movies, and inspect the best spots for lost treasure. In other words, if it's info that few know, you'll find it here. **GUARD THIS KNOWLEDGE WELL. AS YOU'RE ABOUT TO FIND OUT, SPIES ARE EVERYWHERE!**

CRACK THE CODE

LEARN THESE CIPHERS TO **DECODE THE MYSTERIES** OF *TOP SECRET*

As you skulk through *Top Secret*, keep an eye peeled for strange messages printed along the bottom of the pages. They might look like random gibberish, but each is a mystery wrapped in a riddle hidden inside a secret code. Can you decode each message and solve the riddle? You could if you knew each code's cipher, a system for replacing or rearranging letters in the alphabet to conceal messages. Think of a cipher as the key to locking and unlocking any secret code. Spy networks have relied on ciphers for centuries to send and decode secret messages. Now you can use the classic ciphers on these pages to decode the riddles in this book (as well as to send secure messages within your own spy network). Study these ciphers, and then get code-cracking!

THE CAESAR CIPHER

Named for Roman ruler Julius Caesar (who used it in his private letters), the Caesar cipher relies on a simple shift in the letters of the alphabet by a set number of spaces left or right. For example, if you set your Caesar cipher to shift three spaces right, then A becomes D, B becomes E, G becomes J, and so on, in your coded alphabet. Only people who know your cipher can crack the code. Here's how your cipher-shifted alphabet looks compared to the regular alphabet:

CAESAR CIPHER	D	E	F	G	H	I	J	K	L	M	N	O	P	Q	R	S	T	U	V	W	X	Y	Z	A	B	C
REGULAR ALPHABET	A	B	C	D	E	F	G	H	I	J	K	L	M	N	O	P	Q	R	S	T	U	V	W	X	Y	Z

CODED

FDOOLQJ DOO VSLHV

DECODED

CALLING ALL SPIES

THE KEYBOARD CIPHER

This cipher is a cinch to use for anyone familiar with a computer keyboard. Simply place your fingers on the keys as you normally would, and then shift your fingers one space to the right. Begin typing your message, which will appear as gibberish to everyone but your agents. They'll know you're using the keyboard cipher, ar they can decode your message by checking a computer keyboard and looking at each letter to the left of the ones you've written.

CODED

VS;;OMH S;; D[ORD

DECODED

CALLING ALL SPIES

⇦ Look at the letter to the left of these letters on a keyboard to see how the cipher works.

THE KEYWORD CIPHER

This one's a little more complicated—perfect for super-duper top secret orders for agents under deep cover (close friends of your secret crush, for instance). First, you need to choose a keyword—any weird word will do. For this example, we'll go with "sneaky." Now write your keyword down, then write the alphabet after it in normal order while also removing any letters that appear in the keyword. Print the normal alphabet above or below your keyword alphabet as a guide for your secret missives, like this:

KEYWORD CIPHER	S	N	E	A	K	Y	B	C	D	F	G	H	I	J	L	M	O	P	Q	R	T	U	V	W	X	Z
REGULAR ALPHABET	A	B	C	D	E	F	G	H	I	J	K	L	M	N	O	P	Q	R	S	T	U	V	W	X	Y	Z

CODED

ESHHDJB SHH QMDKQ

DECODED

CALLING ALL SPIES

THE CIPHER WHEEL

Here's a cipher you can make yourself. First, cut out two circles—one slightly larger than the other—from a piece of cardboard, and then write the alphabet around the edge of each circle (as shown in the image). Fasten both circles together through the center with a split pin so that the inner wheel can turn independently from the outer wheel. Now simply choose two letters to act as your cipher. Align those letters on the two wheels, then write your secret message based on how the other inner and outer letters align around the wheel. Tell everyone in your spy network the cipher and your code. They can use their own cipher wheels to decode your important message!

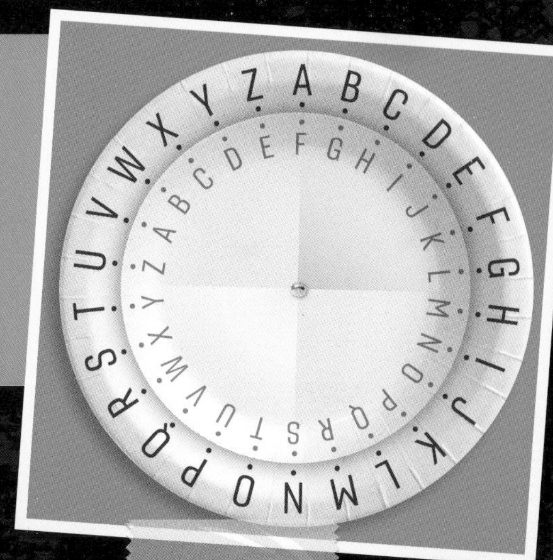

THE ATBASH CIPHER

One of the first and simplest code systems (it debuted in the Old Testament of the Bible), the Atbash cipher works by mapping the alphabet in reverse against its normal order, like this:

ATBASH CIPHER	Z	Y	X	W	V	U	T	S	R	Q	P	O	N	M	L	K	J	I	H	G	F	E	D	C	B	A
REGULAR ALPHABET	A	B	C	D	E	F	G	H	I	J	K	L	M	N	O	P	Q	R	S	T	U	V	W	X	Y	Z

CODED

XZOORMT ZOO HKRVH

DECODED

CALLING ALL SPIES

EGGY-PEGGY

Not so much a code as a nonsense language, Eggy-Peggy works by adding the word "egg" before each vowel in a word. As you'd expect from a language that got its start on English playgrounds, Eggy-Peggy can lead to some bizarre sentences. They're not nonsense if you know the secret, which makes Eggy-Peggy a good encryption system.

CODED

CEGGALLEGGING EGGALL SPEGGIEGGES

DECODED

CALLING ALL SPIES

Cracking Practice

Try out your new decrypting skills on the following secret messages. Each one uses a cipher explained on these pages. Once you figure these out, you'll be ready to crack the coded riddles scattered throughout the book!

1. Yjr d;urdy d[ord eom yjr [toxr

2. Xltp elukp dq nhlvj

3. Wuxvw qr rqh

ANSWERS

1. The slyest spies win the prize (created using the keyboard cipher)

2. Your cover is blown (created using the keyword cipher with "sneaky," as the keyword)

3. Trust no one (created using the Caesar cipher, shifting the alphabet right by three letters)

First day of
spy school a SUCCESS.

SECRET AGENCIES

Learned how to create a
cover story and DECODE
SECRET MESSAGES.

Call them secret agents, case officers, operatives, intelligence assets, or spooks—they're all spies, or professional snoops who try to sniff out secret information from governments, military organizations, and companies (which have their own kind of spying called corporate espionage). Many nations have top secret agencies that employ spies and snooping technology to keep tabs on their rivals. In this chapter, we'll infiltrate shadowy agencies of the present and past, revealing their sneaky history and top secret tactics. Welcome to clandestine operations, where sneakiness is the key to survival.

Just need to figure out how to get INVISIBLE-INK stains out of invisibility cloak.

SPY Q

A BRIEF HISTORY OF **PROFESSIONAL SNOOPING**

Spying is not a new job. Ancient Egypt hired spies to keep an eye on its enemies. So did ancient Greece and Rome. The job description of a spy has changed little since ancient times. Put simply, a spy is anyone who secretly gathers "intelligence," which is just a fancy spy word for information. Intelligence can take the form of an enemy's location, movements, plans, strengths, weaknesses, food allergies, phobias—any scrap of data that gives the spy's employer the upper hand.

Chinese strategist Sun Tzu wrote about the importance of gathering intelligence—and laid out the various types of spies—in his book *The Art of War* more than 2,500 years ago. Informant spies infiltrated an enemy's society or government and gathered information. Disinformation spies spread lies, rumors, and other misinformation to sow chaos and distrust. Both types of spies are still busy today.

SUN TZU

A statue of Nathan Hale stands outside the Central Intelligence Agency (CIA) headquarters in Langley, Virginia, U.S.A.

UNDERCOVER EVERYWHERE

The practice of spying is called espionage, carried out in secret—or "covert"—operations. Although espionage gained momentum in popular culture in the 20th-century because of the Cold War between the United States and the former Soviet Union (more on that later), it was common across many cultures. Warlords in feudal Japan employed ninja to sneak into enemy castles and gather intelligence. The Aztec dressed spies as merchants to infiltrate rival cities and steal their secrets.

WHAT FOLLOWS IS A RIDDLE HIDDEN IN A SECRET CODE. THE ANSWER TO THIS RIDDLE IS A

Many modern techniques of espionage were pioneered in the 16th century by Sir Francis Walsingham, who officially served as the secretary of state for England's Queen Elizabeth I. Unofficially, he was her spymaster. Long before the invention of cameras and recording devices, Walsingham's spies relied on careful "cracking" skills to chip the wax off sealed enemy letters, memorize the information, and then reseal the letters so the enemy believed their secrets were safe. Walsingham also employed "cryptographers" to create secret codes and transmit their findings without fear of discovery. His master forgers created phony documents that got rivals in hot water. Spying then, as always, was tricky work.

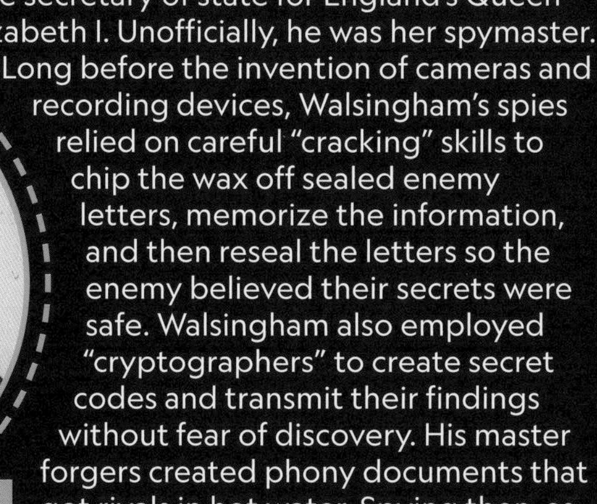

SIR FRANCIS WALSINGHAM

RAVEN

Birds Trained as Secret Agents

Not all spies walk on two legs. Some fly with wings! Espionage agencies have recruited these birds for secret missions:

RAVENS: Among the smartest of the bird species, ravens were taught by the CIA to drop and retrieve listening devices in foreign embassies.

PIGEONS: A CIA researcher trained flocks of pigeons—"squab squads"—to seek out and land near any enemy troops that might be creeping close to home base and planning an ambush.

REVOLUTIONARY WARRIOR

It took a desperate struggle to advance the art of espionage to a point we might almost recognize in today's spy movies. That struggle was America's war for independence from England in 1776. After British forces captured Long Island, New York, and crushed the colonial army in August 1776, General George Washington put the call out for spies to cross enemy lines and snoop on British forces. Nathan Hale, a schoolteacher turned soldier from Connecticut, was the sole volunteer. At just 21 years old, he became America's first spy. Disguised as a Dutch schoolteacher, Hale sailed to Long Island and drew maps of the British redcoats' fortifications. Hale wrote notes in Latin and hid them in his shoes. But his luck soon ran out: America's first spy fell into British hands on September 21, 1776.

After he was captured by the British for spying, Nathan Hale refused to switch sides and become a double agent. He was quickly sentenced to death by hanging and led to the gallows on September 22, 1776. According to the few witnesses to his execution, Hale calmly walked to the noose with dignity. His final words echo through history: "I only regret that I have but one life to give for my country."

A CLOSER LOOK

Nathan Hale's sacrifice was not in vain. The amount of information he gathered before his capture convinced General Washington that espionage was crucial to winning the Revolutionary War. Washington wrote orders to establish a group of spies who were experts in writing secret codes. They became known as the Culper Ring, a group of childhood friends in New York who wrote messages in invisible ink and sent valuable intelligence to Washington via a whale-boat captain. In 1781, the British surrendered, thanks in large part to the Culper Ring. It was the most sophisticated intelligence operation ever until those used during World War II more than 150 years later.

PERSON, PLACE, OR THING DESCRIBED IN THIS CHAPTER. THE CODE IS BASED ON A CIPHER

SPYING 101

THE INS AND OUTS OF **INTERNATIONAL ESPIONAGE**

Modern espionage is the biggest business that barely anyone knows about—and that's just how the people in this line of work like it. It operates in times of war and peace, with its own language, organizations, and special schools for teaching "tradecraft." Some spies work for the money, love of their country, or hatred of a rival nation, but they all have one thing in common: a life full of secrets. Here's your primer on this undercover industry.

SPY VARIETIES

AGENT Your standard spy, paid to snoop on foreign governments.

ANALYST Not a spy in the traditional sense, an analyst gathers information from afar by scouring media sources (newspapers, websites, social media, and TV news), or listens in on phone calls and secretly reads emails. In the United States, analysts work for the National Security Agency to monitor "signals intelligence" (electronic signals such as radar, radio waves, and telecommunication traffic).

ASSET Someone inside a government or organization who secretly provides information. Also known as a confidential informant. Assets are crucial to the business of espionage.

CASE OFFICER A spy who recruits other spies in a foreign country and contacts them for regular reports.

DOUBLE AGENT A spy who works for one intelligence service but is secretly spying on it for an enemy nation.

SLEEPER AGENT A spy who leads a normal life in a foreign country for years—even decades—until he or she receives orders to begin gathering secret information.

TRIPLE AGENT Similar to a double agent, this spy works in secret for three intelligence services.

TROLL OPERATIVE This newest type of spy infiltrates the social-media websites and online forums of other countries to spread false information and stir conflict among citizens. Some nations employ entire agencies of these operatives—known as troll farms—to spread maximum chaos and confusion.

DESCRIBED ON PAGE 8. PERHAPS THAT IS ENOUGH INFORMATION TO SOLVE THIS RIDDL

SPY SCHOOL

In the United States, wannabe snoops recruited for the Central Intelligence Agency begin their training at Camp Peary, a spy school in Virginia also known as "the Farm." Here they learn land navigation to avoid getting lost in strange places, how to drive cars around obstacles on a racetrack, boating skills, hand-to-hand combat, weapons use, and even special skills such as skydiving. After these basics, they take classes in "tradecraft," or mastery of disguises, aliases, surveillance, and other sneaky skills required to succeed in espionage. Most important, they learn the art of deception: living a double life and never letting anyone know they're a spy. Spy students actually practice their cover stories on each other, making the Farm an institution of advanced deception.

Essential Espionage Terms

LEGEND: A spy's cover story while in the field. It's a big bogus identity that includes a phony name, job, and family background. If a spy's legend is discovered as a lie, his or her cover is "blown," or compromised.

INFILTRATE: To slip into a place undetected for the purpose of spying.

EXFILTRATE: To leave that place without getting caught, typically after a spy's cover is blown.

INTELLIGENCE: Another name for the field of spying, as well as the term for any secrets gathered during the course of the job.

COUNTERINTELLIGENCE: The field of battling spies and thwarting each other's snooping activities.

COLD WAR: A golden age of espionage that lasted from the late 1940s to the early 1990s. The Cold War marked a period of intense superpower rivalry between the United States and the former Soviet Union.

SPY AGENCIES ACROSS THE GLOBE

UNITED STATES Central Intelligence Agency (CIA)

CHINA Ministry of State Security (MSS)

ISRAEL Mossad

FORMER SOVIET UNION Komitet Gosudarstvennoy Bezopasnosti (KGB)

MEXICO Centro Nacional de Inteligencia (CNI)

KENYA National Intelligence Service

UNITED KINGDOM Secret Intelligence Service (MI6)

RUSSIA Main Directorate of the General Staff of the Armed Forces (GRU)

PERHAPS NOT. IF YOU'RE STUMPED, YOU WILL FIND A HINT AND THE CIPHER USED AT THE

DO: BLEND IN

When you work in the world of espionage—the business of stealing secrets—standing out from the crowd could get you locked up. Spies who keep a low profile tend to spy longer.

SPY SURVIVAL GUIDE

CLANDESTINE **DOS AND DON'TS**

Imagine moving to a country far from home, having to speak fluently in a foreign language, and trying to convince everyone you meet that you're someone you're not. You might spend your days at a phony job, but your real career is to swipe secrets or convince others to steal them for you. Oh, and you'll suffer a horrible punishment if anyone discovers your true identity. The spy game is no mission for the meek! Intelligent agents of espionage limit their risk with these time-tested rules of tradecraft.

DO: USE DEAD DROPS

These are predetermined spots for passing items (secret photos, documents, cash payments, and the like) between spies, so they don't have to meet and risk getting their cover blown. The best dead drops blend in with the background—trash cans, shrubbery, even doggie doo (it's been done!).

END OF THIS CHAPTER. NOW GET CRACKING! HERE IS THE ENCODED RIDDLE: FKDUJLQJ DKHDG

DON'T: BREAK COVER

Being a spy is a full-time job. Spies always maintain their legend (or cover story) and never do anything to attract attention. Aldrich Ames, a CIA case officer who worked as a double agent for the former Soviet Union, got caught after he began buying jewelry, fancy cars, and an expensive house he couldn't afford on his CIA salary.

ALDRICH AMES

DON'T: TRUST ANYONE

People may not be who they say they are or what they seem.

DO: THINK ON YOUR FEET

Circumstances change rapidly. You have to be able to adapt in a few minutes—or seconds.

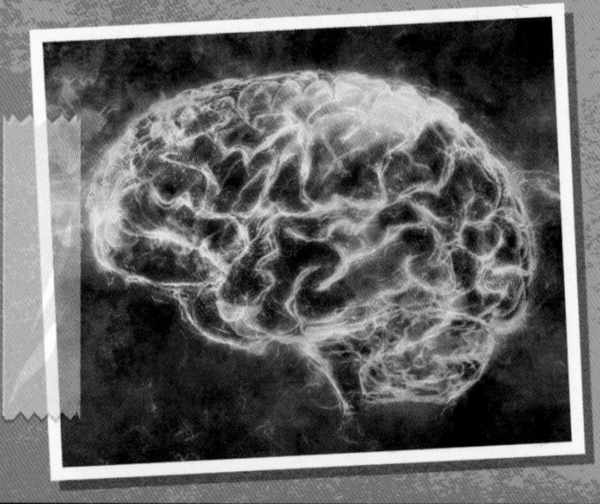

DO: REMEMBER EVERYTHING

Spies don't always have access to a spy camera or photocopiers for swiping secret documents. Sometimes they need to take a photo with their eyes and memorize important details to write down once they are alone.

DO: WATCH FOR TAILS

Spies routinely conduct "surveillance-detection routes," a technique for walking or driving to determine if people or cars are following them. One method is to make only left turns at intersections and see if anyone follows.

DON'T: ADMIT TO ANYTHING

Spies deny, deny, deny everything if caught.

MOSCOW RULES

American agents who worked in Moscow, Russia (which was once part of the Soviet Union)—dangerous territory for foreign spies during the Cold War—followed this set of commonsense guidelines to stay alive:

- **NEVER ASSUME ANYTHING.**
- **IF SOMETHING FEELS WRONG, IT PROBABLY IS.**
- **GO WITH THE FLOW.**
- **ALWAYS HAVE BACKUP OPTIONS READY.**
- **CHOOSE YOUR OWN TIME AND PLACE TO ACT.**
- **NEVER GET COCKY OR TAUNT YOUR ENEMIES.**

A CLOSER LOOK

A spy's risk of getting caught increases during times of war, when even ordinary citizens are on the lookout for potential spies. During World War II, the United States Office of War Information created posters warning the public to keep their mouths shut and their eyes open for anyone who might feed scraps of information to the enemy.

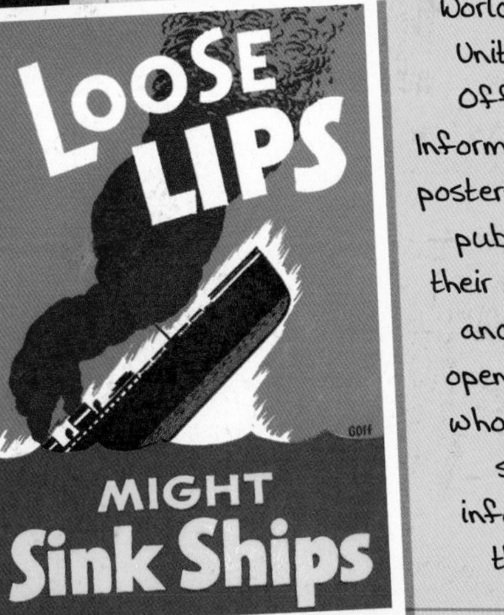

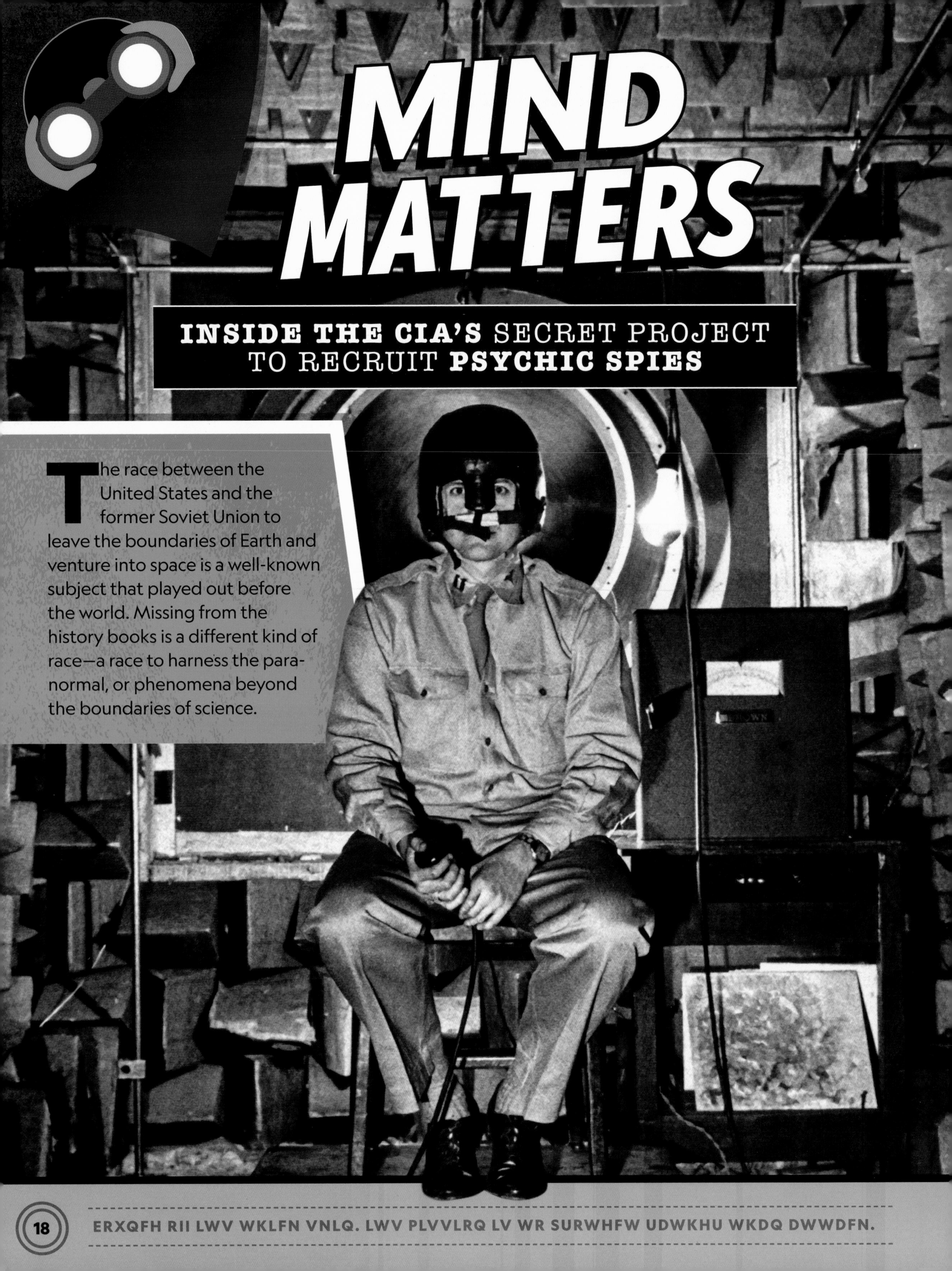

MIND MATTERS

INSIDE THE CIA'S SECRET PROJECT TO RECRUIT **PSYCHIC SPIES**

The race between the United States and the former Soviet Union to leave the boundaries of Earth and venture into space is a well-known subject that played out before the world. Missing from the history books is a different kind of race—a race to harness the paranormal, or phenomena beyond the boundaries of science.

ERXQFH RII LWV WKLFN VNLQ. LWV PLVVLRQ LV WR SURWHFW UDWKHU WKDQ DWWDFN.

Soviet scientists for decades had embraced parapsychology, the study of mental powers. The CIA wasn't about to sit back and let its Soviet rivals win this psychic arms race. In 1972, it launched its own series of secret studies with the help of other shadowy intelligence agencies. These studies all fell under one code name: Project Star Gate.

SNEAK PEEKS

Star Gate scientists recruited volunteers inside and outside the government who claimed they had psychic powers. Swearing themselves to secrecy, the volunteers hoped they had what it took to join this new squad of paranormal spies. They took part in experiments that tested a variety of mental powers. Chief among these: Remote viewing, or the ability to mentally visualize people, objects, or events that are somewhere else—even on the other side of the world. They also studied telepathy, the ability to send mental messages, and psychokinesis, the power to move objects with only your mind.

Star Gate eventually recruited more than 20 test subjects across several intelligence agencies. Most experiments were simple: The subject tried to read a series of cards visible only to the scientist. Some experiments were elaborate. Remote-viewing participants would seal themselves in a chamber that blocked all light and sound, and then try to describe the layout and contents of neighboring rooms and even more distant destinations. At least one subject was asked to describe the surface of Saturn's moon Titan! People involved in these tests reported some success at the time, although this success was later disputed.

FRINGE BENEFITS

Star Gate sounds like the plot of a cheesy sci-fi movie: America's largest intelligence agency recruiting a squad of psychics to help win the Cold War with mental power alone. But the advantages of paranormal espionage were too great to ignore. Agents on mental missions could snoop on military bases in other countries or eavesdrop on heads of state without ever leaving the lab. One declassified Star Gate document listed the main benefit of remote viewing: "No known defense." (After all, the people being snooped on couldn't defend against it if they didn't know it was happening.)

Star Gate was shut down in 1995 after mixed results, and the project's existence was immediately declassified. The reports made clear that Star Gate's spies were never meant to replace agents in the field; they were only intended to provide backup, an extra set of eyes and ears to help gather intel. The CIA claims the project never met its objectives. Whether the United States or the Soviet Union (which dissolved in 1991) scored any victories in the paranormal arms race remains top secret.

POWER STUDY

Star Gate's Mental Gymnastics

PSYCHOKINESIS: Also known as telekinesis, the flexing of mental muscles—not fingers!—to move physical objects (sort of like the Force in the Star Wars movies)

REMOTE VIEWING: The power to perceive people, places, and things from afar

TELEPATHY: The ability to receive the thoughts of others and send mental messages in return

ESP: Extrasensory perception, the blanket term for any perceptions that can't be explained by normal means

A CLOSER LOOK

Beginning as early as the 1920s at Leningrad's Institute for Brain Research, Soviet scientists began studying all sorts of "extrasensory perception." Chief among them was telepathy. The Soviets hoped they could use telepathy to communicate with submarines without relying on radio gear.

Meanwhile, while growing up in Leningrad, in the then Soviet Union, a girl named Nina Kulagina noticed she could make things move when she got mad, and officials in the government took notice. They believed Kulagina might have the power of telekinesis! Soviet officials in the 1960s videotaped her shoving objects on tables and plucking single matchsticks from piles by using only her mind. The Soviets hoped to develop telekinesis to disrupt the guidance systems of enemy nuclear missiles. Skeptics think she faked these feats through a magician's sleight of hand.

MYTHS VS. FACTS

TELLING TRUTH **FROM FICTION**

MYTH: SPIES ARE ALWAYS DOING CRAZY STUNTS.

FACT: If a spy suddenly finds him- or herself in a high-speed chase or clutching the side of an airplane like James Bond, then their mission has taken a turn for the whoops. Even if they survive their stunt, they'll likely get fired. Spies are valuable assets for any government agency—the product of years of expensive training. They're expected to play it safe and lay low rather than risk their lives in dangerous stunts.

MYTH: SPIES ARE MASTERS OF THE MARTIAL ARTS.

FACT: Spies on the big screen can hurl bad guys through windows with just their pinkie fingers. But while real-life spies are trained in defensive driving and the use of firearms, they're not typically experts in offensive fighting moves. They are, however, trained in self-defense and evasion. When push comes to shove and a spy's cover is blown, they rely on their instincts and training to flee rather than fight. To that end, they're taught moves that help them escape—such as kicking a potential captor in the shin—and resist interrogation techniques.

MYTH: SPIES ARE SUAVE AND HAVE IMPECCABLE FASHION SENSE.

FACT: Spies in movies are superhuman, sharp dressers, and smooth talkers. But real-life spies dress just like everyone around them—which helps them blend in. A spy would look like an international model only if he or she was trying to infiltrate an organization of international models.

MYTH: SPIES ARE FLUENT IN MULTIPLE LANGUAGES.

FACT: Speaking a foreign language isn't a requirement for working at the CIA, but language skills are highly valued by the agency, and being bilingual earns spies more interesting assignments. In fact, the CIA has one of the most advanced foreign-language teaching laboratories in the world to keep its agents' smooth-talking skills sharp.

MYTH: SPIES CAN INJECT PEOPLE WITH TRUTH SERUM TO EXTRACT INFORMATION.

FACT: Squeezing information from bad guys in spy movies is easy—just inject them with a special serum and they'll tell nothing but the truth. But although such a substance—called sodium pentothal—really does exist and has reportedly been used in CIA interrogations, it's not the all-powerful "truth serum" portrayed in films. Such substances simply make the subject more talkative and less inhibited about what he or she is saying. Those stuck with the serum might blab for hours, but what they say is likely all nonsense.

MYTH: SPIES DRIVE FANCY SPORTS CARS VERY FAST.

FACT: Spies drive sports cars only if they need to blend in with a group of people who also drive fancy sports cars. It's more likely they'll need to drive an average car—or even a junky one—to avoid standing out, which is a spy's key to success. Spies do get trained to drive fast and carefully to evade pursuers.

MYTH: SPIES USE ALL KINDS OF COOL SECRET GADGETS.

FACT: Actually, this isn't much of a myth. Intelligence agencies really do employ engineers to create nifty devices for gathering intelligence. (The CIA's gadget lab is called the Directorate of Science and Technology.) In some cases, these gadgets are even more advanced than what you see in the movies. Check out a selection of these devices on pages 108–111.

CLASSIFIED CASE

LINDSAY MORAN

ANSWERS FROM A **REAL-LIFE AGENT OF ESPIONAGE**

You've spent enough time reading about secret agents. Now meet a real one: Lindsay Moran, a case officer for the Central Intelligence Agency from 1998 to 2003. After completing her training at "the Farm" CIA spy school in Virginia, U.S.A., she was dispatched to the Republic of North Macedonia (formerly named the Republic of Macedonia) to gather intelligence and recruit other spies. Now an author, Officer Moran has emerged from the shadows to spill her top secrets of the spying profession.

VITAL STATS

NAME	Lindsay Moran
ACTIVE DATES	1998–2003
BEST KNOWN FOR	Posing as a diplomat to recruit a network of spies for the CIA

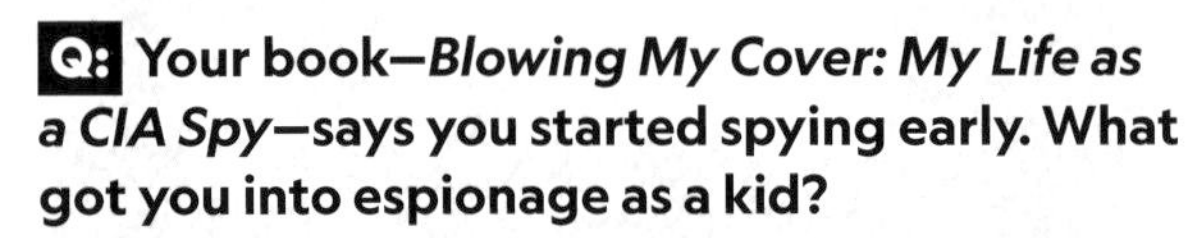

Q: Your book—*Blowing My Cover: My Life as a CIA Spy*—says you started spying early. What got you into espionage as a kid?

Moran: I was obsessed with a series of books about a character named Harriet the Spy. Also, whenever I got in trouble and was sent to my room for a time-out, I would spy on the neighbors and anyone outside. I also communicated in secret code using flashlights with my best friend who lived next door.

Moran, Lindsay

Q: What skills should junior spies focus on?

Moran: You should do well in school because it's very difficult to get into the CIA. Learning other languages is also helpful, especially difficult languages that not many Americans know—like Chinese or Arabic. It's good to know what is going on in the world. But you can start with geography, so you'll know where you are going when you are sent on your first mission.

Q: You went to Harvard and won the hard-to-get Fulbright scholarship for studying abroad. Are all spies as smart as you?

Moran: You don't have to go to Harvard to be a good spy. In fact, the most important attribute is something we call street smarts—or being able to think and act quickly, especially in the face of danger.

Q: You became a case officer for the CIA. Is that the same thing as a secret agent?

Moran: As case officers, or operations officers, we don't call ourselves spies or secret agents. But that's in fact what we were, living undercover in foreign countries and "stealing" secrets!

Q: Did you have a cover story?

Moran: Yes. Mine was that of a diplomat, which is someone who represents their home country overseas. It was good cover because it gave me a lot of access to "targets"—people that the U.S. government is interested in.

Q: So you recruited others to be spies. What did you look for?

Moran: I looked for people whom I could convince that it was in their best interest to give me secrets. Sometimes, they really liked the United States. Other times, they just needed or wanted money. We typically pay our foreign sources of information as a reward for giving us secrets.

Q: Ever accidentally recruit a double agent? How about a triple one?

Moran: Not that I know of! But keeping your agents straight—and especially remembering where and when you are supposed to meet them—is one of the challenges of being a spy.

Q: Was it hard to keep up your cover all the time?

Moran: I never really felt like I was myself, even if I was using my real name—as I did when I wasn't "operational." You tend to become a bit paranoid.

Q: Do spy skills come in handy in everyday life?

Moran: I am a much better driver because of the "defensive driving" training: a weeklong CIA course affectionately called "Crash and Burn."

Q: What are some other differences between make-believe spies and real ones?

Moran: Make-believe spies always have a cool gadget on hand to get them out of tough situations. Real spies more often have to talk their way out of them.

Q: Is being a spy a lonely job?

Moran: Yes, it was very lonely. I couldn't tell anyone where I was working or what I was doing. The only people who knew I was with the CIA were my mother, father, and brother. But all they knew was that they could not tell anyone that. They didn't know what I was doing. That's the nature of being a spy, and I decided I didn't want to spend the rest of my life living that way. But many people do.

Q: How do we know you really left the CIA? Maybe this is all part of your new cover!

Moran: Now you're thinking like a real spy!

THE PRESIDENT'S PROTECTORS

INSIDE A **TOP SECRET** U.S. GOVERNMENT **AGENCY**

Always within arm's reach of the president, their alert eyes keeping watch on every movement, the members of the United States Secret Service provide what is perhaps the most elite protection service in the world. The agency is famous for guarding the president. But you might be surprised to learn how it got its start.

ABRAHAM LINCOLN

HIDDEN HISTORY

The Secret Service was created when Abraham Lincoln was president. He signed legislation for the new agency on April 14, 1865, and that very night he was assassinated. Today that sounds like a bizarre—and unfortunate—coincidence. But back then the Secret Service was not intended to protect the president. Instead, its sole purpose was to stamp out fake money.

At the time, the country was awash with counterfeit currency. According to some estimates, up to half of the money in circulation was fake. Treasury Secretary Hugh McCulloch came up with a solution—a "regular permanent force whose job it [would] be to put these counterfeiters out of business."

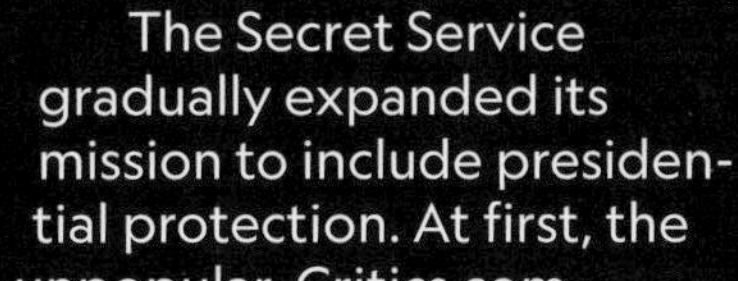

The Secret Service gradually expanded its mission to include presidential protection. At first, the idea was unpopular. Critics complained that the Secret Service would create an unwelcome barrier between the president and the American people. They worried about treating the commander in chief like a king or queen.

But the need for better presidential security became clear after two more presidents—James A. Garfield and William McKinley—were assassinated. In 1901, Congress officially charged the Secret Service with the responsibility of protecting the president, and the agency has done so ever since. Today Secret Service agents watch over the first family and several other political figures, as well as investigate cybercrimes. And they still chase down counterfeiters.

IN THE BUBBLE

The Secret Service employs about 3,200 special agents, but only a small number are assigned to the Presidential Protection division. These agents provide the president with round-the-clock protection, sometimes called "the bubble."

They never leave the president's side, even in the bathroom. The president's meals are prepared under their supervision. And agents have been known to employ sneaky disguises—dressing as priests, soldiers, and even major league umpires—in order to stay close to the president while blending into the background.

The Secret Service faces special challenges whenever the president is on the move. The commander in chief rides in a bulletproof limousine so well armored that it is known as the Beast. Before the president travels anywhere, the agency's advance team combs the site for threats and plans every detail of the president's visit, down to the minute.

The next time you see footage of the president making a speech or meeting with other world leaders, scan the scene for Secret Service agents. Known for wearing earpieces, dark suits, and sunglasses, they try to go unnoticed. But their presence could mean the difference between disaster and just another day.

ANSWERS

1. MOGUL 2. RENEGADE 3. TRAILBLAZER 4. EAGLE 5. TIMBERWOLF 6. RAWHIDE

ROAD WARRIOR

THE FRILLS AND THRILLS OF **THE PRESIDENT'S BEASTLY VEHICLE**

When the president of the United States needs to go places, he or she doesn't take the bus or fly coach. For long trips, the president boards Air Force One or Marine One, the presidential plane and helicopter, respectively. But once the president lands and is ready to scoot around town, he or she climbs inside the Beast. That's the name of a long line of vehicles designed to carry the president in luxurious comfort and safety but also to serve as a mobile command center. The latest model came online in 2018. About 20 spares were built by General Motors at a cost of $15.6 million. It's based off a Cadillac CT6, but the Beast is more like an armored truck. President Barack Obama called it a "Cadillac on a tank frame." And like a tank, the Beast was designed to be nearly indestructible. Many of its security features are top secret, but let's take a sneak peek under the hood.

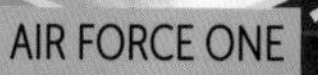
AIR FORCE ONE

MORE THAN FREE WI-FI

The president has access to a state-of-the-art communication system that keeps him or her in the loop of world events. He can contact government and military officials or even place a call to a nuclear submarine on the other side of the world.

WINDOW TREATMENT

Like its armor, the Beast's windows are "ballistics-proof," meaning they can absorb damage from bullets or heavy objects like battering rams. They're composed of layers of special glass and plastics. Each window is five inches (13 cm) thick!

BEASTLY HIDE

The Beast's skin is made of layers of aluminum, steel, and ceramic armors designed to withstand any sort of attack, from bullets to rockets.

LIFTOFF

The Beast travels separately from the president in its own cargo plane and typically is ferried ahead so the commander in chief has his or her ride waiting at the airport.

HEAVY METAL

All that armor and technology adds up. The Beast is estimated to weigh around 10 tons (9 t).

BEHIND THE WHEEL

The beast's most advanced feature isn't any of its high-tech gadgets—it's the human driver, trained for advanced getaways and handling dangerous situations. The driver even has access to night-vision technology to keep on rolling if the headlights go out.

AIR FORCED

The interior of the Beast can be sealed off and supplied with its own air in case of a chemical attack or if the vehicle crashes into water. It can essentially turn into a submarine!

FIRST AID

The interior contains a refrigerated suite equipped with medical gear and even pints of the president's blood type in case he or she is injured.

RIDE SHARE

Up to seven people can ride inside the Beast. Several passengers are Secret Service agents who protect the president in case of an attack. The Beast typically rides in a convoy that includes Secret Service vehicles, a backup Beast, and a communications truck.

FLAT CHANCE

The Beast's tires are called run-flat tires, meaning they're designed to keep rolling even if they're damaged.

DOOR BUSTERS

The Beast's doors are rumored to be at least eight inches (20 cm) thick—about as thick as the doors of a commercial airplane. That's one reason you never see the president open his or her car door. It's too heavy!

FULLY LOADED

Many of the Beast's defenses are classified, but according to reports, it's loaded with James Bond–style tricks, including the ability to create a smoke screen or oil slick as well as launch tear gas.

SECRET SOLDIERS

SPECIAL FORCES ARE THE WORLD'S SNEAKIEST TROOPS

They're the best of the best—handpicked and trained in stealth, survival, and the use of specialized gear. They're special forces: elite soldiers who are dispatched on hard-core military missions, called special operations, or spec-ops. Employed by militaries around the world, they usually strike after sundown, when least expected.

NIGHT WARRIORS

The use of elite troops goes back centuries. The Roman navy crewed sleek camouflaged boats with handpicked sailors for scouting missions. During the Middle Ages, British lords employed "sappers" to dig secret tunnels beneath enemy castles to bring down the walls. But special forces as we know them evolved during World War II with the formation of the British Special Air Service. Each country in that conflict formed elite groups of troops for specialized missions (Canada's Devil's Brigade, for instance, infiltrated enemy alpine wilderness on skis) and for lengthy missions far from home base. Today, spec-ops troops are sent to rescue hostages, sabotage enemy installations, and gather information on the enemy—often in the dead of night.

SELECTIVE SERVICE

The special operations forces don't accept just any regular G.I. Joe or Jane. The U.S. Navy SEALs, for instance, recommend that its applicants can complete 100 push-ups in two minutes and swim 500 yards (457 m) in less than 10 minutes before even applying. And that's just the admittance test for SEAL training. Once accepted, candidates endure a grueling seven-month program that teaches sneaky combat skills and pushes them to their physical and mental limits. Only about 20 percent of the candidates make it through training to become a SEAL.

WORLD WARRIORS

Secret Soldiers Across the Globe

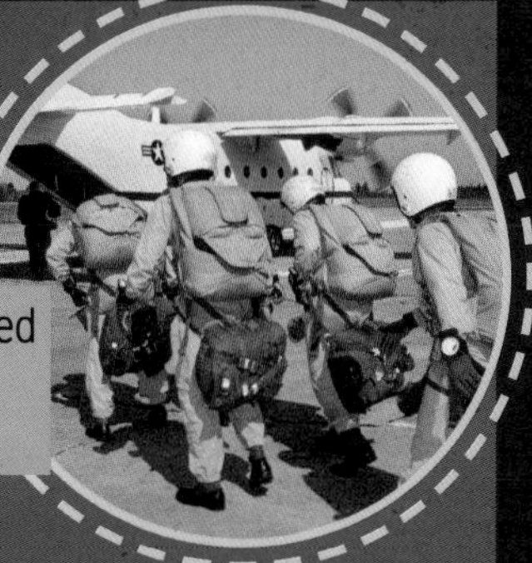

U.S. ARMY DELTA FORCE This highly trained troop of Army specialists is so top secret that its members wear civilian clothes to conceal their identities.

FRENCH SPECIAL FORCES The Commandement des Opérations Spéciales takes the best of the best of France's army, navy, and air force and trains them in hostage rescue and rapid-fire response.

DANISH HUNTSMEN CORPS Formed from hunters and woodsmen in the late 1700s to protect Denmark's borders, the Huntsmen have evolved into the world's sneakiest soldiers, specializing in skydiving behind enemy lines.

BRITISH SPECIAL AIR SERVICE Most modern spec-ops squads are based off the British SAS, which formed during World War II to sabotage the Nazi war machine.

U.S. NAVY SEALS These elite sailors aren't just sneaky underwater—using specialized "rebreather" scuba gear that doesn't leave a trail of bubbles—they're also masters of tactics for use in the air and on land (thus the letters in the SEAL name: sea, air, and land).

NIGHT-VISION GOGGLES

GEAR UP!

Spec-Ops Equipment

Troops in the special operations forces are the best of the best in their nation's military, so it makes sense that they're issued the best of the best in equipment for their sneaky missions. This might include:

NIGHT-VISION/INFRARED GOGGLES: These high-tech goggles amplify all the night's lights—car headlamps, streetlights, the moon, and even starlight—to illuminate the night landscape in an eerie green glow. Some models also detect infrared light to highlight the heat of human bodies far away or even behind concrete walls.

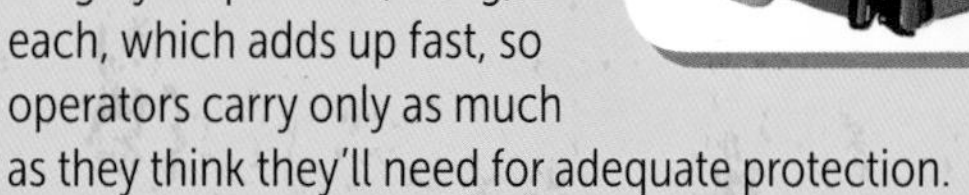

BODY ARMOR: Before they enter dangerous territory, special operations forces members slip on special vests with pockets for plates made of bulletproof material. The plates weigh roughly six pounds (2.7 kg) each, which adds up fast, so operators carry only as much as they think they'll need for adequate protection.

COMMUNICATIONS GEAR: Modern spec-ops forces wear special "bone phones" that transmit sound through the bones in their head and don't "leak" noise like standard headphones.

COMBAT CANINE: Your pooch might know how to sit and roll over, but can she parachute into enemy territory? Highly trained military working dogs often accompany special operations forces on their missions. Typically of the stocky Belgian shepherd Malinois breed, these tough mutts wear bulletproof armor equipped with cameras, so they can scout ahead or send pictures from hard-to-reach places. They even wear protective goggles—called doggles.

UNDERCOVER OPERATION

GET SNEAKY

SET UP YOUR OWN **SPY NETWORK**

Ready to join the ranks of the world's top sleuths but not sure where to begin? Don't worry—we've got you covered with a step-by-step guide to setting up your own spy network.

Part 1: PEOPLE

DIRECTIONS:

STEP 1. RECRUIT A TRUSTED GROUP OF FRIENDS.

What's the key to a successful spy network? The spies, of course! Gadgets are great, but they can't uncover secrets on their own. Come up with a list of potential recruits. Start with classmates, neighbors, and siblings. Make sure to look for people who bring different skills to the table. Recruiting someone who is tech-savvy is a priority. Focus on friends with good observational skills. Younger recruits can start out as trainees.

STEP 2. SELECT CODE NAMES.

Each person will need a code name. One option: Use the code names of former spies. Or have each member pick a name that starts with the first letter of his or her actual name. This will help avoid confusion during missions.

NEED A RIDDLE HINT?

This chapter's code uses a Caesar cipher shifted three spaces right (read about it on page 8).

If you're still at a loss, turn to page 182 for the answer to this encrypted riddle!

HERE'S ANOTHER HINT. ⇧

Part 2: PLACES

STEP 3. FIND A LOCATION FOR "DEAD-DROP" MESSAGES.

The stealthiest spies avoid passing along secrets in person—it's far too risky. You'll need to choose a place where spies can leave each other notes and clues. Maximize sneakiness by selecting a spot that no one would suspect. Is there a loose brick on your house? A rock in the yard that can be shifted and then returned to its place? Make sure messages are concealed so they're not blown away—or spotted by nosy siblings.

STEP 4. PICK THE RIGHT HEADQUARTERS.

You'll need a place to hold meetings and stash supplies. Pick a safe space that is convenient for the group. Tree houses, basements, and bedrooms are all good options.

Part 3: THINGS

STEP 5. COME UP WITH A SECRET HANDSHAKE.

Keep it simple. You don't want to attract unnecessary attention. Ask each person to make a suggestion. Then take a vote.

STEP 6. CHOOSE A CODE.

You'll need to encrypt all top secret messages. Select a cipher (see pages 8 and 9 for ideas) and practice writing and decoding simple notes. Make sure everyone in the network knows how the code works.

STEP 7. CREATE A MISSION LOG.

Keep track of missions in a master log. List the code name for each mission, and record your progress. Once a mission is complete, note results and key takeaways.

Part 4: PLANS

STEP 8. PLAN A PRACTICE MISSION.

Start by hiding an important item, such as a message, a map, or a key. Then plant clues for the group to find. Once the mission is complete, you'll know that your spy network is good to go!

Recovered power source from crashed UNIDENTIFIED FLYING OBJECT.

SECRET HISTORY

Adapted technology to work with microwave oven.

The past might be history, but that doesn't mean we can't solve its mysteries. Did the U.S. government really cover up evidence of alien life? Have secret societies controlled the course of historic events for centuries? What did ancient Egyptians really mean when they covered their kingdom with hieroglyphs? This chapter mines the ages for answers to history's most confounding questions.

Defrosted burritos now appear 30 minutes into the FUTURE.

SECLUDED CELLS

Medieval castles didn't have dungeons (which evolved from the word "donjon," the original name for a castle's innermost tower). Lords, ladies, and knights captured in battle were held in the donjon's uppermost floors until their ransoms were paid. But some castles did have a secret room called an oubliette—accessible via a trapdoor high in its ceiling, which made it nearly escape-proof. Here a castle lord's most hated enemies would be dumped and forgotten.

CHAMBERS OF SECRETS

THE HOLE TRUTH ABOUT HISTORY'S **SECRET SPACES**

History is full of holes: "priest holes," "murder holes," hidden tunnels, and other out-of-sight chambers, accessible only by elaborate trapdoors and passwords. Stealthy construction crews installed such hideaways for all sorts of secret reasons, from stashing treasure to protecting people. Explore them yourself as we unearth undercover architecture.

CONFUSING CORRIDORS

Ancient Egyptians built dead-end hallways and decoy treasure rooms in their towering tombs to throw off grave robbers. Japanese warlords commissioned similar twisting hallways to confuse and corner would-be assassins. In the late 19th century, construction on the Winchester Mystery House in San Jose, California, U.S.A., continued around the clock for decades, resulting in a maze of twisting hallways, stairways to nowhere, dead-end doors, and secret passages. The wealthy widow who lived there hoped to confuse the mansion's resident ghosts.

WHAT FOLLOWS IS A RIDDLE HIDDEN IN A SECRET CODE. THE ANSWER TO THIS RIDDLE IS A

MURDER HOLES

These secret recesses pitted the vaulted ceiling above a castle's gatehouse, letting defenders from above fire arrows and dump boiling water and scalding sand on attackers who breached the gate. Like many European castles built in the Middle Ages, Warwick Castle is a warren of secret passages and hidden rooms, including a defensive "barbican" above the gate complete with murder holes. You can tour these rooms at the castle in Warwick, England.

ESCAPE ROUTES

Hidden passages had many purposes. In more modern structures such as Singer Castle, a mansion built at the turn of the 20th century in New York State, U.S.A., by the president of the Singer Sewing Machine company, they were used to spy on guests through the walls. But in cathedrals and castles they typically served as a means of emergency escape. Medieval castles in particular often had secret exits—called sally ports—that led to underground tunnels. Defenders in a siege could sneak in supplies or launch surprise counter-attacks.

SECRET SANCTUARIES

England's Catholics came under siege beginning with the reign of Queen Elizabeth I in 1558. Declared outlaws, priests fled churches and sought safety within the homes of their followers, who built "priest holes" to hide the clergy from authorities.

REAL ESCAPE ROOMS

Hidden quarters save lives and accommodate spies in times of war. Jewish refugees, for instance, hid from the Nazis in blocked-off attics and secret rooms before and during World War II. Anne Frank and her family famously sought refuge in a secret Amsterdam apartment hidden behind a bookcase. A group of student roommates in Norway, meanwhile, recently discovered a secret attic chamber full of maps and messages. It turns out the room was used to print anti-Nazi newspapers during World War II.

A CLOSER LOOK

Standing nearly half as tall as New York City's Empire State Building, Egypt's Great Pyramid of Khufu held the title of "world's tallest building" for nearly 4,000 years. And it's still giving up its secrets! Scientists studying the behavior of cosmic rays from space used their instruments to look through the pyramid and found a massive hidden chamber inside—the first new room discovered since the 19th century. They haven't been able to explore this area; it's closed off from the rest of the pyramid's interior spaces. But scientists doubt it contains treasure or mummies. Instead, they suspect this chamber, with its steeply sloping floor, was used as a ramp for hauling up the pyramid's titanic building blocks, and then sealed off once the structure was finished. If true, the empty chamber contains its own sort of treasure: insight into how Egypt's massive tombs were built.

PERSON, PLACE, OR THING DESCRIBED IN THIS CHAPTER. THE CODE IS BASED ON SOMETHING

COLOSSAL SECRET

EXPLORE THE **HIDDEN UNDERGROUND** OF HISTORY'S **GREATEST THEATER**

More than 50,000 spectators gathered in Rome's Colosseum in the second century A.D. to witness gory spectacles: reenactments of famous battles, live hunts for exotic animals, and bloody bouts between trained warriors known as gladiators. These events were the blockbuster movies of their day. And like any blockbuster, they relied on dazzling special effects to keep the audience on the edge of their seats. In the Colosseum, the special effects were created by the structure itself. Beneath the sandy floor of this outdoor theater—the world's largest—hid the hypogeum, a warren of hallways and human-powered elevators leading to trapdoors designed to shock audience members right out of their togas. Here's a guide to the Colosseum's subterranean secrets.

THE HIDDEN HYPOGEUM

In its heyday, the hypogeum—or Colosseum underground—hid beneath a wooden stage that was covered with sand, upon which spectacles unfolded on a nearly daily basis. But by the sixth century, the venue fell out of use and became lost to neglect. The hypogeum was raided for its stone and filled in over time. Eventually, it was buried beneath 40 feet (12 m) of dirt. It remained hidden until excavators found it in the 1930s. Archaeologists have been trying to figure out its many secret showstopping features ever since.

GOING UP

Rounded walls within the hypogeum housed capstans, or massive spindles turned by several burly people to power the elevators that raised animals and scenery to the Colosseum floor. You may have seen a capstan in pirate movies; sailors use them to lift the anchors. In fact, much of the machinery of the hypogeum—capstans, winches, ropes, pulleys—resembled equipment used on old square-rigged sailing ships.

CAPSTAN

YOU'VE READ IN THIS BOOK. PERHAPS THAT IS ENOUGH INFORMATION TO SOLVE THIS RIDDLE,

WATERLOGGED

The floor of the Colosseum could be sealed and flooded with water from a nearby aqueduct to stage mock battles between real ships in "seas" at least three feet (1 m) deep!

STARS OF THE SHOW

Gladiators were the professional athletes of their day. But although they were celebrities, most gladiators were enslaved people or prisoners of war forced into fighting for the bloodthirsty crowd's amusement. And they often fought to the death. Rome's emperors hosted these expensive events—which were often free to the public—to make the citizens happy and thus easier to rule.

MISERY BEHIND THE MAGIC

Archaeologists are certain the hypogeum was a horrible place to work: hot, noisy, crowded with workers and surly gladiators, and stinky from animals. And messing up led to a worse fate than getting fired. Many of the Colosseum's shows were hosted by the emperor himself. If a hypogeum staffer missed a cue or caused a technical malfunction, they might be forced to become part of the show—typically a final performance.

TRAPDOORS

Many of the Colosseum's thrills were delivered through trapdoors in the wooden floor. As many as 60 were in operation during the venue's most mind-blowing productions. Forty were large enough to accommodate tigers and even elephants, while another 20 around the perimeter opened to reveal scenery, such as groves of trees that turned the stage into a forest.

PERHAPS NOT. IF YOU'RE STUMPED, YOU WILL FIND A HINT AT THE END OF THIS CHAPTER.

SECRET STONE

THE ROSETTA STONE CRACKED ANCIENT EGYPT'S CODE

Learning your ABC's is a breeze nowadays, but imagine if the 26 letters of the alphabet were replaced with more than 700 pictures of plants, birds, boats, and other animals and objects. Ancient Egyptians invented just such a script—later called hieroglyphs by the Greeks—around 3100 B.C. Inspired by the natural world, these famous symbols are etched across Egypt's ancient temples, tombs, and monuments.

But after the Romans took control of Egypt around 30 B.C., hieroglyphs began to fade from use. By the fifth century A.D., nobody knew how to read them. To anyone who wanted to learn about Egypt's ancient past, the pictures plastered across the tombs and temples presented a maddening mystery.

Four feet (1.2 m) long and weighing nearly a ton (0.9 t), the Rosetta Stone is inscribed with the same royal decree in three scripts: hieroglyphs, a shorthand version called demotic, and ancient Greek.

JEAN-FRANÇOIS CHAMPOLLION

CODE BUSTED

The mystery started to get solved in 1799 when the French army discovered a granite slab near the Egyptian village of Rosetta. The stone—later named the Rosetta Stone after the location of its discovery—was engraved with a royal decree from 196 B.C. written in both hieroglyphs and Greek. Scholars who knew Greek set to work translating the Egyptian script, and by 1822, a French genius named Jean-François Champollion had cracked the code. Suddenly, Egyptologists could make sense of the symbols scattered across Egypt. The kingdom's tombs, temples, and monuments became an open book.

NOW GET CRACKING! HERE IS THE RIDDLE:

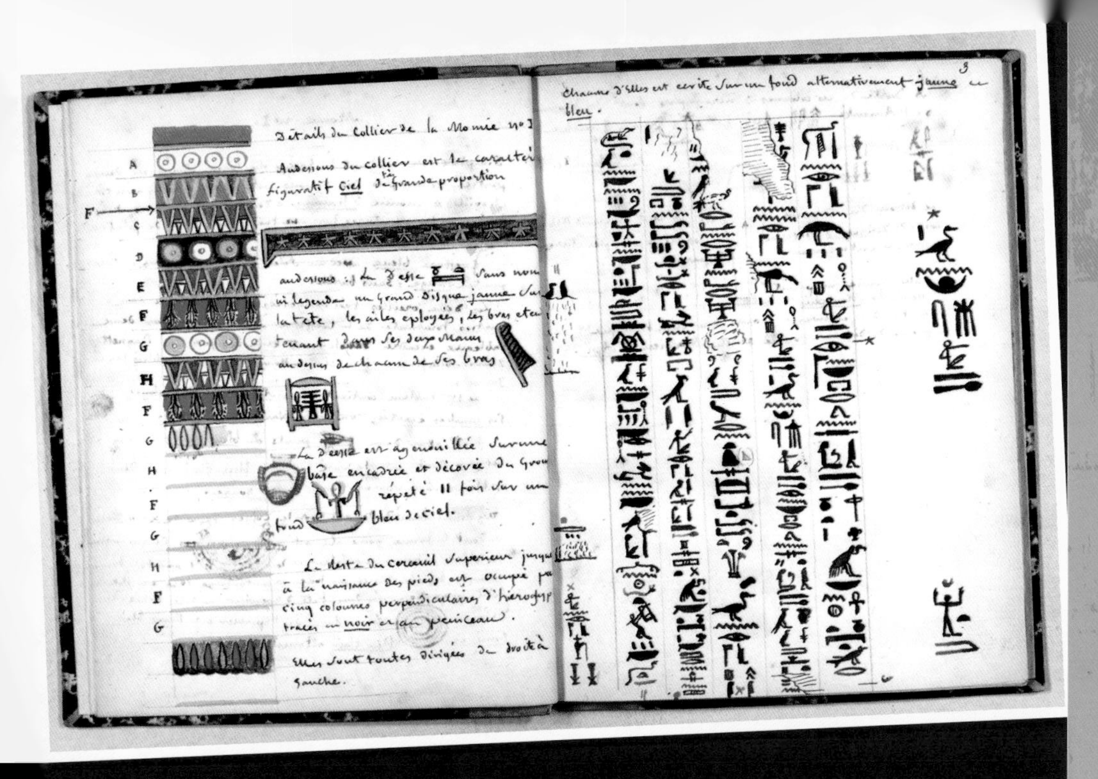

DECODING HIEROGLYPHS

Some hieroglyphs portrayed precisely what they pictured, or just simple ideas. A symbol of a woman represented a woman. A pair of legs implied motion. But writers soon realized these hieroglyphs had limits. How do you draw a picture of jealousy? Or faith? So the ancient Egyptians developed symbols to spell out more complex thoughts.

Hieroglyphic script was as complex as it is beautiful. Only one percent of Egyptians could read it. Children lucky enough to become scribes—the civil servants who etched spells on tomb walls, collected taxes, and kept records—began their education at a young age. They spent four years learning in a temple, copying and recopying Egyptian tales and prayers on scraps of pottery or flakes of stone. Apprenticeship to a scribe came next. The entire training process might last more than a decade, but it was worth it. Smart scribes became important officials and had the cushiest careers in the kingdom. They didn't even have to pay taxes!

A CLOSER LOOK

Archaeologists use special lights to reveal the bumps and indentations left by ancient text in manuscripts that have since been reused. These markings are photographed and scanned into a computer program that reassembles the old manuscripts in digital form.

OF THE LOST

You'd think lost books would be bad for any library. But for the oldest continuously operating library in the world, lost books are a source of priceless knowledge. Built at the foot of Mount Sinai in modern-day Egypt around 1,500 years ago, Saint Catherine's Monastery contains thousands of ancient manuscripts. About 160 of these are extra special. They're palimpsests, or books that were scraped clean long ago and reprinted with new text, creating many layers of writing. The practice was a necessity at this desert monastery, where parchment supplies were hard to come by.

But such recycling is good news for modern archaeologists. Teams of them are using scanners and computer programs to digitally peel away each palimpsest's ancient layers of writing without physically harming the paper. The process makes these lost books legible again, turning one priceless book into many. Archaeologists studying these manuscripts have found a trove of lost knowledge dating from 1,500 years ago, including new poems of Greek mythology, ancient medical cures, and manuscripts written in languages that disappeared centuries ago. These lost books also fill in gaps in history, offering a glimpse of how people lived way before the invention of books, magazines, or online social networks. The study continues, making Saint Catherine's Monastery one of the few libraries where lost books are returned on a regular basis.

PALIMPSEST

ALIENS UNDERCOVER

A HUSH-HUSH HISTORY OF **FLYING SAUCERS**

If you've spotted something soaring high above and didn't know what it was, then congrats! You've seen an unidentified flying object, or UFO. But whether that streaking smudge was actually an alien spaceship is a question for the ufologists, or people who study mysterious objects in the sky. Some ufologists believe otherworldly craft have buzzed around humanity for centuries and continue to do so today, but we never hear about such sightings because governments around the globe hide evidence of alien visitation. It might sound like an outrageous claim, but it's rooted in truth: Since World War II, government officials have commissioned classified reports on UFO activity. Let's map out the milestones of these out-of-this-world studies.

1940 — 1945 — 1950

1940: CHURCHILL'S SECRET

British prime minister Winston Churchill was celebrated for his defiant leadership in the face of Nazi Germany's overwhelming military might at the start of World War II. He was less known for his interest in alien visitors. Churchill wrote essays about the possibilities of life on other planets and was fascinated by reports of UFO sightings. According to secret files declassified in 2010, Churchill once ordered that a reported encounter between a British bomber and a UFO be kept classified because news of extraterrestrial visitors "would create mass panic among the general population."

1944: FOO FLYERS

While on night missions, fighter pilots in World War II reported seeing balls of red, orange, and green light chasing their aircraft and skimming along the ground. Believing these strange lights were some new type of weapon, the pilots named them "foo fighters" after a nonsense term borrowed from an American comic strip popular in the 1930s. Secret CIA studies commissioned after the war never determined what the foo fighters were.

JUNE 1947: FLYING SAUCER MARK 1

While flying near Mount Rainier in Washington State, U.S.A., pilot Kenneth Arnold spotted several unidentified objects skipping through the sky. From his description of the craft as saucerlike, the press invented the term "flying saucer." Sightings of similar craft soon began popping up across the country.

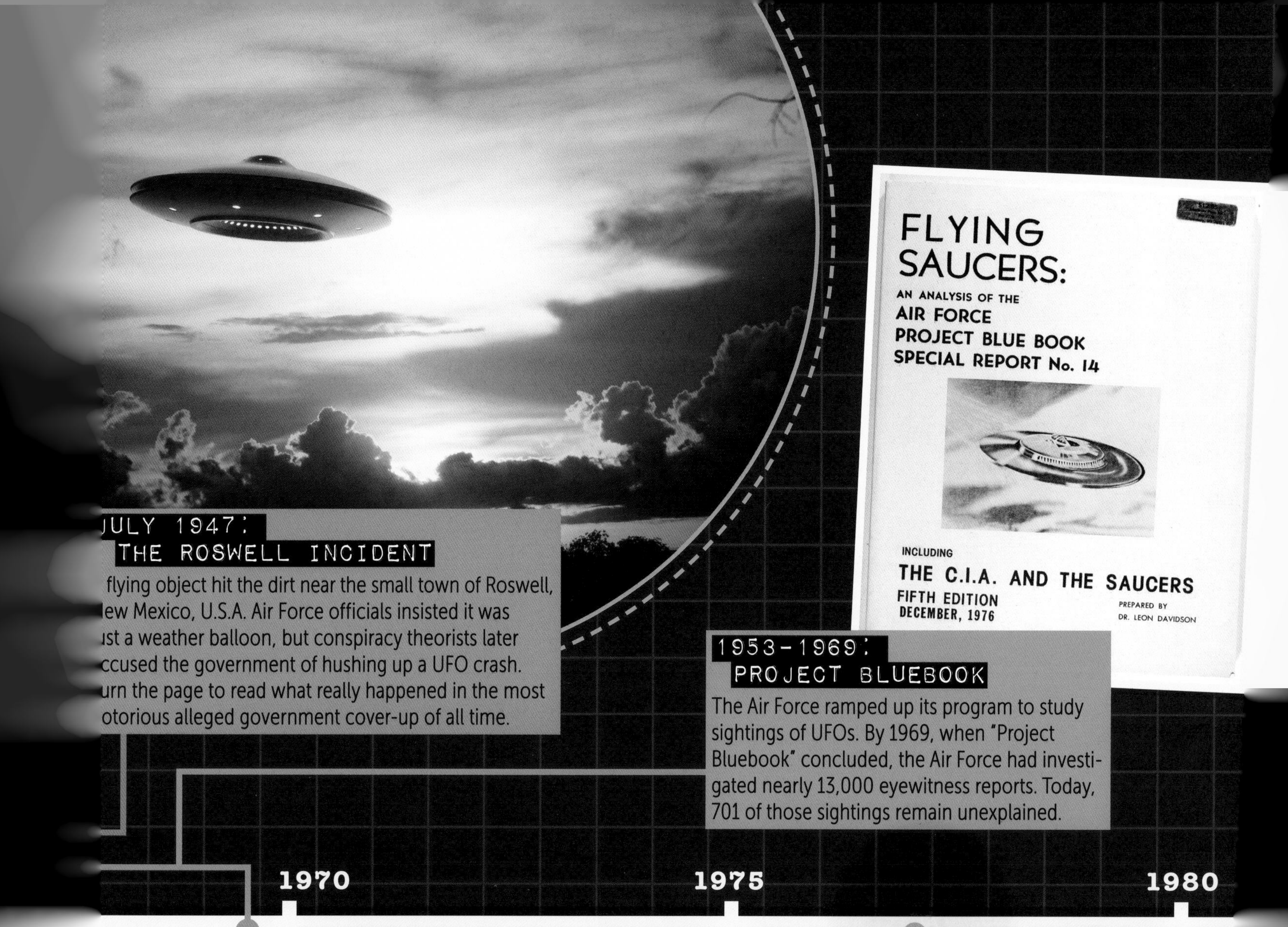

JULY 1947:
THE ROSWELL INCIDENT

flying object hit the dirt near the small town of Roswell, lew Mexico, U.S.A. Air Force officials insisted it was ıst a weather balloon, but conspiracy theorists later ccused the government of hushing up a UFO crash. urn the page to read what really happened in the most otorious alleged government cover-up of all time.

1953-1969:
PROJECT BLUEBOOK

The Air Force ramped up its program to study sightings of UFOs. By 1969, when "Project Bluebook" concluded, the Air Force had investigated nearly 13,000 eyewitness reports. Today, 701 of those sightings remain unexplained.

1970 — 1975 — 1980

JULY 1948:
PROJECT SIGN

The United States Air Force began "Project Sign," an in-depth investigation of UFO reports, particularly sightings reported by airline and military pilots. One especially convincing claim of a near collision with a "torpedo-shaped object" played a large role in Project Sign's final report, later that year, that alien craft were the best explanation for UFOs.

1977 TO PRESENT:
THE SECRET'S OUT

An activist group called Citizens Against UFO Secrecy formed in 1977 to fight for the release of classified government documents pertaining to UFOs. By using freedom-of-information laws and filing lawsuits, the group has uncovered a trove of once secret reports and studies. Still, the declassified documents are often so "redacted" (or released with crucial words blacked out) that they raise more questions than answers.

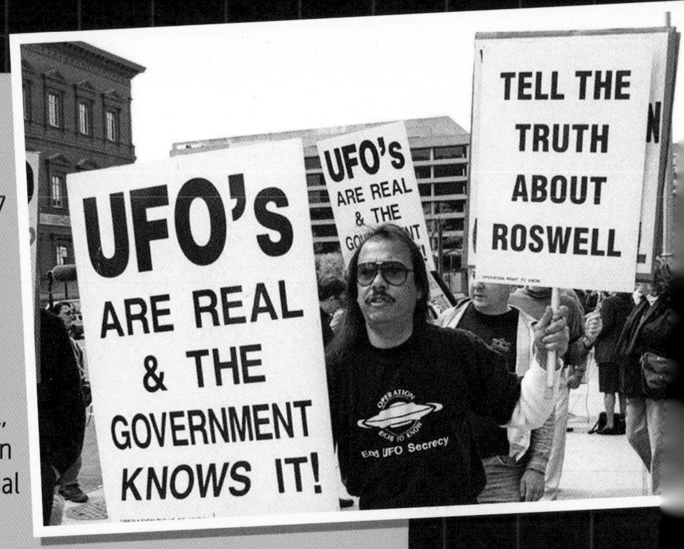

CLASSIFIED CASE

THE ROSWELL INCIDENT

DID THE U.S. GOVERNMENT COVER UP **A UFO CRASH?**

A wrecked spaceship. Alien bodies pulled from the wreckage. Government agents dispatched to cover up the evidence. Even if you can't pinpoint the town of Roswell on a New Mexico map, you might've heard the details of its famous 1947 "incident." Or at least you *think* you've heard the details, which have been distorted by conspiracy theorists and Hollywood storytellers. For the real story, we need to separate fact from science fiction.

UNIDENTIFIED FALLING OBJECT

Yes, a UFO did crash outside the town of Roswell in the summer of 1947. A rancher named William "Mac" Brazel discovered the wreckage. Linking it to a recent rash of flying saucer sightings, Brazel reported the debris to the sheriff, who in turn called the nearby Roswell Army Air Field (RAAF). After investigating the wreckage, Army officials issued a press release saying they recovered a "flying disc."

HOT SAUCER

That doozy of an announcement led to a startling headline in the local paper: "RAAF Captures Flying Saucer on Ranch in Roswell Region." According to the story, residents spotted a glowing object in the sky before the crash, and Air Force personnel confiscated the wreckage. As newspapers across the country began reporting on the Roswell incident, military officials quickly changed their story. The Roswell debris wasn't a flying disc after all, they said. It was a high-altitude balloon used to study the weather. The explanation fit with Brazel's description of the debris: bits of rubber, tinfoil, some sticks, and tough paper. The Roswell incident was quietly forgotten for the next 30 years.

ALIEN TALES

Although no longer in the spotlight, the Roswell case wasn't even close to closed. Eyewitnesses in the 1970s came forward with crashed-saucer stories. Some claimed they saw tiny alien corpses recovered from the wreckage, spirited away to military bases for secret experiments. Others insisted the debris contained impossibly strong metal alloys not of this world. At least one former Air Force officer swore there was not one, but *two* crashes. The conspiracy grew deeper with each new witness.

IDENTIFIED FLYING OBJECT

The U.S. government released a report in the mid-1990s that put all those conspiracies to rest. It revealed that the 1947 debris was actually a crashed balloon in its top secret "Project Mogul," which used high-altitude sensors to monitor for enemy nuclear missile tests. And those supposed alien corpses? They were crash-test dummies dropped from miles in the sky to check parachute technology.

SPOILER ALERT

Alien Autopsy

THE CLAIM: The Roswell conspiracy resurfaced in 1995 when grainy black-and-white footage aired on television showing scientists slicing open a dead extraterrestrial and plucking out its organs. The film's producer claimed he obtained the 17-minute clip from a secret military contact involved with the 1947 UFO crash near Roswell. The deceased alien in the footage was supposedly one of the pilots pulled from the downed saucer, and the autopsy became a ratings sensation.

THE TRUTH: Autopsy director Spyros Melaris, an English magician and filmmaker, later admitted the footage was faked. He and a team of special-effects experts staged the autopsy in a London apartment, stuffing a foam alien body with animal organs and pig brains.

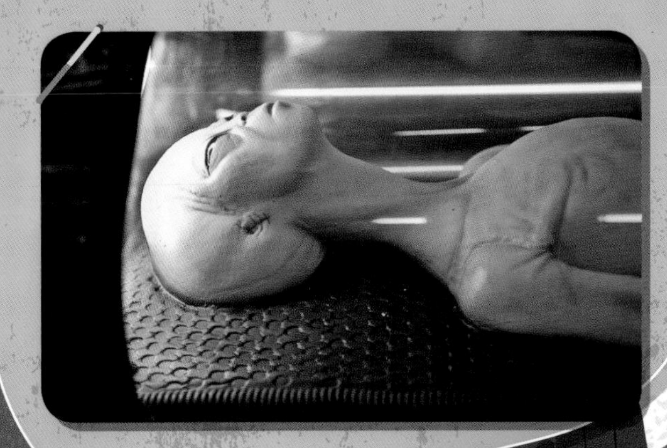

TOP SECRET

TWISTED PLOTS

THE FICTION AND THE FACT BEHIND **KOOKY CONSPIRACY THEORIES**

You are being lied to! Or so conspiracy theorists insist. They believe shadowy agents are meeting behind closed doors to hatch secret plots to harm us, control us, make a bunch of money—or all of the above! Here are four of the kookiest conspiracy theories—and the truth behind them.

CONSPIRACY THEORY 1: EXTRATERRESTRIAL REPTILES CONTROL THE WORLD!

Humanity's most powerful people aren't people at all! Our politicians, movie stars, pop singers, and billionaire executives are actually members of a secret race of cold-blooded extraterrestrial reptiles called the Annunaki, who voyaged from the constellation Draco long ago to enslave humanity. Working behind the scenes, these lizard overlords orchestrate wars and natural disasters to sow global grouchiness, which to them is a sort of energy.

Or so goes the theory of the "reptile elite," first proposed by English author, conspiracy theorist, and former pro soccer player David Icke in his 1998 book *The Biggest Secret*. In it he laid out the Annunaki's hidden history on Earth and their experiments in crossbreeding with humans to create a new race. The book contained interviews with supposed eyewitnesses to reptilians finagling with global events. And don't bother looking for scaly tails or slit pupils on your favorite movie stars: The Annunaki can assume human shape to blend in with the locals.

THE FACTS: Icke's theory of shape-changing aliens is conveniently hard to disprove—especially to anyone already prone to distrusting the powers that be. Still, you have to think it's pretty silly that Taylor Swift is secretly an extremely talented lizard lady from some dragon-shaped constellation sent to lull us into a peaceful state suitable for easier conquest.

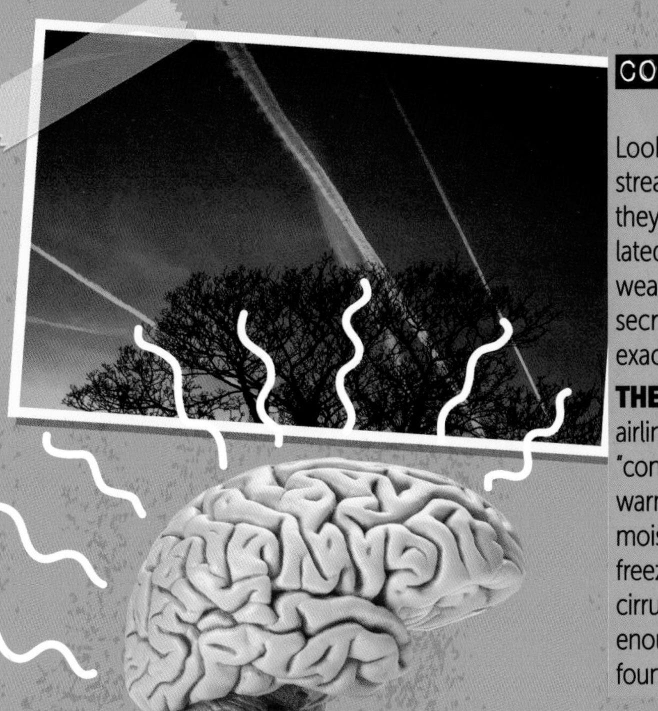

CONSPIRACY THEORY 2: CHEMTRAILS ARE CONTROLLING US!

Look, up in the sky! It's a plane! It's a misty trail! It's a chemtrail! Those poofy white streaks you see lingering in the air behind commercial airliners aren't smoke—they're trails of mind-controlling chemicals. Or maybe they're a toxic fog formulated to shorten our lives. Or maybe they're a misty agent designed to control the weather. Believers in the "chemtrail" conspiracy are convinced the government is secretly using airplanes to spritz citizens with chemicals. They can't agree on the exact purpose of these chemicals, except it's sinister and top secret!

THE FACTS: One thing is true: Those white lines you see lingering in the air behind airliners aren't smoke. But they're not trails of dangerous chemicals, either. They're "contrails," or trails of condensation that form when the hot exhaust of jet engines warms the freezing air around them at high altitudes. The engine heat sucks the moisture out of the air—a process called condensation—and this moisture then freezes into a trail of tiny ice crystals (the same types of crystals found in high-altitude cirrus clouds). Contrails only form in moist air, and not all plane engines are hot enough to create them. A 2016 study conducted by leading atmospheric scientists found no evidence of any secret chemical-spraying program using airplane contrails.

CONSPIRACY THEORY 3: THE EARTH IS FLAT!

According to the Flat Earth Society, that spinning globe in your social studies classroom has it all wrong. Our planet is shaped more like a pancake than a basketball. Earth's landmasses and seas are all squished onto the surface of an enormous disc bordered at its rim by the icy wilderness of Antarctica. Flat-earthers have concocted all sorts of theories to explain a world that isn't round. The sun and moon, they say, are actually artificial light sources whirling through the sky to create the illusion of a spherical, spinning planet. NASA's space missions were all faked on elaborate movie sets.

THE FACTS: People have known the Earth is round for more than 2,000 years. A Greek mathematician named Eratosthenes even managed to calculate the distance around the planet some 1,700 years before Columbus set sail! But you don't need to be a Greek mathematician to prove the flat-earthers wrong. Ships traveling over the horizon, for instance, disappear from the hull up as the curvature of the Earth obstructs our view from shore. During lunar eclipses, the Earth's shadow on the moon is obviously round. Then there's the straightforward fact that a flat Earth doesn't square with the laws of physics. Gravity would tug everything toward the center of the disc, crunching it back into a spherical shape—which is precisely why all planets are round and not flat.

CONSPIRACY THEORY 4: NEW COKE WAS A CROCK!

Cola aficionados faced a crisis in April 1985 when the Coca-Cola Company debuted its new, sweeter formula—aka New Coke—to compete with rival Pepsi, whose pop was exploding in popularity. Coke's new pop flopped. Less than 80 days after the announcement of New Coke, Coca-Cola brought the original soda back. Called Coke Classic, its reintroduction made the front page of newspapers and put the company back in the lead in the Cola wars, a position it has maintained ever since. Believers in the New Coke conspiracy claim Coca-Cola intentionally released its inferior new flavor as a marketing gimmick to drum up demand for the classic formula and retake the lead in the soda skirmish.

THE FACTS: Coca-Cola's flavor scientists actually expected New Coke to dominate the market. Its flavor was preferred in taste tests of nearly 200,000 soda fans. Coke braced for a boost in sales and certain victory in the Cola wars. The new formula certainly caused a stir—just not the type that Coca-Cola executives wanted. The company's phone lines were flooded with calls from outraged soda fans demanding a return of the original formula. Groups such as the "Old Cola Drinkers of America" formed to protest the new soda. New Coke was a disaster for one of America's most successful companies. When Don Keough, the company's president, was confronted about whether New Coke was secretly intended as a marketing ploy, he scoffed: "The truth is, we're not that dumb, and we're not that smart."

SECRET STASHES

LOST TREASURES JUST WAITING TO BE FOUND

Finding pirate treasure and long-buried artifacts is easy in books and movies. X always marks the spot! But such troves in the real world are rarely so easy to find, their secret resting spots lost in the mists of history. Here are four famous examples.

THE AMBER ROOM

ST. PETERSBURG, RUSSIA

Built in the early 18th century in Prussia, this priceless piece of architecture was assembled from sculpted panels of amber set against gold and mirrors. It moved from palace to palace before disappearing in World War II. Some believe it was destroyed by bombs; others think it was hidden in a bunker or a long-lost mine. The room has since been re-created in Catherine Palace in St. Petersburg, Russia, but the original is still waiting to be found.

CLEOPATRA'S TOMB

ALEXANDRIA, EGYPT

Born in Egypt in 69 B.C., the brilliant and bewitching Cleopatra became one of Egypt's most famous pharaohs—as well as its last. She was the first in her line of foreign rulers to learn the Egyptian language, and she expanded the temples of knowledge in the Egyptian city of Alexandria. It's in Alexandria, or thereabouts, where she was likely laid to rest, along with her famous husband, the Roman general Mark Antony. As with the tombs of other Egyptian kings—such as the famous boy king Tutankhamun—Cleopatra's resting place is no doubt a trove of priceless artifacts buried to keep her occupied during the afterlife. Egyptologists are still searching for her tomb today.

THE COPPER SCROLL
ISRAEL

Found in a Middle Eastern cave among the famous Dead Sea Scrolls—a trove of more than 800 documents about Christianity and Judaism written around 2,000 years ago—the Copper Scroll is the closest thing archaeologists have found to a treasure map. It's a list of 64 treasures—mostly gold and silver—stashed two millennia ago around what is now modern-day Israel. Treasure hunters have had little luck tracking down these treasures for a few reasons. For one, the scroll is written in ancient Hebrew and difficult to decipher. But the greater obstacle is the sheer passage of time. The shrines, staircases, and other hidey-holes described in the scroll no longer sit at their described locations, which are likely long demolished or buried by 2,000 years of historical and geological events.

THE SPANISH TREASURE FLEET
TREASURE COAST, FLORIDA, U.S.A.

Riding low in the water, their holds laden with gold and silver worth $300 million in today's U.S. dollars, Spanish treasure ships, or galleons, set sail for home from Cuba on July 25, 1715. The galleons were part of the world's most powerful navy, heavily armed against the pirates prowling the Caribbean. But cannons were useless against the monster that bore down on the treasure fleet a week later off the coast of Florida. Furious gales ripped apart the rigging. Two-story waves smashed the ships to splinters. One by one, the galleons succumbed to a hurricane that seemed endless. Of the eleven ships that set out, only one made it home. Although millions in gold and silver have been recovered in the three centuries since, much of the treasure still remains lost off the Atlantic Coast of Florida, along a stretch known as the Treasure Coast.

LOST TREASURES... FOUND!

The most successful treasure hunters are also amateur archaeologists, piecing together historical records and scraps of maps to pinpoint the secret spots for buried hoards. But even armed with local knowledge (and powerful metal detectors), fortune hunters don't strike it rich unless they have one key component: luck. Meet three of the luckiest:

GOLD RUSH: A California couple was walking their dog on their property in 2013 when they spotted something shiny in the dirt. Digging deeper, they unearthed eight cans containing more than 1,400 gold U.S. coins from the mid-1800s.

VALUE: $10 million

ANGLO-SAXON TREASURE: An Englishman sweeping a metal detector over a freshly plowed field in 2009 hit the jackpot when he discovered enough gold and silver artifacts from seventh-century England to fill nearly 250 bags.

VALUE: $5.3 million (split with the farmer who owned the field)

PIRATE PLUNDER: Underwater explorer Barry Clifford discovered the first authenticated pirate shipwreck off of Cape Cod, Massachusetts, U.S.A., in 1984. The hold of the ship—named the *Whydah*—was crammed with treasure looted from other vessels during the golden age of piracy.

VALUE: $200 million

A CLOSER LOOK

The rule of "finders keepers, losers weepers" doesn't always apply to lost treasure. Depending on where you find these treasure troves, you'll either get to keep the entire hoard or turn it over to the owner of the property (or split the find fifty-fifty with that owner). In England, for instance, all troves more than 300 years old belong to the crown. The hunters are rewarded for their efforts, however, and paid a fair value.

SPACE BASE

INSIDE THE U.S. ARMY'S TOP **SECRET PLAN** TO BUILD A FUTURISTIC **OUTPOST ON THE MOON**

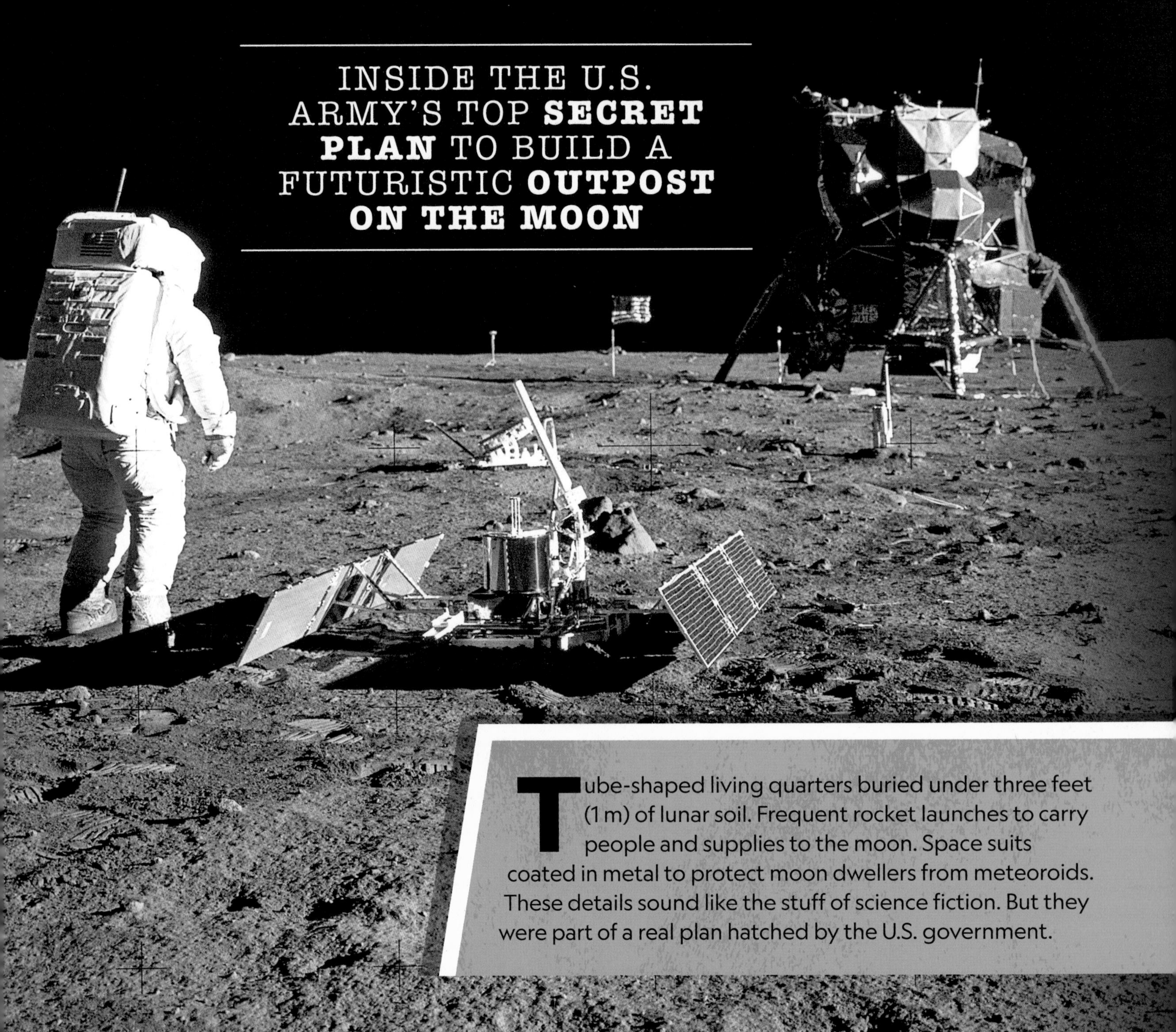

Tube-shaped living quarters buried under three feet (1 m) of lunar soil. Frequent rocket launches to carry people and supplies to the moon. Space suits coated in metal to protect moon dwellers from meteoroids. These details sound like the stuff of science fiction. But they were part of a real plan hatched by the U.S. government.

In 1959, the United States Army drew up top secret plans to build a permanent base on the moon. At the time, the United States and the Soviet Union—Russia today—were competing to outdo one another in space exploration. Two years before, the Soviets had launched Sputnik, the first human-made satellite to orbit Earth. Then they broadcast plans to hold a celebration for their government's 50th anniversary. The party was to take place in 1967—on the moon!

Americans took notice. "To be second to the Soviet Union in establishing an outpost on the moon would be disastrous," wrote the authors of the secret U.S. Army report. They concluded that there was only one thing to do: Set up an American base on the moon—and fast—before the Soviets could build one of their own.

A special team from the U.S. Army got to work, developing meticulous plans for constructing a lunar outpost. They called the top secret mission Project Horizon. Their report included diagrams of rockets, space suits, lunar vehicles, and underground living quarters. It said construction could be finished by the late 1960s.

The project never made it past the planning stages. The visions were beyond the reach of the technology of the time. But in 1969, the United States sent Neil Armstrong and Buzz Aldrin to walk on the lunar surface. The whole world watched as the astronauts became the first people to set foot on the moon.

Today, scientists are setting their sights on a more permanent return to Earth's closest celestial body. There's talk of a lunar village where people could either live or visit as temporary tourists. Will the moon base of the future look anything like the one that was planned in the past? Perhaps you will have a chance to see for yourself.

NEIL ARMSTRONG

PROJECT HORIZON

The Project Horizon planners wrote that rockets would blast off from Earth every few days, carrying supplies, and eventually people, to the moon. The mission called for 149 rocket launches just to set up the base.

HELP WANTED: The base would be occupied by 12 people at a time. Each crew would stay on the moon for one year before returning to Earth. Who would be selected for the adventure of a lifetime? According to the U.S. Army report, candidates chosen for the mission would be male, between 21 and 45 years old, and no more than six feet (1.8 m) tall. "All individuals must have some of the characteristics of the explorer, the adventurer, and the inventor," the report noted.

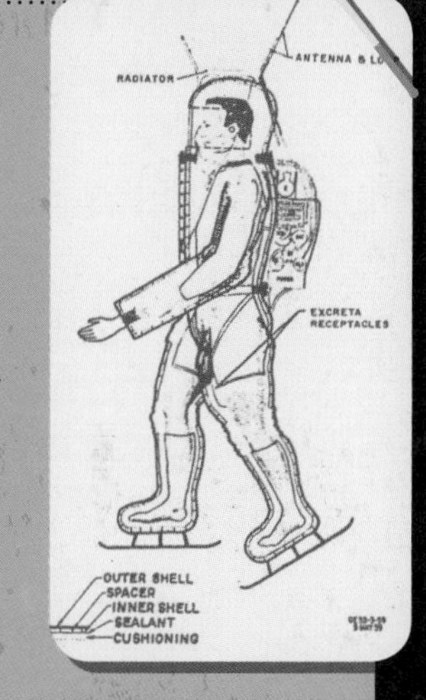

WHAT TO WEAR: Lunar suits would be coated in metal for protection from meteoroids and the rough surface of the moon. The suits would be unwieldy on our planet but not on the moon since lunar gravity is one-sixth that of Earth's. "If a man and his lunar suit weigh 300 pounds [136 kg] on Earth, they will only weigh 50 pounds [23 kg] on the moon," the Project Horizon team noted. An artificial hand would be operated from inside the suit arm. And a backpack would hold an oxygen tank and a temperature-control system.

HOME, SWEET HOME: Moon residents would live in tube-shaped metal tanks buried three feet (1 m) under the lunar surface. There they would be shielded from meteorites and drastic temperature swings. The team would use multipurpose moon trucks to dig ditches in the soil where their living quarters would be placed. The trucks would also be used to move the heavy tanks into the trenches and then cover them with lunar soil.

THE ILLUMINATI

The most mysterious of secret societies, the Illuminati (the Latin word for "enlightened") has its roots in an 18th-century German sect that rejected superstition and embraced the pursuit of knowledge. Although it was quickly disbanded, the Illuminati lives on in popular culture and conspiracy theories as a shadowy organization that controls the world from behind the scenes. Some point to the eye-and-pyramid symbol on the one dollar bill—a supposed secret Illuminati icon—as proof that the sect has meddled in the United States' affairs.

MEMBERS ONLY

TAKE A SNEAK PEEK INTO FIVE **SUPERSECRET SOCIETIES**

Their members mingle in plain sight exchanging secret handshakes and speaking elaborate code phrases. They meet behind closed doors to study forbidden knowledge or meddle in world affairs. And some would prefer you didn't know they existed. Let's shine the light on five societies with something to hide.

THE FREEMASONS

It's one of the world's oldest and largest fraternities, but the Freemasons don't have a website or make public appeals for new members. Instead, potential initiates must earn an invitation from high-ranking Freemasons and commit to memory elaborate rituals. This ancient men's club spawned in the Middle Ages as a professional organization for skilled carvers of stone (although some believe they originated from ancient druids or a mysterious group of warriors called the Knights Templar). Freemason ranks include George Washington, automobile pioneer Henry Ford, and composer Wolfgang Amadeus Mozart—all powerful and influential men.

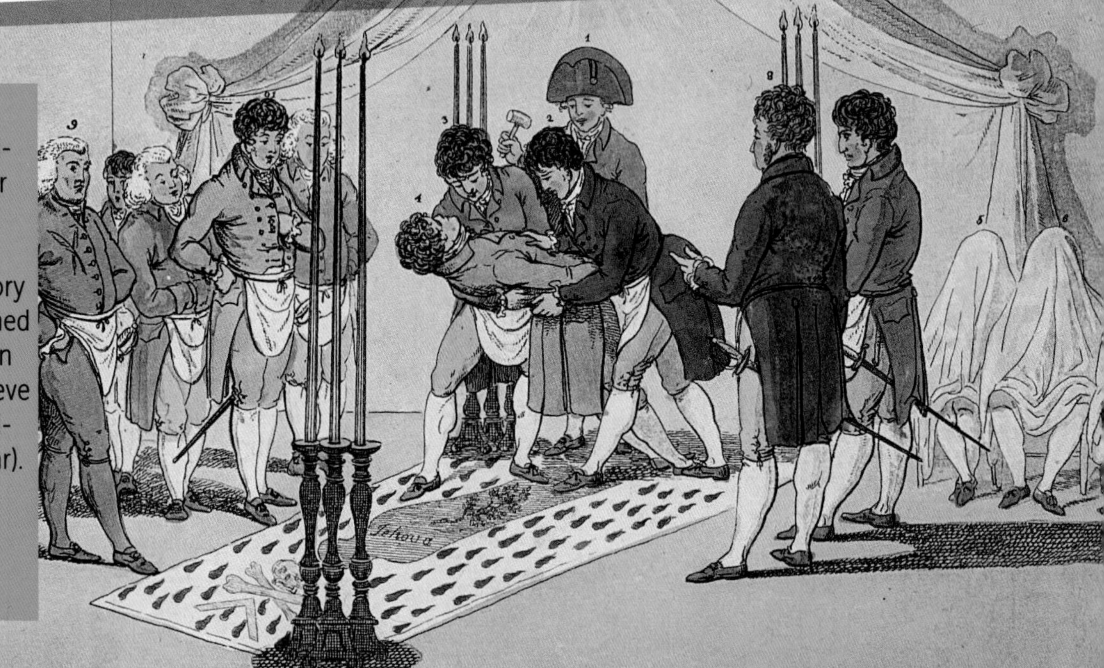

THE SENTINELESE

The most secretive society in the world lives on an island just 31 miles (50 km) from a bustling port city off the coast of Myanmar in the Indian Ocean. Outsiders have named this society the "Sentinelese" after their home, North Sentinel Island (a territory of India). No one knows what the Sentinelese call themselves, or what language they speak, or even how many members are in the tribe (estimated to be fewer than a hundred). They've lived in isolation for tens of thousands of years; outside contact is potentially fatal for the islanders because their bodies haven't developed immunity to the diseases we face every day. As commercial airliners soar overhead, the islanders fish from canoes carved from trees and wield bows and arrows to hunt. Their only modern technology is what washes ashore. Stepping foot on the island is against Indian law. It's also a bad idea. The Sentinelese are quick to defend their territory.

HERMETIC ORDER OF THE GOLDEN DAWN

Witchcraft and wizardry are far from fictitious according to the members of this secretive group, which formed in Great Britain in the 19th century to study magic, paranormal activities, and all other unexplained phenomena. The men and women who joined studied for years to rise through its ranks. Starting members were called neophytes. A well-learned master finally became a Magus. In many ways, the Hermetic Order of the Golden Dawn was like a real-life Hogwarts from the Harry Potter novels.

A member of the Hermetic Order of the Golden Dawn in ceremonial regalia, circa 1895

SKULL AND BONES

Despite its scary name—and the fact that its members meet in a secretive hall called the Tomb—Skull and Bones isn't some sinister organization. It's an exclusive social club formed by students at Yale University in 1832. Members (called Bonesmen) include former presidents, Supreme Court justices, famous writers, movie stars, and captains of industry. Conspiracy theorists claim that Skull and Bones membership is a first step to becoming a spy for the Central Intelligence Agency—a claim that the CIA denies.

UNDERCOVER OPERATION

READ LIKE AN EGYPTIAN

CRACK THE HIEROGLYPHIC CODE!

Earlier in this chapter, you learned how the Rosetta Stone helped historians decode hieroglyphs, the symbols chiseled and painted across ancient Egypt. Now you can try to translate these symbols yourself with the help of your own decoding stone presented on this page.

Like the real Rosetta Stone, this simplified version is engraved with the same message in more than one language: hieroglyphs and English. Study it well and see if you can match the Egyptian symbols with their corresponding English letters.

KEEP IN MIND:

- Hieroglyphic sentences don't have punctuation or spaces.
- They can be read in either direction.
- The animal symbols always face the start of the sentence. If they're looking left, read to the right!

NEED A RIDDLE HINT?

This chapter's code uses Egyptian hieroglyphs.

If you're still at a loss, turn to page 182 for the answer to this encrypted riddle!

HERE'S ANOTHER HINT. ⇨

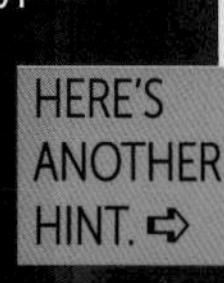

GIVE IT A TRY:

Decoding the symbols is only half the challenge here. Once you have them figured out, see if you can rewrite this 4,000-year-old message from an Egyptian scribe in hieroglyphs (then check your answer to the right):

"IF YOU HAVE ANY SENSE, YOU WILL BE A SCRIBE!"

ANSWER

Tested out new COVER STORY on colleagues at fast-food restaurant.

SECRET IDENTITIES

MET WITH SKEPTICISM, particularly the part about being an international hot-dog-eating champion.

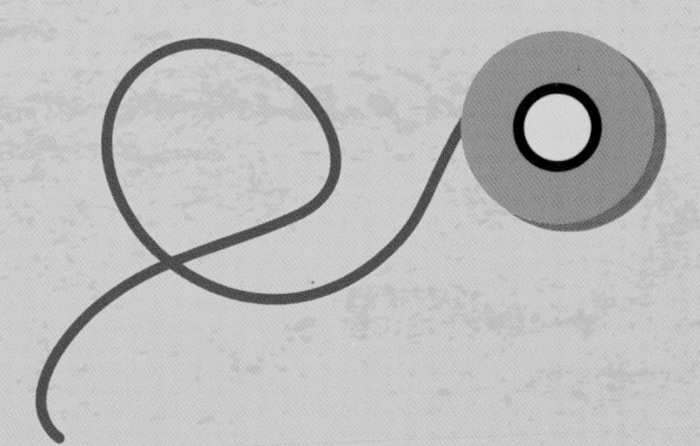

WILL REVISE.

For some professional fibbers, keeping secrets isn't just a job—it's a way of life! Spies disappear into their cover identities. Assassins blend into the night. Con artists pose as anyone who'll help make them a buck. This chapter slips into the sneaky shoes of master spies, ninja, identity thieves, pirates, and even some real-life costumed crime fighters. Some are heroes, some are villains, but they're all about to have their double lives exposed.

FADE TO BLACK

THE NINJA WERE HISTORY'S FIRST **MASTERS OF DISGUISE**

It's midnight in 16th-century Japan, and a ninja is on a mission. He must sneak into a castle and spy on the Japanese warlord who lives inside. It's dangerous work. The warlord is guarded by his loyal samurai warriors. Sliding from shadow to shadow in the moonlight, the ninja approaches the castle unseen and unheard.

The fabric of a ninja's suit was dark navy instead of true black, the better to blend in with the moonlight.

SILENT BUT VIOLENT

The roots of the ninja stretch back to the eighth century—to secretive Japanese mountain clans trained since childhood in survival, self-defense, assassination, and stealth. In one early legend, a 13-year-old ninja escaped his pursuers by climbing a bamboo tree until it swayed to the opposite bank of a river. These secretive warriors, also known as *shinobi*, emerged from the shadows in the 16th century, when hundreds of power-hungry warlords squabbled over control of Japan.

WHAT FOLLOWS IS A RIDDLE HIDDEN IN A SECRET CODE. THE ANSWER TO THIS RIDDLE IS A

During this violent "feudal" era, warlords relied on their armies of samurai—noble warriors whose code of battle forbade sneaky tactics—to defend their lands and attack rivals. But when they needed to spy on, assassinate, and create confusion among rivals, the warlords hired ninja.

SNEAK AND DESTROY

Two villages in central Japan—Iga and Koga—were centers of ninja training. The shinobi business boomed in the 16th century, as ninja hired themselves out to the highest bidder. A ninja might work for a warlord one year, and then spy on that same warlord the next. Ninja on a mission needed to blend in anywhere, from a bustling village to a castle rooftop at midnight. That meant he or she (women trained for the job, too) was a master of disguise. Ninja would dress as farmers, merchants, or musicians to slip unnoticed through the countryside. In one famous siege, a team of ninja dressed as the castle's guards and marched right through the front gate, set fire to the fortress, and then escaped as the inhabitants bickered over who started the flames.

ARMY OF ONE

The ninja on tonight's mission is infiltrating the castle solo. Slinking through the dark, with only moonlight as his guide, he carries with him all the tools he needs for tonight's dirty duty. Using a bamboo tube as a snorkel, he crosses the castle's moat like a ghost, and then unrolls his *tobibashigo*—a throwable rope ladder with hooks on the end—to scale the sheer wall. Finally, he's inside and ready to snoop. This ninja's work has just begun.

A CLOSER LOOK

Ninja were feared and despised for their sneaky tactics and supposed supernatural powers. According to legend, ninja could walk on water, vanish, and even fly. These myths were likely rooted in ninja ingenuity. They really did walk on water, using bucketlike shoes to cross castle moats. Early masters of gunpowder, ninja wielded smoke bombs to hide their escape. Their supposed flight abilities are pure myth, although ninja supposedly mastered a secret speedy walk that required no more energy than a regular pace.

DRESSED TO KILL

Ninja Gear

COWL: Two pieces of dark fabric covered a ninja's hooded face except for the eyes.

SUIT: A ninja's jacket and pants—an ensemble of dark fabric called a *shinobi shozoku*—were kept tidy by a long cloth belt, with no dangling clasps to snag on obstacles while climbing, fighting, or fleeing. Some ninja wore chain-mail armor under their outfit to blunt blows from blade-wielding foes.

SHOES: Ninja boots—called *tabi*—were stuffed with cotton for stealthy stepping and had a split toe that made climbing easier.

KATANA: A ninja's standard blade was similar to a samurai's sword but shorter. That made it easier to swing in cramped quarters and left room in the scabbard to stash blinding powder that could be flung at an enemy's eyes.

SHURIKEN: These blade-tipped metal discs—aka throwing stars—have become the ninja's calling card in karate movies. In reality, they were used only to slow pursuers.

TEKKO-KAGI: When it came time to climb, ninja slipped iron spikes onto the palms of their hands and the soles of their boots, granting them scaling skills rivaling Spider-Man's. The claws also worked as weapons and could deflect sword attacks.

SHINOBI BLOCKERS

Anti-Ninja Defenses

Japanese warlords "ninja-proofed" their castles with floors that squeaked under sneaky feet. Nails arranged along the underside of each creaky floorboard rubbed against metal clamps to produce a chirping sound (which is why the floors were called nightingale floors). Halls leading to important chambers twisted and turned to slow down and confuse intruders. These mazelike corridors cost ninja precious time in which they were more likely to be captured.

But when all else failed and the fear of ninja attacks became unbearable, many warlords simply packed up their households and fled to secret hot springs far from their castles. A soothing soak cured their ninjaphobia, but many warlords had a tricky time ruling their lands while on vacation.

CAPTAIN JANE SPARROW

PIRATE QUEEN **MARY READ** KEPT A SECRET ON **THE HIGH SEAS**

In a golden age of sneaky pirates (the late 17th and early 18th centuries), Mary Read was one of the sneakiest. She took a liking to disguises early, impersonating her late brother at a young age to weasel money from their grandmother. She maintained this ruse into adulthood, when she joined the military and fought fiercely alongside male soldiers who thought she was just one of the guys. Eventually she sailed to the Caribbean and picked up a new career after siding with mutineers: piracy.

A PIRATE'S LIFE FOR SHE

Still dressed in dude's duds, Read joined the crew of John "Calico Jack" Rackham, a charming, swashbuckling freebooter (another word for pirate). At first Calico Jack didn't suspect that Read was a woman. Pirates, a superstitious bunch, considered females aboard their ships bad luck. Read relished the pirate's life alongside her captain and Anne Bonny, another famous female pirate who dressed as a man during pillaging and plundering (when skirts got in the way).

Read's secret was safe until Bonny, dressed in women's clothes, began to flirt with her—which made Calico Jack jealous. The buccaneer captain was delighted when Read revealed she was really a

THIS BOOK. THE CODE IS BASED ON A CIPHER DESCRIBED ON PAGE 8. PERHAPS THAT IS

Mary Read (right) and Anne Bonny (left) were two of history's most famous pirates.

woman. From that point on, he opened his ship's charter to female and male freebooters alike.

THE JIG IS UP

When a pirate hunter pulled alongside Calico Jack's ship during a raucous pirate party, only Read and Bonny were brave enough to stand on deck and face their captors. Both women were sentenced to be hanged—the punishment for piracy—but they claimed they were pregnant to escape death. Read survived in prison until 1721, fading out of history near the end of the golden age of piracy.

Daring Women Dressed as Dudes

HUA MULAN (AROUND A.D. 500): Disney's 1998 animated movie *Mulan* tells the story of a girl who disguises herself as a boy to go to war in place of her aging father—and she may have been a real person (or at least inspired by a real person; in Chinese history, she looms large as a legendary figure). In most Chinese families, the sons answered the emperor's call to take up arms. Mulan had no brothers, and her father was too elderly to fight, so she dressed as a man and shouldered the family duty. Clutching an ancient sword passed down through her family for generations, Mulan headed off to fight an army of invaders known as the Huns. Her dad had taught her spectacular combat skills, which won the respect of her fellow soldiers.

CHARLEY PARKHURST (1812–1879): Navigating before GPS, fighting off bandits, controlling a team of horses—stagecoach drivers in the U.S. Wild West had it rough. The job wasn't too tough for Charley Parkhurst, aka "One-Eyed Charley" (after losing the use of an eye to a horse's kick), one of the finest stagecoach drivers around. It wasn't until Parkhurst's death that the secret came out: This daredevil driver was a woman!

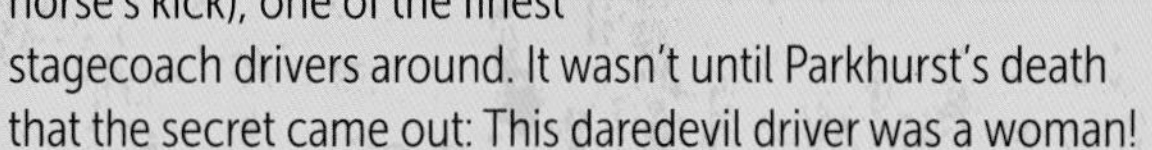

DOROTHY LAWRENCE (1896–1964): British-born Dorothy Lawrence wanted to be a journalist during World War I and report from the front lines, but the only way she could get there was in disguise. Lawrence clipped her long hair, wore bulky clothes to conceal her figure, roughed up her smooth skin, and then traveled toward the battlefields of Somme, France. There she joined soldiers who were digging underground to the German lines to plant bombs. Worried she would be discovered, Lawrence finally confessed to the commanding officer and was forced to sign a document saying that she wouldn't write about her experiences. Nevertheless, she published her fascinating account of the war after it was over.

ENOUGH INFORMATION TO SOLVE THIS RIDDLE, PERHAPS NOT. IF YOU'RE STUMPED, YOU

STARS AND SPIES

THESE CELEBS LED **DARING DOUBLE LIVES**

A celebrity who lives in the spotlight may seem an unlikely candidate for a job as a secret agent. But some leading ladies and men have used their fame to open doors—and uncover secrets. Others worked as spies before moving on to careers in the public eye. You may be surprised to learn that these famous folks were, at one time or another, agents of espionage.

ONSTAGE AND UNDERCOVER: JOSEPHINE BAKER

Josephine Baker was an American jazz singer and dancer who took Paris by storm in the 1920s. The Jazz-era icon dazzled audiences all over the world but made France her home. When Germany invaded France during World War II, Baker took action—as a spy. She helped French military officials by passing along secrets she overheard while performing throughout Europe. Her sheet music served as a cover, as she used it—and invisible ink—to smuggle her secret messages! After the war, Baker was given a military medal and inducted into France's prestigious Legion of Honour.

WILL FIND A HINT AND THE CIPHER USED AT THE END OF THIS CHAPTER. NOW GET

Look, it's a jellyfish! Wait, now it's a stingray! No, it's actually a deadly sea snake! Watching the Indo-Malayan mimic octopus is like playing a game of submarine charades. This amazing master of disguise can imitate as many as 15 dangerous sea creatures! It needs to keep up its quick-change act to survive. The mimic octopus is only two feet (60 cm) long and completely harmless—a bite-size snack for a hungry fish. But that same fish would think twice before nibbling on what it sees as a poisonous sea snake or a spiny lionfish!

Like other cephalopods (squid, octopus, and cuttlefish), the mimic octopus is covered with tiny color-shifting cells called chromatophores. It's also able to change the texture of its skin by flexing a complex network of muscles to create ridges and horns. But while many cephalopods are known to blend in with rocks and corals, only the mimic octopus copies the behaviors and appearances of living creatures. Scientists credit the little octopus's environment for these amazing powers of mimicry. It lurks on the bottom of drab Indonesian river mouths that lack rocks or corals to copy. Forced to hide in plain sight, the clever mimic imitates the next best thing—its dangerous neighbors.

SEE CREATURES

The Mimic's Masterful Disguises

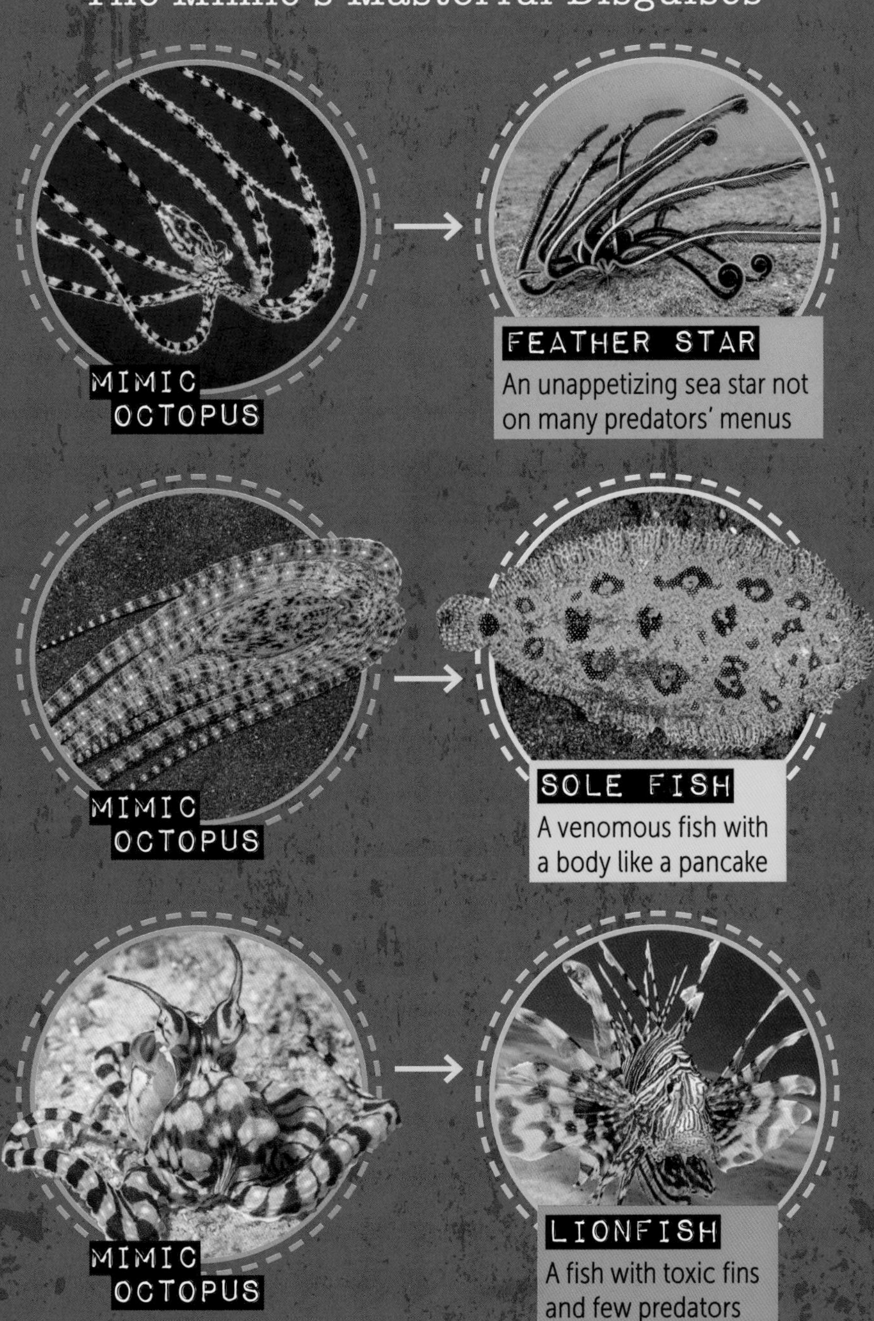

MIMIC OCTOPUS → FEATHER STAR: An unappetizing sea star not on many predators' menus

MIMIC OCTOPUS → SOLE FISH: A venomous fish with a body like a pancake

MIMIC OCTOPUS → LIONFISH: A fish with toxic fins and few predators

HIDE AND SNEAK

Secrets of Animal Camouflage

The mimic octopus's secret identities are a type of camouflage, or physical characteristics that disguise an animal's appearance. It's what helps predators sneak up on prey and enables prey to hide from predators, and it can take many forms.

BLENDING IN: This tactic involves blending into the environment. Polar bear fur matches the surrounding snow, for example. A tiger's stripes blend with the tall grass of its hunting range. Some animals' appearances change with the season. The arctic fox's fur shifts from brown to white in wintertime.

ARCTIC FOX

STANDING OUT: Standing out from the crowd is a bad thing for animals that live in herds or schools, so they often sport camouflage that makes them blend in with each other rather than the environment. A zebra's vibrant stripes serve two functions: They break up the animal's shape (a tactic known as disruptive coloration) as well as match the fur of its herd neighbors, making it hard for a lion to see where one zebra ends and the next one begins.

COPYCATTING: Some animals are mimics, or look-alikes of other animals or objects. A Southeast Asian insect called the walking leaf looks just like a tree leaf. It even sways while it walks to imitate a leaf blowing in the wind! Many creatures copy the appearance of toxic animals that share their habitat. Predators mistake these mimics for the real thing and back off to avoid deadly bites or upset bellies.

WALKING LEAF

CLASSIFIED CASE

MEET THE SNEAKIEST SPY OF ALL

THE DOUBLE AGENT WHO **DOUBLE-CROSSED HIS DOUBLE-CROSSERS**

During World War II, on the night of December 16, 1942, a mysterious man parachuted out of a plane over England, carrying a radio transmitter, a pistol, and some invisible ink. He was a spy for the Germans, and he had an assignment. He had been told to disappear into the criminal underworld and plan the explosion of an aircraft factory where British military planes were being built. But the spy did not follow those orders. Instead, he immediately turned himself in to the British and made them an offer. He would pretend to keep working for the Germans while actually serving the British. They agreed to his plan, and Eddie Chapman, double agent, reported for double duty.

FROM THIEF TO SPY

Chapman was British himself. So why did he work for the Germans? Before he was a spy, he was a thief with a knack for breaking open safes. While on a trip to the Channel Islands, not far from England, he was arrested and sent to prison. Soon after, the Germans invaded and occupied the area. When Chapman's jail term was over, he wanted to go home to England. So he offered to work there for the Germans—as a spy. He was sent for training and given the code name Fritz.

VITAL STATS	
NAME	Eddie Chapman
CODE NAMES	Fritz (German); Zigzag (British)
BEST KNOWN FOR	Faking the explosion of an aircraft factory where British military planes were being built

A year later, upon landing in England and switching to the British side, he got a new code name: Zigzag. The first order of business was to fake the explosion at the aircraft factory. The British arranged for a story to appear in the newspaper, reporting an "explosion at a factory on the outskirts of London." They created a scene of Chapman's supposed success, scattering debris from a bogus blast and painting the roof to make it look as if it had been badly damaged. Their ruse worked. The Germans were so pleased with Chapman, in fact, that they awarded him a military medal called the Iron Cross. And they continued to trust the false reports that he shared with them.

LIFESAVING LIES

A few months after the fake explosion, the Germans instructed Chapman to plant a bomb on a British ship. He followed orders, but promptly informed the ship's captain, foiling the Germans' plan. Then, in 1944, the Germans wanted to know whether their missiles were reaching their targets in England. Chapman tricked them again, and his misleading information ensured that Germany would direct its bombs to areas with fewer people. Chapman's lies likely saved many lives.

Chapman was eventually pardoned for the crimes he committed before the war. He died in 1997 at the age of 83. Four years later, the British declassified his file, revealing countless details about his time as both Fritz and Zigzag—and proving that a double agent really is twice as sneaky as a standard spy.

Chapman foiled the Germans' plan to destroy a British ship, like the one pictured here.

TOP SECRET

JAMES ARMISTEAD

DARING OR DECEITFUL?

When it comes to double agents, it depends on whom you ask.

JAMES ARMISTEAD, a slave from Virginia, was a double agent in the Revolutionary War who helped the American colonists defeat the British. He signed on to spy for both sides, but he was loyal to the colonists, providing key information in advance of the critical Battle of Yorktown. Armistead served under General Marquis de Lafayette, who later petitioned for Armistead's freedom. Armistead was emancipated, and in gratitude, he adopted Lafayette's surname.

OLEG PENKOVSKY was a Soviet intelligence officer who secretly aided both the United States and Britain during the Cold War. The information he passed along helped the United States avoid a nuclear conflict with the former Soviet Union. To the American and British officers he assisted, he was known by the code name Hero. But to the Soviets, he was a traitor. In 1963, they sentenced him to death.

ROBERT HANSSEN is considered to have been one of the most damaging spies in U.S. history. He joined the Federal Bureau of Investigation (FBI) in 1976. Three years later, he started selling secrets to Russia, which was known as the Soviet Union up until 1992. After he gave them the names of Russian agents who were secretly spying for the United States, at least two were arrested and executed. He also shared that the U.S. government had dug an eavesdropping tunnel underneath the Russian embassy in Washington, D.C. Hanssen continued to spy for the Russians, off and on, until he was caught in 2001. The following year, he pleaded guilty to espionage, claiming, "I am ashamed." He was sentenced to life in prison.

THE MAN WITH EIGHT LIVES

HOW ONE **MASTER IMPOSTOR** HAD EVERYONE **FOOLED**

Poster for the movie *Catch Me If You Can*

An airline pilot, teacher, doctor, and lawyer—all before the age of 21—Frank Abagnale, Jr., had a résumé that seemed too busy to be true. And it was! Abagnale was a master of making things up. After swindling banks by writing phony checks, he decided to impersonate an airline pilot so he could get free airfare. And this was before he even turned 17! His career as a master of bogus identities had just begun. Within five years, it would end in a way you'd never expect.

Frank Abagnale, Jr., posing as a pilot

FLIGHT OF FANTASY

Posing as a pilot, Abagnale traveled the world for two years in the 1960s, charging hotel rooms and food to the airline. But soon he decided he needed a new identity to stay one step ahead of the law. Abagnale went on to impersonate a pediatrician and, after forging a transcript from Harvard Law School, an attorney. He even got a job at the Louisiana State Attorney General's office before his 20th birthday. Eventually he had assumed at least eight identities, none of them legit. An escape artist as well as a master of disguise, Abagnale gave police the slip twice. After one capture, he relied on his impostor skills to convince the guards he was a prison inspector. They cut him loose. Then his luck finally ran out.

SWITCHING SIDES

The master con artist was caught in France in 1969. He had to answer for fraud committed across the globe, serving sentences in French and Swedish prisons before getting sent back to the United States for more time behind bars. In 1974, the U.S. government made Abagnale an offer he couldn't refuse. They let him go if he agreed to become one of the good guys, serving the FBI as an expert on criminals who had led an impostor lifestyle, too. Today he runs his own security firm. The former fraudster now helps banks and other businesses avoid people just like him. His life story was turned into the 2002 Steven Spielberg movie *Catch Me If You Can.*

FBI OFFICIAL SEAL

POSER PARADE

Famous Phony-Balonies

PRINCESS CARABOO: Mary Willcocks, a shoemaker's daughter from Devon, England, knew that the key to a foolproof secret identity was a good backstory—and she had a whopper. In 1817, she put on strange clothes and invented an exotic language to convince people in the English countryside that she was a princess from an island off the coast of India. She claimed she had escaped from pirates and used her exotic tale to make a comfortable living among the rich and famous.

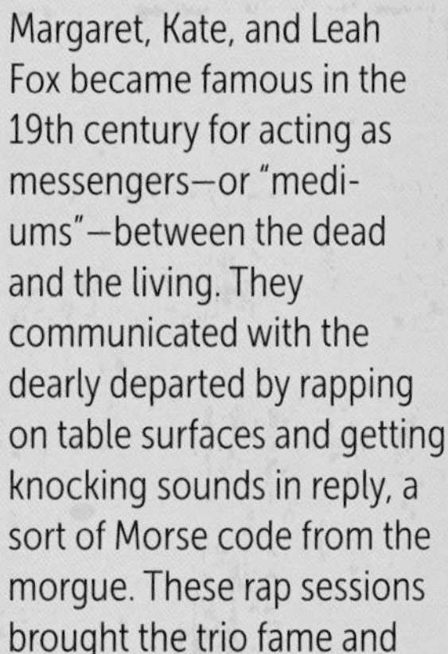

THE FOX SISTERS: Margaret, Kate, and Leah Fox became famous in the 19th century for acting as messengers—or "mediums"—between the dead and the living. They communicated with the dearly departed by rapping on table surfaces and getting knocking sounds in reply, a sort of Morse code from the morgue. These rap sessions brought the trio fame and followers. In 1888, however, Margaret Fox confessed that the whole thing was a sham. The girls were making the knocking noises by cracking their toes and knuckles. Despite her admission, belief in mediums continues today.

BRIDGE SALESMAN: George C. Parker seemed like the ultimate salesman in the 1900s, especially if you were newly arrived in the "land of opportunity." He gained fame for approaching tourists and immigrants in New York City and selling them some of the city's most amazing landmarks. The Brooklyn Bridge, the Statue of Liberty, Grant's Tomb, the Metropolitan Museum of Art—all were up for sale, and Parker found plenty of buyers. There was just one problem: He didn't own these landmarks. He had forged documents and worked from a phony office to gain the trust of his victims. Some weeks he managed to sell the Brooklyn Bridge twice! Eventually, Parker's ruse ran its course. He was caught and sentenced to life in New York's Sing Sing Prison in 1928 for his many swindles.

HISTORY'S MYSTERY PEOPLE

WHO WERE THESE FAMOUS INDIVIDUALS? **NOBODY KNOWS.**

A prisoner, a bystander, a spy, and a fugitive all have left their mark on history without leaving a single fingerprint. The true identities of these famous figures have eluded expert and amateur sleuths alike. So we can reveal their stories, but not their names.

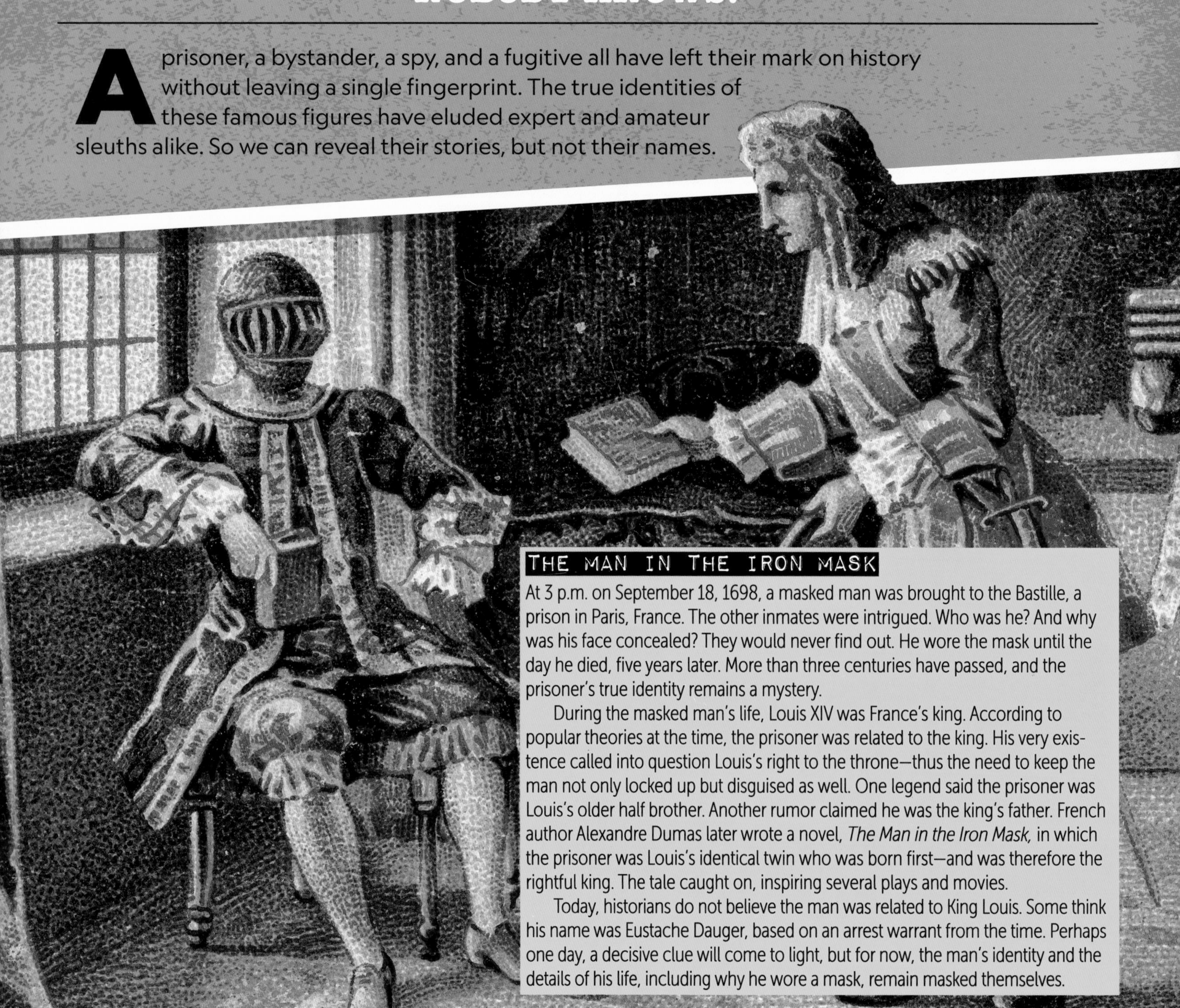

THE MAN IN THE IRON MASK

At 3 p.m. on September 18, 1698, a masked man was brought to the Bastille, a prison in Paris, France. The other inmates were intrigued. Who was he? And why was his face concealed? They would never find out. He wore the mask until the day he died, five years later. More than three centuries have passed, and the prisoner's true identity remains a mystery.

During the masked man's life, Louis XIV was France's king. According to popular theories at the time, the prisoner was related to the king. His very existence called into question Louis's right to the throne—thus the need to keep the man not only locked up but disguised as well. One legend said the prisoner was Louis's older half brother. Another rumor claimed he was the king's father. French author Alexandre Dumas later wrote a novel, *The Man in the Iron Mask,* in which the prisoner was Louis's identical twin who was born first—and was therefore the rightful king. The tale caught on, inspiring several plays and movies.

Today, historians do not believe the man was related to King Louis. Some think his name was Eustache Dauger, based on an arrest warrant from the time. Perhaps one day, a decisive clue will come to light, but for now, the man's identity and the details of his life, including why he wore a mask, remain masked themselves.

THE BABUSHKA LADY

After President John F. Kennedy's assassination in 1963, authorities tracked down as many witnesses as they could find. But one woman who showed up in several photos of the crowd could not be identified. She was nicknamed Babushka Lady because of her Russian-style headscarf. (*Babushka* is the Russian word for grandmother.) She wore sunglasses; a long, tan coat; and appeared to be holding a camera. Even after gunshots were fired and the crowd fled, she stayed in one place and—it seems—kept taking pictures. She has never been found, and unlike other witnesses, never came forward, leading some to wonder if her coat and scarf were part of an elaborate disguise.

In 1970, a woman named Beverly Oliver claimed that she was the Babushka Lady and that agents from the Federal Bureau of Investigation (FBI) had confiscated her camera. But many aspects of her story did not add up. For example, she claimed to have been using a type of camera that had not yet been released in 1963. To this day, nobody knows who the Babushka Lady really is—or what clues may be hidden in the pictures she did not share.

PERSEUS THE SPY

During World War II, a group of American scientists worked to develop the world's first atomic bomb. The project was top secret, but the Soviet Union (now Russia) found out about it anyway. How? Some of the scientists leaked classified information to Soviet agents.

The FBI uncovered the identities of some of those scientists. But in the 1990s, a former Soviet spy wrote about a high-level source who was never caught. The spy claimed that the source was a physicist who went by the code name Perseus. Who was he? Over the years, the scientific community has raised suggestions and even accusations. But Perseus's identity—if there even was a Perseus—remains a mystery.

D.B. COOPER

A neatly dressed man identifying himself as Dan (aka D. B.) Cooper boarded a Boeing 727 at Portland International Airport in Oregon, U.S.A., in 1971 and soared into the night to become history's most mysterious fugitive. Claiming he had a bomb in his briefcase, Cooper demanded that the plane land at Seattle's airport, where he was to receive $200,000 and four parachutes.

When his demands were met, Cooper released the passengers and ordered the pilots to take off and fly him to Mexico at the lowest speed and altitude possible. Once in the air, Cooper lowered the plane's rear stairs and parachuted into the rainy night over the wilderness of southwestern Washington.

Although no body was found, FBI investigators believe that the hijacker who called himself Dan Cooper didn't survive his jump. A boy hiking near the jump site in 1980 stumbled upon $5,800 of the ransom cash, but the fate of the mysterious skyjacker and his money are still a mystery. The FBI closed its case on Cooper for good in 2016. Amateur sleuths, authors, and TV producers continue digging for clues, hoping to reveal the man behind the legend, dead or alive.

UP AND AWAY!

REAL-LIFE SUPERHEROES LEAD DOUBLE LIVES TO SAVE THE DAY

Billionaire Bruce Wayne dons a utility belt and cowl to become Batman. Brainy Peter Parker web-swings as Spider-Man. Clumsy Clark Kent soars as Superman. The secrets have long been spilled on the alter egos of heroes in comic books. If you want to find a superhero with his or her secret identity intact, you need to look in an unlikely place: real life. Costumed crusaders are out there, not up in the sky, but patrolling the neighborhood, visiting children's hospitals, helping the helpless. They're members of the "real-life superhero movement," a worldwide unofficial brother- and sisterhood of average citizens inspired by comic-book legends to dress up, head out, and make the world a better place.

CAPES OF GOOD HOPE

By day they're accountants and security guards, teachers and gardeners. By night, real-life superheroes don capes and cool costumes before taking to the streets on the prowl for people in need. Although they lack superpowers, these Good Samaritans in spandex share some characteristics with their comic-book inspirations. They carry utility belts and backpacks filled with essential neighbor-helping tools: flashlights, cell phones, sturdy cameras, and laser pointers. They have cool superhero names: KnightVigil, The Crimson Fist, and Master Legend, to name a few. They've created their own origin stories and personas. Their real-life identities typically remain a secret.

COSPLAY CRUSADERS

The real-life superhero movement's origin story begins in the late 1990s, when a masked Mexican folk hero calling himself Superbarrio donned red tights and a yellow cape to organize rallies and protests in support of poor families. Today, real-life superheroes swing to the rescue everywhere from Argentina to the United States, handing out food to the homeless, walking people home in dangerous neighborhoods, changing tires, carrying groceries for the elderly, reporting crimes, and engaging in other helpful activities. Some have even formed leagues of like-minded do-gooders, including Team Justice, which takes donations to buy toys for needy children. The Avengers would be proud.

SUPERB

SECRET IDENTITIES

The League of Extraordinary People

NYX

BASE OF OPERATIONS: New York City and New Jersey, U.S.A.

SUPERPOWER: Powerful intuition and deep sense of empathy. She organizes patrols to look after homeless people in her area of operation.

CIVITRON

BASE OF OPERATIONS: Salem, Massachusetts, U.S.A.

SUPERPOWER: Amazing marketing skills. Organizes events for charity and street cleanups.

THANATOS

BASE OF OPERATIONS: Vanco
British Columbia, Canada

SUPERPOWER: Extreme gene
Hands out dry socks, rain slick
and canned food to people li
on the streets.

LIFE

BASE OF OPERATIONS: New York City

SUPERPOWER: Outstanding organizational skills. Co-founded Superheroes Anonymous to unite other real-life superheroes in making a difference.

DC GUARDIAN

BASE OF OPERATIONS: Washington, D.C.

SUPERPOWER: Extreme courage and super patriotism. Co-founded Skiffy-Town League of Heroes to provide costumed assistance for the Make-A-Wish Foundation, Juvenile Diabetes Research Foundation, and other organizations that help children.

UNDERCOVER OPERATION

MAKING CHANGE

HOW TO BECOME A **MASTER OF DISGUISE**

When movie spies need a new look fast, they slip on a high-tech latex mask or a holographic disguise and—voilà—instant makeover! You don't have access to such movie magic, but you can raid greater resources: your closet and your imagination. Here's a guide to using both to create a look that might not exactly fool your friends but will make them look twice (and maybe make them laugh).

PLAYING THE PART

Hats and headbands can change up your look in a pinch, but don't neglect the fashion accessory on your head: your hair! Do your do in a way that doesn't look like you. Part it a different way. Make a bun. Braid it. Even don a wig if you really want a new look!

FACING FACTS

A good spy needs to fit in, not stand out. That means you'll want to stay away from phony beards and eye patches, unless you're blending in with a crew of hairy pirates. Dark sunglasses are an easy way to disguise your eyes, one of your most recognizable features.

DITCH THE FAKE STUFF

NEED A RIDDLE HINT?

This chapter's code uses a keyboard cipher shifted one space right (read about it on page 8).

If you're still at a loss, turn to page 182 for the answer to this encrypted riddle!

HERE'S ANOTHER HINT.

DON'T DRESS FOR EXCESS

When you go raiding your closet, don't dress up—dress for successful spying. Look for outfits that won't look out of place with the group or event you're trying to snoop on. Wear a superhero T-shirt if you're going to a sci-fi convention, for instance. You'll want clothes you don't normally wear, too, so borrow duds from an older sibling or close buddy. If you have a shirt you can wear inside out, wear it! You might need to flip it to give counter-operatives the slip!

COVER STORY

Your disguise should go beyond your physical appearance. You'll want to hide your past, too, so people won't know you're you. Invent a backstory (aka your legend). Say you're a distant relative in your family or a student from far, far away. You want a legend that's believable but forgettable. Make it more convincing by highlighting specific phony experiences or maybe talking with an accent.

WALK THIS WAY

Your friends will likely recognize you up close, but you can throw them off from far away by walking in a new way. Try moving your arms with a little more gusto or taking longer steps than usual. If you tend to slouch, stand up straight or vice versa. Practice your new walk before you hit the field. A clumsy stumble would be worse than embarrassing—it might blow your cover!

CHARM OFFENSIVE

Adapt your personality to blend with the group you're snooping on. If you're at a sporting event, cheer for the home team. If you're with a quiet group and you're normally the life of the party, clam up and fit in. Being a spy involves more than just playing a part. You'll need to live the role.

PLAY ALONG

Escape set for MIDNIGHT TONIGHT.

SECRET PLANS

HACKSAW HIDDEN in meatball sandwich. Meatball sandwich was particularly DELICIOUS.

Think about the biggest secret anyone's ever told you. Now consider what would happen if you let it slip. Maybe you'd embarrass a buddy or lose some cool points within your social circle. Now imagine if spilling the beans cost someone's freedom or life or the fate of a nation at war. This chapter is crammed with such high-stakes secrets. Few once knew the plots we're about to reveal to you. They were hatched in hidden bunkers, the back rooms of government agencies, or behind the bars of prison cells. Desperate times call for supreme acts of sneakiness, as you'll see in the following tales of great escapes and daring schemes.

ESCAPE POSTPONED until new hacksaw procured.

SNEAK ATTACKS

FAMOUS **VICTORIES** THROUGH **DECEIT**

You'd expect a book called *The Art of War* to offer lots of tips about waging big battles. Instead, this 2,500-year-old tome—written by a Chinese tactician named Sun Tzu—teaches how to *avoid* battles by outwitting the enemy using sneakiness and smarts. Sun Tzu would approve of these four famous victories.

THE TROJAN HORSE
ANCIENT CITY OF TROY, CIRCA 1200 B.C.

After laying siege to the city of Troy for a decade with nothing to show for it, the armies of Greece packed up their camp, boarded their ships, and headed for home. But they left a parting gift: a titanic wooden horse parked right outside Troy's gates.

You probably know what happened next. The Trojan horse is the most famous case of a "ruse of war," or the use of deceit to achieve victory. Relieved that the long siege was over, the citizens of Troy hauled the horse into their city and partied late into the night. As the Trojans slept off their celebration, Greek soldiers hidden in the horse's belly emerged and opened the city gates. The Greek army, which had only pretended to sail home, swarmed into Troy and conquered it.

Whether the horse really existed or is just a tale from Greek mythology, its legend has inspired popular phrases, pieces of art—and even our software. A Trojan horse is the name for any computer program that's supposed to do one thing but secretly attacks your computer.

WHAT FOLLOWS IS A RIDDLE HIDDEN IN A SECRET CODE. THE ANSWER TO THIS RIDDLE IS A

OPERATION GREIF
BELGIUM, 1944

When Germany's Adolf Hitler wanted to take control of crucial bridges in Belgium, he hatched one of World War II's sneakiest schemes: Operation Greif. Led by Nazi commando Otto Skorzeny, the mission involved dressing German troops in the uniforms of American soldiers (their foes) and sneaking them behind enemy lines, along with captured U.S. tanks and vehicles.

Skorzeny was unable to gather enough vehicles and English-speaking troops to succeed in capturing the bridges, but his disguised men still managed to confuse U.S. forces. They messed with road signs, passed along phony orders, and spread paranoia among their foes. U.S. soldiers began to question whether any allies they met were secretly Germans in disguise, which resulted in fatal cases of mistaken identity and at least one high-ranking U.S. officer being grilled at gunpoint until he could prove who he was.

OTTO SKORZENY

WASHINGTON'S GAMBLE
TRENTON, NEW JERSEY, U.S.A., 1776

Dodging floating chunks of ice in the dark and paddling through bone-chilling sleet, General George Washington led his force of roughly 2,400 Continental Army soldiers across the freezing Delaware River—and into the history books—on Christmas night in 1776. The general was desperate for a victory to inspire his troops, many dressed in rags and weary from defeat, and he thought a surprise attack via this dangerous route might just catch the enemy off guard.

The tactic worked. Washington's men managed to surprise and defeat an encampment of British-paid German mercenaries in Trenton, New Jersey. Victory at the Battle of Trenton boosted morale and recruitment for the Continental Army. It's one of history's most famous sneak attacks.

ARMY OF NONE
EUROPE, 1944

Tanks clashed and artillery blasted across the battlefields of World War II, but for the 1,100 men of the 23rd Headquarters Special Troops, it was all a big game of pretend. This contingent of artists and actors, special-effects experts and set designers was tasked with staging battles using inflatable tanks and jeeps, wooden cannons, and phony planes poised on painted runways. Audio engineers blared the sounds of skirmishes—explosions, screaming tank engines, and infantry commands—from speakers across the bogus battlefield, while radio operators broadcast phony chatter. What was the point of all this pretend combat? To convince the German army that a 30,000-man Allied force was in their midst, thus distracting their attention from real soldiers and vehicles. The 23rd logged 21 operations, some so successful that German soldiers surrendered to the dummy tanks!

BUSY BODY

THE BURIAL PLOT THAT **HELPED WIN A WAR**

Major William Martin of the British Royal Marines managed to sneak behind enemy lines, fool one of Germany's top spies, and clear the way for an Allied invasion in World War II.

Not bad for a dead guy.

Martin wasn't some zombie super-soldier. He was the central figure in Operation Mincemeat, one of the most successful deceptions in the history of sneaky warfare. William Martin wasn't even his real name.

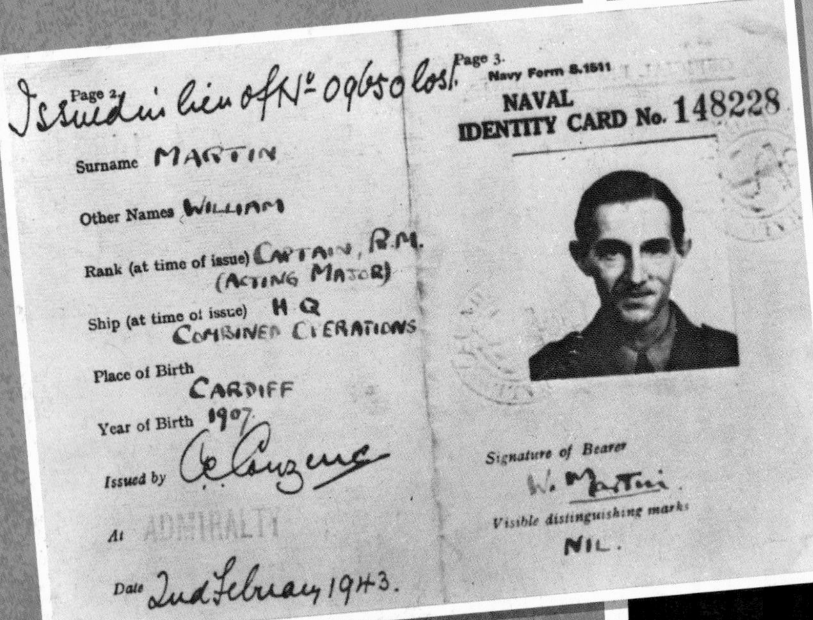

Page 2. Issued in lieu of No 09650 lost.

Surname MARTIN

Other Names WILLIAM

Rank (at time of issue) CAPTAIN, R.M. (ACTING MAJOR)

Ship (at time of issue) H Q COMBINED OPERATIONS

Place of Birth CARDIFF

Year of Birth 1907.

Issued by [signature]

At ADMIRALTY

Date 2nd February 1943.

Page 3. Navy Form S.1511

NAVAL IDENTITY CARD No. 148228

Signature of Bearer W. Martin

Visible distinguishing marks NIL.

His identity—and the entire operation—was devised in 1943 by two cunning English intelligence officers, Charles Cholmondeley and Ewen Montagu. Their big idea: Find a recently deceased man who looked like he had perished at sea, dress him in a British military uniform, equip him with secret—but bogus—military documents, and set him adrift so the Germans would find him. Pulling it off required a vast cast of characters, intense planning, and loads of luck.

DESCRIBED ON PAGE 9. PERHAPS THAT IS ENOUGH INFORMATION TO SOLVE THIS RIDDLE,

NEW LIFE

After tracking down the perfect corpse (Welshman Glyndwr Michael) and renaming him William Martin, Cholmondeley and Montagu set about giving the body a life of his own. They filled his wallet and pockets with personal letters and receipts, fake IDs and photographs. They even included a picture of Martin's phony fiancée, Pam (actually a clerk in the intelligence office). With his background built, Martin was ready for his most essential accessory—a briefcase stuffed with military plans for an invasion of Greece, handcuffed to his cold wrist. Sealed in a casket of dry ice to stave off rot, Major Martin was ready for his mission.

PAM, THE PHONY FIANCÉE

TAKING THE BAIT

A Royal Navy submarine dumped Martin near the port of Huelva, Spain, home of a notorious German spy named Adolf Clauss. A local fisherman found Martin, and soon the body and his briefcase caught Clauss's attention. When Spanish authorities returned Martin's body to the British, it was clear that the secret documents had been seen. Intelligence officials dispatched a message to British prime minister Winston Churchill, who had been following the operation: "Mincemeat swallowed whole."

German leaders—including Adolf Hitler—fell for the trick. They dispatched their troops to the decoy invasion point detailed in the phony documents. That left Sicily, site of the real invasion, lightly defended. Countless Allied forces were spared from a brutal battle. And all because of a bobbing mystery major named William Martin.

Knowing that German spies read England's newspapers, British intelligence reported the death of Major William Martin in the *Times* of London—just another bit of backstory for the make-believe major.

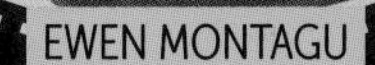

EWEN MONTAGU

A CLOSER LOOK

Cholmondeley and Montagu worked for the Twenty Committee, the British intelligence team in charge of recruiting double agents. The Committee's name was inspired by the Roman numerals XX, or "double cross." Clever, huh?

PERHAPS NOT. IF YOU'RE STUMPED, YOU WILL FIND A HINT AND THE CIPHER USED AT THE

POCKET THAT ROCKET

THE CIA **STOLE A SOVIET SPACECRAFT ...** AND GAVE IT RIGHT BACK

It was early evening, and the truck was on its way to the railroad station. It was carrying an enormous crate that was supposed to be loaded onto a train. But just before the truck reached its destination, a group of government agents intervened.

They pulled over the vehicle, and escorted its driver away. A new driver jumped in and drove the truck—and its cargo—to a nearby junkyard surrounded by a 10-foot (3-m)-high fence. He backed in through a narrow alley, and the gates slammed shut.

END OF THIS CHAPTER. NOW GET CRACKING! HERE IS THE ENCODED RIDDLE: SNSJALJ SHH

All was silent for 30 minutes as the agents waited to make sure they had not been followed. Then two men got to work opening the crate. With several planks removed, they could now see inside. There lay their stolen prize: the Lunik, a Soviet spacecraft. If they wanted to avoid getting caught, they would have to work quickly. The team—officers in the U.S. Central Intelligence Agency (CIA)—braced themselves for a busy night.

RACE TO THE MOON

In 1959, the United States was racing to outdo the Soviet Union (now Russia) in the field of space exploration. The Soviets were winning the race. They had already sent up an Earth-orbiting satellite called Sputnik, and had built a new type of spacecraft to explore the moon. Though it became widely known as the Lunik, its official name was Luna, the Russian word for "moon." Multiple Lunik spacecraft were to be developed. Some would orbit the moon, and others would land on it. (See "To the Moon" below.) All would be uncrewed, meaning that no people would ride inside.

The Soviets were so proud of their Lunik moon explorers that they included one in a special exhibition about the Soviet Union that traveled to several countries, including the United States. A team of CIA officers went to the show to check out the competition. They expected to see just a model of the Lunik but were stunned to discover an actual spacecraft on display. To get a closer look, they hatched a plan to take the Lunik for one night only. If all went according to plan, the Soviets would not suspect a thing.

FROM NOSE TO TAIL

The agents kidnapped the Lunik as it was being transported from one city to another. They learned that the spacecraft was scheduled to sit on a parked train overnight and figured nobody would miss it if it spent the night at the junkyard instead. They would make sure to return the Lunik to its train car before its scheduled departure the next morning.

On the eve of the heist, the four agents tasked with examining the Lunik got to work around 7:30 p.m. After dropping ladders over the side of the crate, they climbed in. Two people focused on the nose of the space probe, and two studied the tail.

The agents dissected the spacecraft carefully, knowing they would need to reassemble it. One window was pried off, as was the cap of the engine compartment. The engine was not inside—it had been removed for the exhibition—but there was still plenty to examine. The agents took meticulous notes and dozens of photos.

Once the spies had all the information needed, they repaired what they had taken apart. Then they double-checked each compartment, making sure that not even a scrap of paper was left behind. By 4 a.m., they had closed up the crate. They drove it to the train station and sent the moon craft on its way.

The mission was a success. The team had a chance to examine the Soviets' prized moon probe inside and out, and they managed to do it without leaving a trace. In 1967, a CIA report concluded: "To this day, there has been no indication the Soviets ever discovered that the Lunik was borrowed for a night."

TO THE MOON

Between 1959 and 1976, the Soviets launched multiple Luna space probes. Some of those launches made history.

JANUARY 1959
Luna 1 misses the moon, but becomes the first spacecraft to fall into orbit around the sun.

SEPTEMBER 1959
Luna 2 becomes the first spacecraft to reach the moon.

OCTOBER 1959
Luna 3 takes the first photos of the far side of the moon.

FEBRUARY 1966
Luna 9 becomes the first spacecraft to land on—rather than crash into—the moon.

NOVEMBER 1970
Luna 17 delivers a robot vehicle to explore the moon.

1959 1962 1965 1968 1971

CLMK LY KQESMK, XK VCL KJRKP RCDQ YLPRPKQQ DJ RCK NSX. DR DQ S PLEG QTPPLTJAKA NX

ESCAPE ACADEMY

COLDITZ CASTLE **COULDN'T HOLD** WORLD WAR II'S **BREAKOUT STARS**

Soldiers taken prisoner during World War II might have lost their battles, but they could still help win the war. Allied troops were under orders to escape by any means necessary, a tactic that tied up the enemy's time and resources. Prisoners even had a term for a successful getaway: a home run. The Germans locked up the Allies' most habitual jailbreakers in Oflag IV-C, a camp walled inside a 15th-century fortress called Colditz Castle. But by imprisoning so many home-run plotters in one spot, the Germans had unwittingly created a training ground for escape artists, a sort of Hogwarts for the sneaky arts. The result: Colditz captives scored more than 30 home runs.

A KEEP FOR SAFEKEEPING

The medieval castle of Colditz was built on a rocky outcrop overlooking the River Mulde near Leipzig, Germany. It served as a residence, hunting lodge, and mental hospital before the Germans turned it into a prisoner-of-war camp in 1939. Surrounded on three sides by precipitous plunges and staffed by more guards than it had captives, Colditz was deemed escapeproof.

ESCAPE ARTISTS

Oflag IV-C was home to more than 600 Allied prisoners during its run as a prison camp. They hailed from Great Britain, France, Belgium, Poland, and the United States, but the captives all had one thing in common: a knack for breaking out. The prisoners pooled their talents for document forgery, toolmaking, map-reading, tunnel engineering, and lock-picking to orchestrate escape after escape.

QCSPG-DJYKQRKA VSRKPQ. JLNLAX BKRQ LTR SHDUK TJRDH RCK QKJRKJEK KJAQ.

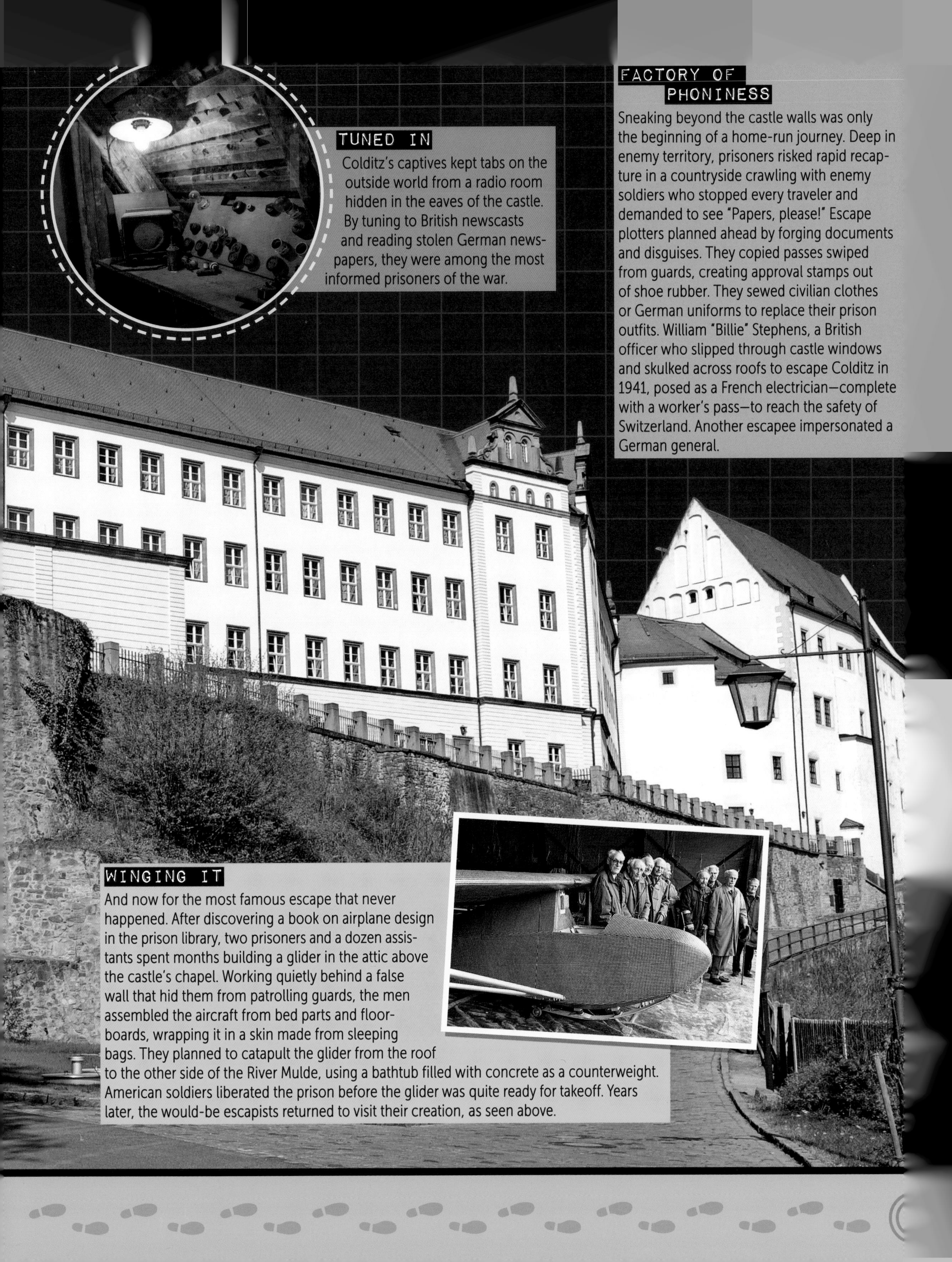

TUNED IN

Colditz's captives kept tabs on the outside world from a radio room hidden in the eaves of the castle. By tuning to British newscasts and reading stolen German newspapers, they were among the most informed prisoners of the war.

FACTORY OF PHONINESS

Sneaking beyond the castle walls was only the beginning of a home-run journey. Deep in enemy territory, prisoners risked rapid recapture in a countryside crawling with enemy soldiers who stopped every traveler and demanded to see "Papers, please!" Escape plotters planned ahead by forging documents and disguises. They copied passes swiped from guards, creating approval stamps out of shoe rubber. They sewed civilian clothes or German uniforms to replace their prison outfits. William "Billie" Stephens, a British officer who slipped through castle windows and skulked across roofs to escape Colditz in 1941, posed as a French electrician—complete with a worker's pass—to reach the safety of Switzerland. Another escapee impersonated a German general.

WINGING IT

And now for the most famous escape that never happened. After discovering a book on airplane design in the prison library, two prisoners and a dozen assistants spent months building a glider in the attic above the castle's chapel. Working quietly behind a false wall that hid them from patrolling guards, the men assembled the aircraft from bed parts and floorboards, wrapping it in a skin made from sleeping bags. They planned to catapult the glider from the roof to the other side of the River Mulde, using a bathtub filled with concrete as a counterweight. American soldiers liberated the prison before the glider was quite ready for takeoff. Years later, the would-be escapists returned to visit their creation, as seen above.

CLASSIFIED CASE

THE REAL-LIFE WILLY WONKA

MEET THE **CHOCOLATE MAKER** WITH A **STRIKING RESEMBLANCE** TO THE FICTIONAL **CANDY MAN**

Nobody ever goes in, and nobody ever comes out. So says the tinker in a famous scene from *Willy Wonka and the Chocolate Factory*. In the movie, as in the Roald Dahl book it is based on, Wonka locks up his factory after spies dressed as workers steal his secret recipes. He gets back to candymaking, with the help of workers called Oompa Loompas, but he keeps the factory's great iron gates closed to everyone else—that is, until the day he invites five golden-ticket winners inside.

Wonka is a fictional character. But the real-life head of a famous chocolate company was known for being just as secretive. Italian entrepreneur Michele Ferrero ran his family's sweets business for 66 years, launching Nutella, Kinder treats, and other confectionary favorites. Under his leadership, the candy company was wildly successful. It was also shrouded in mystery, leading many to compare Ferrero with Wonka.

VITAL STATS	
NAME	Michele Ferrero
LOCATION	Italy
BEST KNOWN FOR	Running the secretive company that makes the popular chocolate-hazelnut spread Nutella

THE CANDY MAN

Ferrero was born into the chocolate-making business. In the 1940s, his father, Pietro, invented a chocolaty treat that he sold around town. At the time, cocoa—chocolate's key ingredient—was very expensive. Pietro cut costs by combining a small amount of cocoa with lower-priced items, including hazelnuts and molasses. The result was thick, creamy, and more affordable than other chocolaty treats. It was so popular that in 1946 the Ferrero family started a company to manufacture and sell it.

When Pietro died just three years later, Michele took his father's place. He grew the company, adding factories throughout Europe and eventually around the world. In the early 1960s, he updated his father's chocolate-hazelnut concoction and relaunched it as Nutella. The spread was an instant hit. By the end of the decade, the company was selling Kinder treats and Tic Tacs, too. Ferrero Rocher, boxed chocolates wrapped in shiny gold paper, were added in 1982.

COVERT CONFECTIONERY

Like Willy Wonka, Ferrero was fiercely protective of his recipes. He banned tours of company headquarters. He wore dark glasses whenever he went out and refused to talk to reporters. And to ensure that no competitor could replicate his candymaking processes, he had an in-house engineering department build every machine. In 2010, a Ferrero employee spoke about the company's secretive policies to a reporter from the *Guardian*, a British newspaper. Ferrero's rules required the person to remain anonymous. "Don't quote me by name, I beg of you," the employee said.

Unconventional as they were, Ferrero's tactics seem to have paid off. His candy company's success made him the richest person in Italy. And though there are other chocolate-hazelnut spreads, there is only one Nutella.

In 2015, on Valentine's Day—when sweet treats are exchanged around the world—Ferrero, candymaker extraordinaire, died at the age of 89. A bittersweet goodbye, indeed, for the real-life Willy Wonka.

CANDY WARS

The chocolate business isn't always as sweet as the candies it creates. Chocolatiers are known for being extraordinarily competitive. In the early 20th century, British candy companies routinely sent spies to work in rival factories. Recipe stealing was such a big problem that chocolate firms hired detectives to keep track of their own workers.

Even in more recent times, the snooping has continued. In the 1990s, after giant candy company Nestlé introduced a chocolate egg treat with a toy inside, the U.S. government banned the product for safety reasons. Nestlé suspected that its rival, Mars, had worked to sink the product, and hired spies to prove it. In an effort to crack the case of the chocolate egg, the agents dug through trash from Mars headquarters. The spies were so careful that they replaced each garbage bag they searched with "new" trash!

BIG BREAK

THE SECRET PLOT TO **ESCAPE THE "INESCAPABLE"** ALCATRAZ PRISON

Built on a rocky island in the middle of the San Francisco Bay in California, U.S.A., battered on all sides by blood-chilling seas and treacherous tides, Alcatraz Federal Penitentiary was supposed to be an escape-proof prison for America's most hardened criminals. But that was before Frank Lee Morris, a career crook who practically grew up behind bars, stepped off the island's ferry in 1960 to become inmate #AZ-1441. He set to work masterminding a top secret escape plan with three fellow inmates. Two years later, they broke out of "The Rock."

FRANK LEE MORRIS

CHIP OFF THE OLD ROCK

Using spoons and nail clippers, Morris and his co-conspirators chiseled away the concrete around ventilation grills at the backs of their cells to gain access to hidden passages in the walls. The salty air had softened the concrete, but it still took the men several months to chip through it. They replaced the missing concrete with papier-mâché so the guards wouldn't notice their progress.

Once in the wall passage, the men skittered up plumbing pipes to reach the roof of the cellblock, but their exit was still blocked by a ventilation fan. They needed to drill out the screws that held the fan in place—another painstaking process that took months. A broken vacuum, which one of the escape plotters volunteered to fix, provided the motor for a makeshift drill. They could only use their noisy tool during the prisoners' music practice, which covered up the drilling racket. Meanwhile, each man crafted a papier-mâché dummy of his head using soap, toilet paper, flesh-colored paint from the art room, and hair from the prison barbershop. These phony heads would be crucial to their plan.

BEDHEAD: made from papier-mâché and hair

ARTS AND RAFTS

The men knew they couldn't swim to freedom if they managed to get outside. (In addition to its cold waters and the treacherous tides, San Francisco Bay is a habitat for great white sharks.) So they set about fashioning rafts using rubber cement and raincoats borrowed from other inmates. The rafts were stored atop the cellblock until the night of the escape.

Morris and the other men chose June 11, 1962, as the date of their big break. Shortly after lights-out (prison slang for bedtime), they tucked the phony heads into their bunks so that guards walking their rounds wouldn't notice the men missing. One escape plotter couldn't get through the ventilation grill in his cell, but the other three slipped into the hidden passageway, grabbed the rafts, and climbed to the roof through the loosened ventilation fan. Once they reached the water's edge, the men used a modified accordion to inflate the floats and set sail. Morris and the two other inmates were never seen again, leading prison officials to declare that they were swept to sea and drowned. Their bodies, however, were never found. Some speculate that inmate #AZ-1441 and his two accomplices are still at large.

BREAKOUT STARS

More Secret Escapes

ESCAPE ARTIST: In the early 1700s, Jack Sheppard became England's most wanted man—and its biggest star for his sheer escape artistry. A carpenter by day and burglar by night, he'd slipped out of prison three times before his 23rd birthday. Authorities finally locked Sheppard in an especially secure Newgate Prison cell known as "the Castle." He was shackled in manacles, his leg irons padlocked to the floor. It wasn't enough. Sheppard used a nail to pick the locks, and then pulled an iron bar from a chimney in his cell. Still hobbled by leg irons, Sheppard used the bar to break through no less than six heavily secured doors before reaching the roof of the prison. He climbed atop a neighboring house, tiptoed down its stairs without waking the residents with his clanking chains, and escaped into the night and the countryside.

MOVIE MAGIC: When the Central Intelligence Agency needed to rescue six Americans from Iran in 1980, the spy agency concocted an escape plan right out of a movie—literally! Tony Mendez, a CIA master of disguise and expert at exfiltration (remember the word "exfiltrate" from chapter 1?), devised bogus identities for the six Americans: that of a Canadian film crew scouting for movie locations. To give the story credibility, he set up a fake studio office in Hollywood and placed ads for a phony science-fiction film called *Argo* in Hollywood publications. Mendez then flew to Iran and delivered the fake identification documents to the Americans, who were hiding out in the home of the Canadian ambassador. Posing as members of the Canadian film crew, the Americans boarded a plane and escaped the country. The audacious rescue—which became known as the "Canadian Caper"—was later portrayed in a real Hollywood movie.

MAILED MAN: While many enslaved people during the American Civil War used the Underground Railroad—a vast network of secret routes and safe houses—to find freedom in the North, Henry "Box" Brown concocted his own escape plan by thinking outside the box. Or, rather, inside it. Brown asked a carpenter in 1849 to build a wooden crate 3 feet long by 2 feet wide (1 m by 0.6 m). After poking ventilation holes and packing some water, Brown squeezed into the box and had friends nail it shut. They mailed this very special delivery to the Anti-Slavery Society in Philadelphia, Pennsylvania. The trip took more than a day, and Brown spent most of it upside down (despite writing "right side up with care" on the box). He arrived safely and became active in Philadelphia's anti-slavery movement.

EMPEROR EVER AFTER

UNEARTHING THE **SECRET KINGDOM** OF CHINA'S FIRST EMPEROR

Qin Shi Huang had grand plans in life. By 221 B.C., he had unified a land of squabbling kingdoms to become the first emperor of China. He then went on to connect his empire with roads and canals and protected it with the first version of the Great Wall. Qin Shi Huang had grand plans for his afterlife, too, but those remained secret until 1974, when workers digging a well outside of Xi'an, China, uncovered a human-size clay soldier looking ready for battle.

GREAT WALL OF CHINA

Chinese archaeologists arrived to continue the digging and unearthed one of the greatest archaeological discoveries in the world—and one of history's great mysteries. They found another 2,000 life-size clay action figures, complete with their weapons and teams of horse-drawn chariots. Craftsmen more than two millennia ago created this army to protect Qin Shi Huang (pronounced chin shu wang) in his afterlife. But this "terra-cotta army"—named after the ceramic material it's made from—hints at a much larger secret: a buried kingdom that has yet to be revealed.

QIN SHI HUANG

LOST LAND

Much like the pharaohs of ancient Egypt, the first Chinese emperors viewed death as the start of a great journey, and they didn't want to go unprepared. For Qin Shi Huang, the clay figures would serve as his army in the hereafter. Archaeologists suspect they've unearthed only a fraction of his forces, which they believe number around 8,000. More intriguing is what archaeologists haven't found but suspect is buried beneath a nearby mound: the emperor's tomb.

ETERNAL ARMY: Emperor Qin Shi Huang's artisans crafted thousands of life-size guardians.

According to ancient accounts by Qin Shi Huang's court historian, the emperor ordered the construction of a vast mausoleum, or complex of tomb structures, that re-created China in scaled-down form. It sprawled across mountains of bronze, palaces of gold, rivers of the toxic liquid metal called mercury, and a re-creation of the sky inlaid with pearls and other precious stones to represent the stars and planets. The account claims more than 700,000 workers labored on this tomb, creating a treasure-filled mini kingdom that Qin Shi Huang could rule over for eternity.

ETERNAL SECRET

But for the foreseeable future, Qin Shi Huang's tomb will remain a mystery, buried and undisturbed. Archaeologists in China don't want to unearth the suspected burial site. It's not that they fear the rivers of poisonous mercury or the deadly traps hinted at in historical accounts (which describe crossbows rigged to fire at tomb raiders). Chinese historians simply don't want to risk damaging the priceless artifacts with digging machinery or even exposing them to the air, which could cause them to fade and rot.

MERCURY

But modern technology has let the archaeologists dig in other ways, and they know *something* is down there. Soil around the site contains high levels of mercury. Remote-sensing equipment has detected an underground chamber with four stairlike walls. Pits dug around the tomb revealed more life-size clay figures. Instead of warriors, these were dancers, musicians, and acrobats in fun poses: terra-cotta entertainers putting on an eternal show for their emperor.

LOCH NESS SUBMARINE

A London surgeon supposedly photographed the slender neck of "Nessie" poking from Scotland's Loch Ness in 1934, and the photo became the longest-standing piece of photographic proof that a serpent lurks in the lake. Sixty years later, a person involved with the picture admitted it's a hoax—just a plastic model glued to a tin toy submarine.

DIRTY SECRETS

ASTOUNDING **DISCOVERIES** THAT WERE **TOTAL HOAXES**

BOGUS BIGFOOT

After claiming they discovered a Bigfoot (aka Sasquatch) carcass in the wilderness of Georgia, U.S.A., in 2008, two hunters put the body on ice and submitted it for scientific study. Turns out the "body" was just a rubber gorilla costume. Supposed Bigfoot tissue samples were actually from a possum. And the hunters just happened to co-own a company that offered Bigfoot tours.

GIANT LIE

A 10-foot (3-m)-tall stone man uncovered by workers digging in a well in 1869 became an instant tourist attraction in Cardiff, New York, U.S.A., luring thousands of visitors who paid to see the rock colossus. Debate raged over whether the giant was a petrified man from biblical times or a century-old statue created to impress the locals. Truth be told, the "Cardiff Giant" was actually a sculpture commissioned by a tobacco grower and buried as a prank. Its "discovery" was no accident, either, and the prankster earned a small fortune from all the hubbub.

MADE-UP MERMAID

Circus showman P. T. Barnum displayed the long-dead body of a so-called "Fiji Mermaid" in the 1800s. Such mummified mermaids were once common curiosities, but they were nothing more than creepy craft projects made from stitched-together animal parts and papier-mâché.

FAIRY FAIL

In 1917, a pair of mischievous girls in Cottingley, England, posed in photos with card-board cutouts of fairies clipped from a popular children's book. The pictures became a sensation across England. Even Sherlock Holmes creator Sir Arthur Conan Doyle was convinced the fairies were real. The girls admitted to the hoax much later in life.

CROCK CIRCLES

When intricate swirls started appearing in English cornfields in the 1970s, believers in the paranormal hailed them as evidence of artistic visitors from outer space. Crop circle fever gripped the nation—until two pranksters in 1991 admitted they used ropes and boards to press at least some of the mysterious designs into the fields.

A CLOSER LOOK

Sometimes "hoaxes" turn out to be real. When naturalist George Shaw saw the first preserved platypus specimen in the late 18th century, he thought the duck-billed creature was a fake stitched together from other animals. Nope! Today we know these odd egg-laying mammals really exist!

UNDERCOVER OPERATION

THE ABC'S OF ABRA-CADABRA

ESSENTIAL **TRICKS** FOR THE STARTING **SORCERER**

You don't need a secret spell to try our magical moves, but these few suggestions will help you perfect the art of illusion. First, show confidence. You'll never convince an audience that magic is before their eyes unless you believe it's magic yourself. Second, keep talking. Your audience is less likely to spot your sneaky maneuvers if they're watching your face. And finally, try to distract your audience's attention from the action happening in your hands. Oftentimes just a snap of the fingers from your free hand will do.

THE PINKIE BREAK

ESSENTIAL FOR: Card tricks

Before you start asking people to "pick a card, any card," you need to know this fundamental trick for marking a spot in the deck. Why is deck marking so crucial? It will help you find and retrieve any card slipped back into the deck by audience members. Here's a breakdown of the pinkie break, complete with a trick to illustrate its potential.

DIRECTIONS:

STEP 1. While holding the deck face down in your dominant hand and fanning it open, ask an audience member to choose a card at random.

STEP 2. Ask the audience member to memorize the card, and then slip it back into your deck in a random spot. Hold the deck tight so the chosen card sticks out a little bit.

STEP 3. Here's where the pinkie break comes into play. With your free hand, split the deck above the card that was chosen by the audience member. Fit the card flush with the rest of the deck beneath it, and then place the top half of the deck onto the audience member's card, while sticking the tip of your deck hand's pinkie in between the two halves of the deck. This will create a break—the pinkie break!—between the cards on top of the audience member's card.

NEED A RIDDLE HINT?

This chapter's code uses a keyword cipher with the keyword "sneaky." (Read about it on page 9.)

If you're still at a loss, turn to page 182 for the answer to this encrypted riddle!

HERE'S ANOTHER HINT. ⇧

STEP 4. Cut the deck a few times to give the impression that you're shuffling. Create a new pinkie break each time you place cards on top of the audience member's card. Keeping a sneaky pinkie break isn't easy, so make sure to practice, practice, practice!

STEP 5. When you're ready to reveal the audience member's card, cut the deck above the pinkie break, which will put the chosen card on top. Reveal the card to your audience and bask in the stunned stares and applause.

THE COIN PALM

ESSENTIAL FOR: Vanishing tricks

Your success as a magician depends on your mastery of "sleight of hand," or the ability to manipulate objects in such sneaky ways that the audience can't tell what you're doing. The coin palm is a classic example. Do it right, and you can make coins vanish right before your audience's eyes. It's also good practice for more complicated sleight-of-hand tricks.

DIRECTIONS:

STEP 1. Ask for a coin from your audience. Once you have it, put it in the center of your non-dominant hand and show your audience.

STEP 2. Clasp your hands together (with the coin in the middle).

STEP 3. Open your hands, but before you do, pinch the coin tightly between the side of the thumb and index finger of your dominant hand.

STEP 4. Turn your hands upside down and voilà! Your hands look like they're empty, but the coin is still locked in, not visible to your audience. Make a big deal of showing your audience that your other hand is empty.

STEP 5. You have many options for magic tricks once you have the coin successfully palmed. You can drop it into your opposite hand while passing your hands over one another, or drop it into your lap while no one is looking, then hold both palms up to show that you've made the coin disappear. You can pretend to pull the coin from someone's nose or ear.

Sawed in Half ... Solved!

THE CLAIM: The magician locks the cheery assistant into a coffin-like enclosure before sawing the box in two. Slicing implements vary, from simple rectangular blades to roaring buzz saws, but the result is always the same: The assistant spends a few seconds neatly halved before emerging, smiling and unhurt, from the reassembled box. Thrilling? Certainly. But this famous illusion is a triumph of sneakiness rather than magic.

THE TRUTH: While the magician distracts the audience by readying the cutting implement, the assistant—typically a skilled contortionist—draws his or her legs to the top half of the box. Those feet wriggling from the holes at the other end? They're animatronic tootsies made to match the assistant's feet. The magician thrusts the cutting tool through the box, neatly slicing it in two. The bottom and top halves are pulled apart as the assistant's head, hands, and (robotic) feet wriggle. The magician then connects the two halves and removes the blade. Inside, the assistant stretches his or her legs to the bottom of the box. Just before the magician undoes the latches and opens the box, the assistant pulls the robot feet back inside along with his or her head and hands. Up comes the lid and out springs the smiling assistant.

First test of ROCKET SHOES a painful failure.

SECRET GADGETS

Developing fire-proof socks now a PRIORITY.

And fire-proof pants.

Secret agents in spy movies always enlist the aid of a gadget specialist—a tech-savvy sidekick who equips the hero with laser-firing watches and poison-injecting pens. Turns out that's not just movie make-believe! This chapter is stocked with actual classified devices that real spies have used—and in some cases are still using—to gather intel, foil foes, and make stealthy escapes. Some tech is designed to protect. (Scrap passwords: an eye-opening scanner safeguards your identity.) Some is made to conceal. (Slip on a real-life invisibility cloak and vanish into thin air.) All of it would make James Bond jealous.

CAUGHT ON FILM!

THE SECRET HISTORY OF **SPY CAMERAS...** AND **SPY PHOTOS**

Spies are trained to remember everything they see, but not even photographic memories can capture little details as well as an actual photograph. That's why the most valuable gadget in a spy's bag of tricks is a camera, preferably small enough to hide or disguise as an ordinary object.

Spy agencies came up with all sorts of disguises for the Minox, which was so small it could be hidden nearly anywhere. This custom brush box saw action during the Cold War in the 1960s.

STRAIGHT SHOOTER

The first widely used spy camera was manufactured by a German company named Minox in the late 1930s. Not much bigger than a pack of gum, the Minox "subminiature camera" was a savvy spy's hidden camera of choice for half a century. The little camera could snap 50 pictures on a single roll, and its special lens captured the tiniest details, such as the fine print in classified documents. It is still made today, although it doesn't see nearly as much espionage action as in the days of the Cold War.

WHAT FOLLOWS IS A RIDDLE HIDDEN IN A SECRET CODE. THE ANSWER TO THIS RIDDLE IS A

MINOR DETAILS

But just as tiny spy cameras can capture the big picture for analysts back home, tiny photos can help spread secret messages to spies abroad. The Microdot Mark IV camera could shrink images down to an itty-bitty photo called a microdot, about the size of the period at the end of this sentence. For instance, a spy using the Microdot camera could snap a photo of a piece of paper with a message of 300 words, develop the photo into a microdot, and then smuggle the dot to a spy behind enemy lines inside of a peanut shell or hollowed-out coin or box of tea (all have been used). The spy can then insert the microdot into a special lens about the size of a grain of rice and read the message. Microdots were used to send secret messages to spies on both sides of the Cold War and even to captured spies held as prisoners during the Vietnam War.

PIGEON CAMERA

Spies often passed microdot photos and microfilm, another type of tiny photos that could hold even more information, inside specially made hollowed-out coins that could be hidden with other spare change.

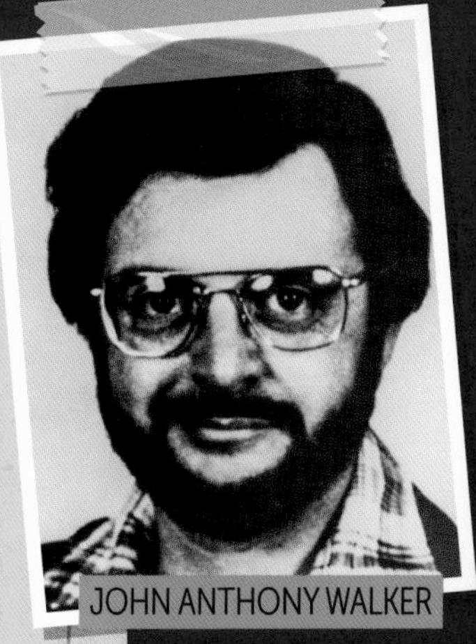
JOHN ANTHONY WALKER

A CLOSER LOOK

One of the many spies to use the Minox camera was John Anthony Walker, an American who used his position as a communications specialist in the U.S. Navy to photograph plans for secret submarine technology and sell his secret pics to the former Soviet Union. By the time he was caught in 1985, Walker had recruited family members into his espionage business and sold enough secrets to give the Soviet Union an edge in the Cold War.

Ingenious Real Gadgets for Snapping Secret Pics

BUTTONHOLE CAMERA: The lens of this tiny camera was tucked behind the right middle button of an ordinary coat, perfectly positioned for photographing unsuspecting subjects. Snapping a picture was easy: The coat's wearer squeezed a shutter cable hidden in the coat pocket, which caused the fake button to open and snap a picture. Several types of buttonhole cameras were widely used in the former Soviet Union, Europe, and North America during the early 1970s.

PIGEON CAMERA: You've heard of carrier pigeons? How about pigeon spies! In 1918, intelligence offices outfitted pigeons with tiny cameras and released them over military sites. As the birds flew, the cameras continuously clicked away, snapping pictures that were developed and scrutinized for intel when the pigeons reached their destination.

PEN CAMERA: A tube-shaped camera called the Tropel was disguised as several ordinary objects, including a pen, as well as a key chain and lighter. It was used by CIA spies in the late 1970s.

MATCHBOX CAMERA: Camera company Eastman Kodak made this special camera disguised as a matchbox for the Office of Strategic Services (OSS), the WWII-era spy agency that later became the CIA. The matchbox camera could be customized with labels for the country where it would be used.

BYE, PASSWORDS

HIGH-TECH DEVICES THAT CAN **CONFIRM** THAT **YOU ARE YOU**

In 2018, a suspect in China was picked out of a crowd of 60,000 people at a concert. Facial recognition technology identified the man and alerted police. He was arrested before the concert even began.

Biometrics—the process of using the body (including the face) to identify a person—is not new. Police have been using fingerprints for more than 100 years. But other methods are quickly gaining traction. And they are not just for law enforcement. Cutting-edge identity scanners let you unlock your phone just by staring at the screen ... or step onto a plane after having your eyes scanned. Fans of the tech say it is convenient, but many people worry that the updates could amount to an invasion of privacy. Are the newest gadgets cool or creepy? Take a look and judge for yourself.

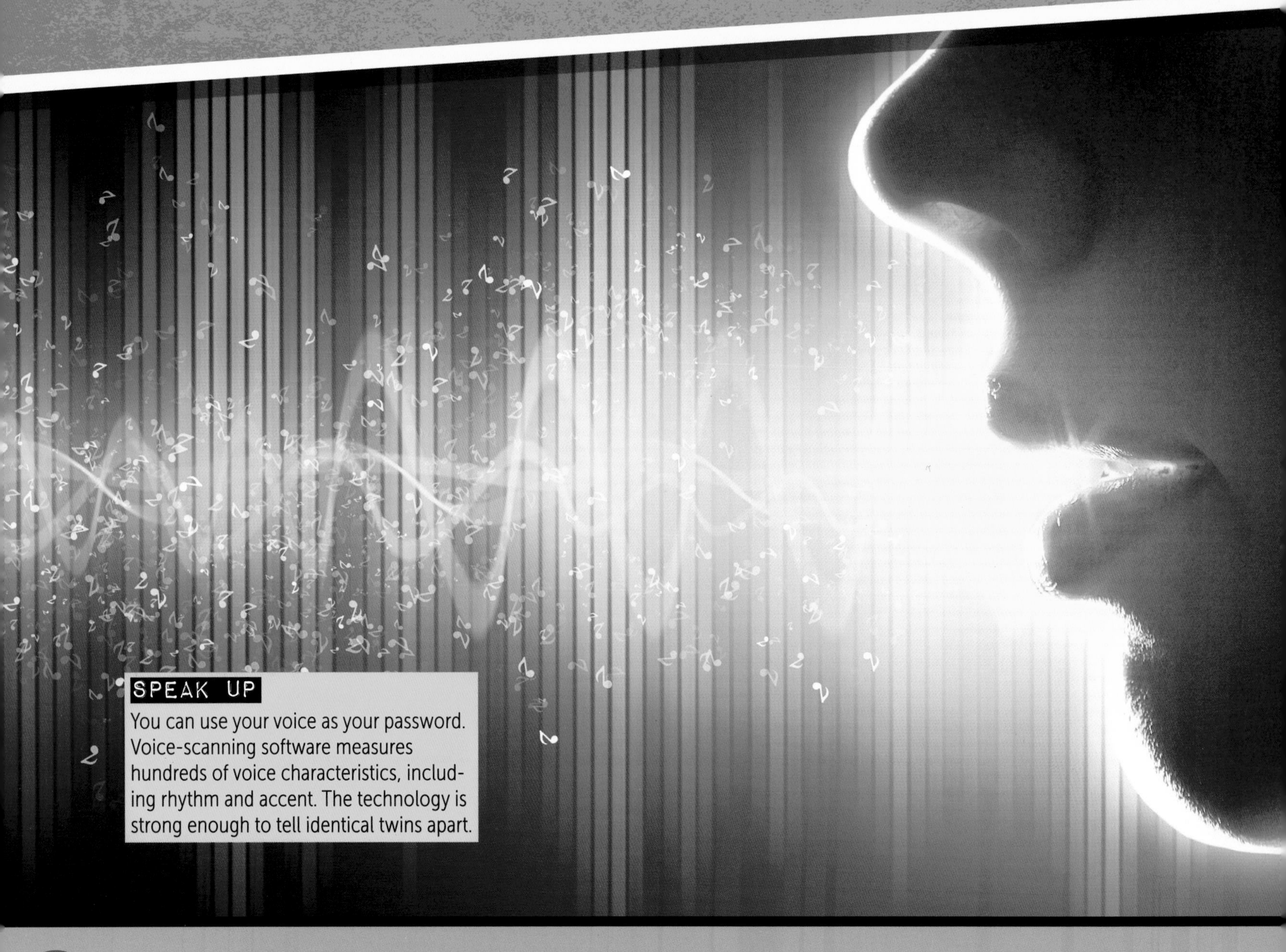

SPEAK UP

You can use your voice as your password. Voice-scanning software measures hundreds of voice characteristics, including rhythm and accent. The technology is strong enough to tell identical twins apart.

DESCRIBED ON PAGE 9. PERHAPS THAT IS ENOUGH INFORMATION TO SOLVE THIS RIDDLE,

QUICK PRINTS

A mobile device lets officers scan fingerprints at the scene of an incident. If the print matches up with one in the police database, a suspect's photo can be pulled up in an instant.

EYE-D

An iris scanner can recognize you based on unique features in the colored portion of your eye. The devices have appeared in banks, hospitals, and even on smartphones.

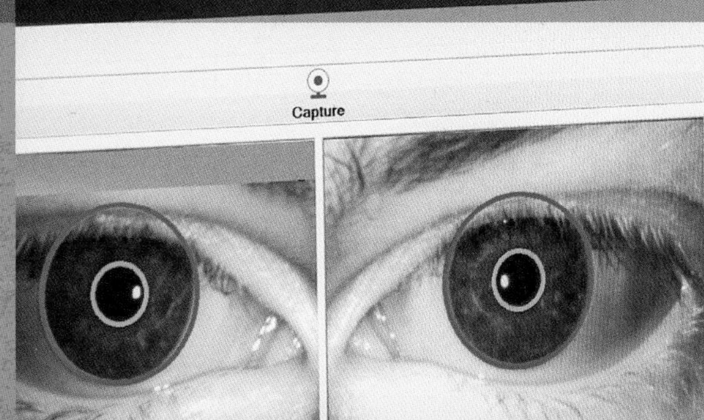

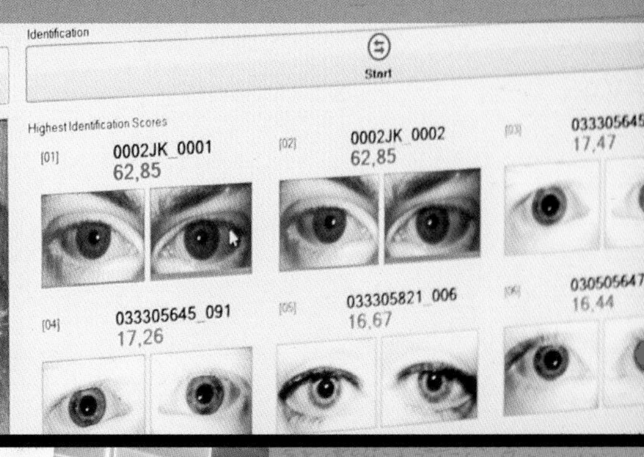

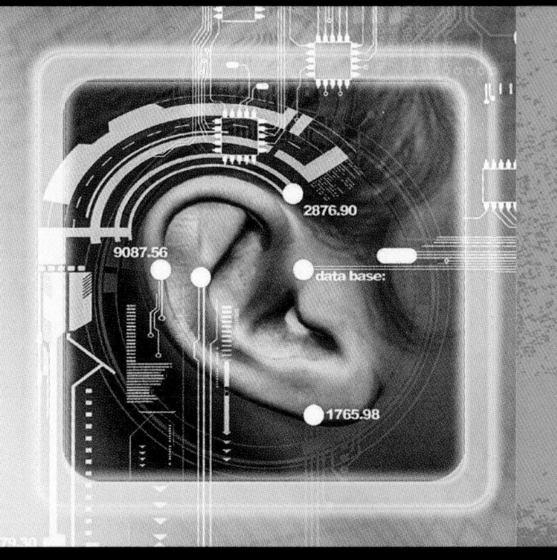

ALL EARS

Like fingerprints, ears are unique. The Helix system can verify your identity with a simple scan of your ear.

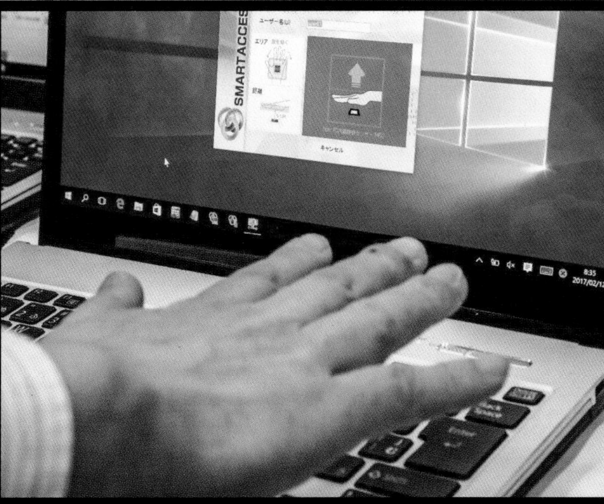

PALM READER

A device scans the squiggly vein patterns in your palm ... and you're in!

SAY CHEESE (BURGER)

A burger restaurant uses face-scanning technology to recognize customers and keep track of their favorite orders.

FACE VALUE

Apple's Face ID projects a grid of 30,000 invisible dots onto a person's face to create a 3D model.

PERHAPS NOT. IF YOU'RE STUMPED, YOU WILL FIND A HINT AND THE CIPHER USED AT THE

CORONA PROGRAM

DECLASSIFIED

LAUNCHED IN: 1959

SPY-PHOTO QUALITY:
Could reveal structures down to 40 feet (12 m).

Built at the beginning of the U.S. space program, the Corona series of spy satellites was so top secret that even its code name had a code name: Discoverer. As far as the public knew, the Discoverer payloads included probes, primates, and experiments essential to planning human exploration of outer space. Instead, each craft carried two nine-foot (2.7-m)-long cameras and up to six miles (10 km) of film. Nearly 150 Corona satellites were launched to spy on the former Soviet Union and the People's Republic of China in the 1960s.

CORONA SATELLITE

Recovering pictures from orbit wasn't easy in the days before digital photography and wireless downloading. Each finished roll of Corona film ejected from the satellite aboard a tiny capsule shielded to survive the fiery reentry into Earth's atmosphere. Air Force planes trailing long hooks caught the parachute-equipped capsules in midair over the Pacific Ocean—before they could fall into enemy hands.

SAY "CHEESE"

TOP SECRET EYES IN THE SKY

Next time you feel like you're being watched, trust your gut. You probably are! Constellations of imaging satellites swarm the heavens, snapping high-definition photos of the terrain far below for scientists, city planners, mapmakers, government agencies, and the web-based virtual globe of Google Earth. But while most of these eagle-eyed "birds" are easy to track on websites (and even on an app for your smartphone), an elusive few soar in secret to snoop on various countries from low Earth orbit. We track the telemetry of these sneaky spacecraft.

HEXAGON PROGRAM

DECLASSIFIED

LAUNCHED IN: 1971

SPY-PHOTO QUALITY: Could resolve details down to two feet (0.6 m), such as home plate on a baseball field.

Nicknamed "Big Birds" (each satellite was the size of a bus), Hexagon spacecraft were an upgrade from the Corona satellites, equipped with powerful cameras that captured larger patches of terrain at much greater resolution. By the time the last of the Big Birds rocketed into orbit in 1986, they had photographed the entire surface of Earth. These craft ejected their film in capsules just like the Corona satellites.

END OF THIS CHAPTER. NOW GET CRACKING! HERE IS THE ENCODED RIDDLE: THEGGEREGGE

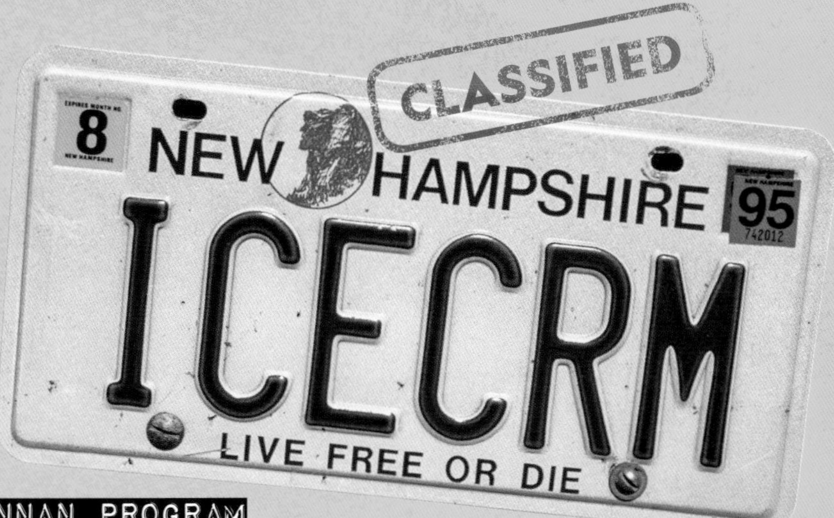

KENNAN PROGRAM

LAUNCHED IN: 1976

SPY-PHOTO QUALITY: Could reportedly resolve details as small as the digits on a license plate.

Although the Corona and Hexagon satellites gave the United States valuable sneak peeks at its rivals, both systems suffered from one major flaw: They were useless once they ran out of film. (Considering each satellite cost hundreds of millions of dollars to build and launch, these were the world's most expensive disposable cameras!) The top secret Kennan satellites—still in use and classified to this day—solved this problem. They were reportedly the first satellites that carried digital cameras, and they could broadcast their images live through a top secret network of communication satellites to intelligence agencies around the world.

ORION PROGRAM

LAUNCHED IN: 1995

SPY-PHOTO QUALITY: These sneaky satellites listen rather than look. They can eavesdrop on your phone calls!

Reconnaissance satellites are more than just eyes in the sky for spy agencies. They're their "ears," too! The Orion satellites carry enormous radio dishes that gather signals intelligence—or electronic signals such as radar, radio waves, and telecommunication traffic.

PREDATOR DRONES

LAUNCHED IN: 1995

SPY-PHOTO QUALITY: Able to capture the big picture better than space-based satellites, drone cameras can track moving objects—such as cars and people—in an area about half the size of San Francisco, California, U.S.A., and then zoom in to see what everyone's up to.

When spy agencies and the military need eyes in the sky but don't have time to reposition a spy satellite, they send in the drones. Unmanned aerial vehicles (UAVs) like the Predator are small aircraft that carry cameras and sensors instead of pilots and crew. They're flown at altitudes around 20,000 feet (6,100 m) by remote control from anywhere in the world—or even by automatic pilot. Drones have become a popular snooping tool in clandestine operations, which have changed drastically since the days of the Cold War. They're the closest equivalent to the high-tech monitoring systems seen in modern spy movies.

A CLOSER LOOK

When the parachute on a Hexagon satellite's film capsule failed to open on reentry in 1971, the U.S. Navy sent its deepest-diving submarine to recover the film from three miles (5 km) down in the Pacific Ocean.

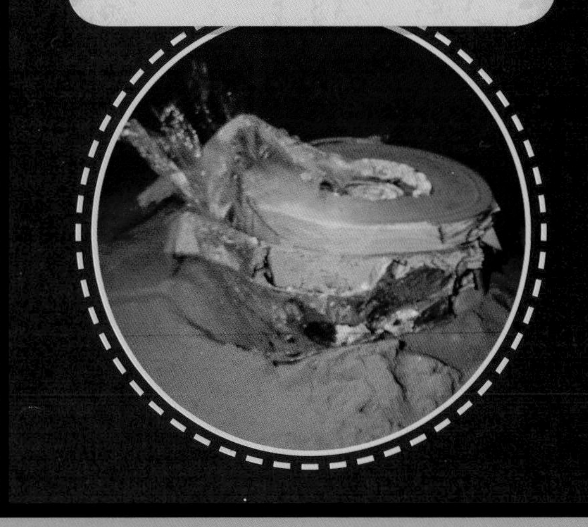

OUT OF SIGHT!

THE TOP SECRET TECH OF CLOAKING DEVICES

Surveys show that invisibility ranks near the top of people's most wanted superpowers. Soon, kid wizards and comic-book heroes may not be the only ones who can disappear with the swish of a cape. At this moment, in laboratories around the world, scientists are trying to make objects vanish before their eyes. They're working on cloaking technology: devices that hide people, places, and things in plain sight. And they're succeeding! The technology goes by the more technical name of "active camouflage," and it involves materials that change color to blend in with the environment (as opposed to "passive camouflage," which is simply colors or patterns that naturally blend in with the background). To understand how these devices fool your eyes, you need to know how your eyes work in the first place.

NOW WE SEE YOU ...

It's not easy being sneaky when all that light bounces off your head, shoulders, knees, and tennis shoes. That's how vision works: Light travels from the sun (or some other light source like a lightbulb or campfire) and reflects off objects in the environment into our eyes, which focus the light in a way our brains can process and perceive as colors, curves, and angles. Cloaking technology plays tricks with the light and fools our eyes.

NOW WE WON'T.

The ability to cloak and hide in plain sight already exists in the wild. Color- and texture-shifting cells in the skin of octopuses, squid, and cuttlefish, for instance, allow them to blend seamlessly with rocks and morph into coral-like shapes. Researchers studying these marine masters of disguise have begun to understand their tricks. Already scientists in California have developed a type of color-shifting "squid tape" that soldiers can wrap around their uniforms to add another layer of camouflage.

CUTTLEFISH

Cloaking devices are bulkier and more complex. The simplest prototypes use cameras and displays to project a background onto an object, making the object disappear or completely blend in with the background. More complex cloaking systems rely on lenses to bend light around objects, rendering them invisible if you look from a certain and precise angle.

The most advanced invisibility cloak is made of metamaterials that—like a charmed object from the world of Harry Potter—defy the laws of nature. In fact, metamaterial isn't made from any material found in nature. It's composed of an artificial fabric that creates an electrical field to bend light around it rather than reflecting or scattering light like a normal fabric would. So, anyone looking at the metamaterial-wrapped object would see right through it, making it invisible. Someday metamaterials might be woven into a real-life invisibility cloak. Today, they can only be manufactured on a small scale, not even large enough to cloak a grain of sand.

A CLOSER LOOK

Invisibility is just the beginning with so-called metamaterials, which have a wide range of uses beyond fooling the human eye. They can manipulate sound and heat as well as light, meaning these materials could be used for everything from communication systems in deep space and ultra-fast computers to tumor-zapping devices for the human body.

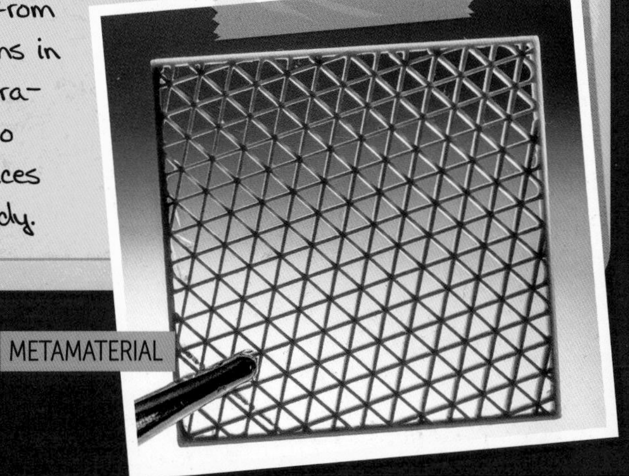

METAMATERIAL

Real-Life Uses for Cloaking Technology

Elaborate magic tricks, sneaky spy missions, the world's best surprise parties—the list of functions for a real-life invisibility cloak is endless. But uses for such spiffy technology go way beyond pranks and hocus-pocus. All the cloaking concepts listed below are real prototypes based on a variety of "active camouflage" technologies.

SAVING ENERGY: House walls and roofs could be switched into transparent mode to let in natural light and help heat the house with sunlight on cool, sunny days.

SEE-THROUGH SURGERY: As they operate, surgeons could drape a fabric over their arms and hands for an unobstructed view of their patients.

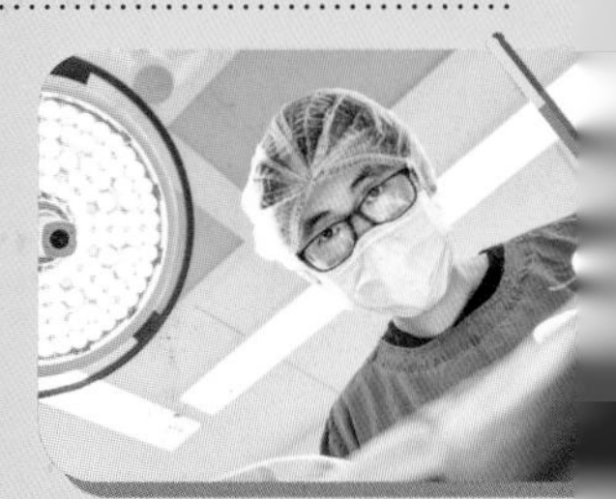

TRANSPARENT TRAVEL: Airline pilots and automobile drivers could make the hulls of their planes and cars see-through to eliminate blind spots or avoid backing into light poles (or people).

FOR APPEARANCE'S SAKE/DRESSING UP: Any material capable of hiding a person or object would also be able to disguise it. Invisibility cloaks could transform eyesore cell-phone towers into majestic redwood trees or turn construction sites into 3D previews of the buildings to come. A scientist working on a cloaking fabric in Berkeley, California, U.S.A., envisions cloaking bandages that hide pimples, and shirts that make a full tummy look like six-pack abs!

SECRET WEAPONS

FLY **UNDER THE RADAR** WITH STEALTH TECHNOLOGY

The first combat planes were camouflaged with color schemes that hid them from eyes on the ground and in the skies above, but that only worked until the invention of radar. This decades-old technology uses invisible beams of light to detect intruders on the ocean, in the sky, and even in space. Radar beams bounce off objects and paint a simple picture of these "intruders" on the operator's screen back at the radar-broadcasting station. With such systems in place, every country can keep an eye on its coasts and airspace for uninvited guests.

Unless those guests use stealth technology. Since the 1940s, engineers have been working in secret to develop materials and designs that make certain vehicles—especially planes, helicopters, and even ships—invisible to radar. Here's a guide to these once classified craft.

U-2 SPY PLANE

FIRST FLIGHT: 1955

USED BY: U.S. Air Force, the Central Intelligence Agency, NASA, Taiwanese military

One of the first planes designed to spy on other countries undetected, the U-2 soars so high that its pilots must wear pressurized space suits. The U-2's designers thought radar couldn't track planes above 70,000 feet (21,000 m). They were wrong. Several were shot down.

LEAST STEALTHY

SR-71 BLACKBIRD

FIRST FLIGHT: 1964

USED BY: U.S. Air Force, NASA

Test-flown at the mysterious Area 51 government facility in the Nevada desert, the Blackbird is designed to fly higher (up to 90,000 feet [27,400 m]) and faster—three times the speed of sound—than any other plane. It carries high-tech cameras for capturing detailed, close-up photos of military bases and other strategic sites worth snapping. The Blackbird is named after its special black paint that soaks up radar beams.

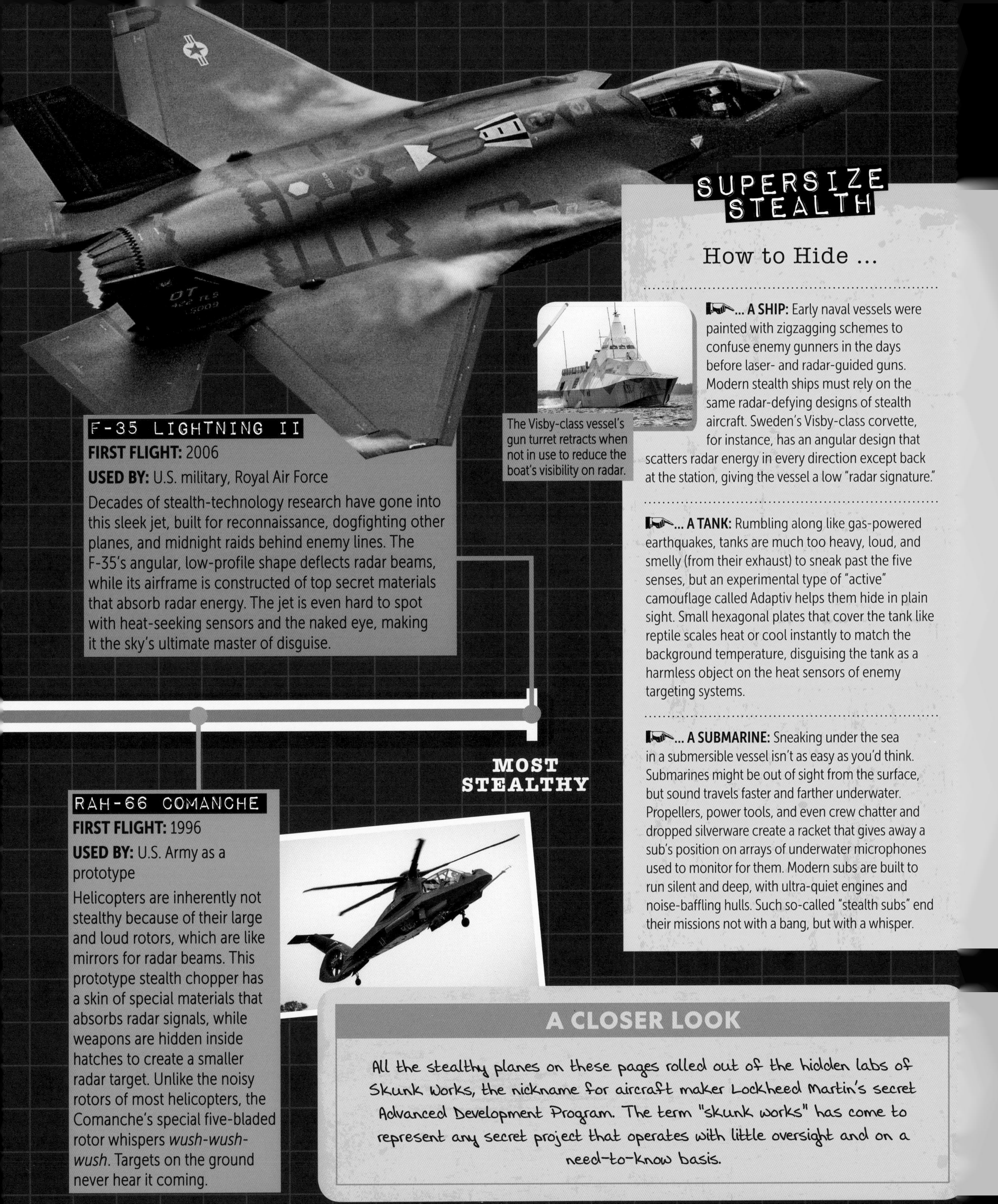

SUPERSIZE STEALTH

How to Hide ...

... A SHIP: Early naval vessels were painted with zigzagging schemes to confuse enemy gunners in the days before laser- and radar-guided guns. Modern stealth ships must rely on the same radar-defying designs of stealth aircraft. Sweden's Visby-class corvette, for instance, has an angular design that scatters radar energy in every direction except back at the station, giving the vessel a low "radar signature."

The Visby-class vessel's gun turret retracts when not in use to reduce the boat's visibility on radar.

... A TANK: Rumbling along like gas-powered earthquakes, tanks are much too heavy, loud, and smelly (from their exhaust) to sneak past the five senses, but an experimental type of "active" camouflage called Adaptiv helps them hide in plain sight. Small hexagonal plates that cover the tank like reptile scales heat or cool instantly to match the background temperature, disguising the tank as a harmless object on the heat sensors of enemy targeting systems.

... A SUBMARINE: Sneaking under the sea in a submersible vessel isn't as easy as you'd think. Submarines might be out of sight from the surface, but sound travels faster and farther underwater. Propellers, power tools, and even crew chatter and dropped silverware create a racket that gives away a sub's position on arrays of underwater microphones used to monitor for them. Modern subs are built to run silent and deep, with ultra-quiet engines and noise-baffling hulls. Such so-called "stealth subs" end their missions not with a bang, but with a whisper.

F-35 LIGHTNING II

FIRST FLIGHT: 2006

USED BY: U.S. military, Royal Air Force

Decades of stealth-technology research have gone into this sleek jet, built for reconnaissance, dogfighting other planes, and midnight raids behind enemy lines. The F-35's angular, low-profile shape deflects radar beams, while its airframe is constructed of top secret materials that absorb radar energy. The jet is even hard to spot with heat-seeking sensors and the naked eye, making it the sky's ultimate master of disguise.

MOST STEALTHY

RAH-66 COMANCHE

FIRST FLIGHT: 1996

USED BY: U.S. Army as a prototype

Helicopters are inherently not stealthy because of their large and loud rotors, which are like mirrors for radar beams. This prototype stealth chopper has a skin of special materials that absorbs radar signals, while weapons are hidden inside hatches to create a smaller radar target. Unlike the noisy rotors of most helicopters, the Comanche's special five-bladed rotor whispers *wush-wush-wush*. Targets on the ground never hear it coming.

A CLOSER LOOK

All the stealthy planes on these pages rolled out of the hidden labs of Skunk Works, the nickname for aircraft maker Lockheed Martin's secret Advanced Development Program. The term "skunk works" has come to represent any secret project that operates with little oversight and on a need-to-know basis.

TOOLS OF THE TRADECRAFT

REAL-LIFE **SPY GADGETS**

With the help of the International Spy Museum in Washington, D.C., and secret sources at the Central Intelligence Agency, we gather nine of the coolest, sneakiest—and even deadliest—spy tools.

International Spy Museum, Washington, D.C.

LIPSTICK PISTOL

CIRCA 1965

Wielded by female agents of the former Soviet Union's espionage agency during the Cold War, this little lip-gloss canister hid a big surprise: a 4.5-mm single-shot pistol. "It delivered the ultimate 'kiss of death,'" says Peter Earnest, the International Spy Museum's executive director and a 36-year career CIA operations officer. Agents fired the mini-pistol by twisting the tube—the same motion that extends the gloss in a regular lipstick applicator. The agent wouldn't want to forget this gizmo in their makeup bag!

BELLY BUSTER DRILL

CIRCA 1950S AND 1960S

This sneaky tool drilled tiny holes in walls so spies could implant hidden listening devices. It was powered by hand and held against the stomach, which allowed a spy to use his or her bodyweight to help drive the drill through tough masonry—hence its "belly buster" nickname. The kit was packed with accessories to clean up any mess and patch the hole once the bug was planted.

LETTER REMOVER

CIRCA 1940S

In the days before the internet, hacking someone's mail meant secretly removing their letters from their envelopes and then returning them without any trace of tampering with the envelopes' seals. This tweezer-like device was inserted into the tiny unsealed gap of each envelope's flap. It gripped the letter inside and wound it into a tight tube shape that could be pulled through the gap. Once the letter was read, it could be re-inserted into the envelope's gap and unwound to its original flat shape. Voilà! Message received!

"THE THING"

CIRCA 1950S

The U.S. ambassador to the Soviet Union (now Russia) was delighted when Soviet schoolchildren gave him this hand-carved wooden replica of the Great Seal of the United States in 1945. Told it represented friendship between the two nations, he displayed it proudly in his Moscow study for years. But less than a decade later, technicians discovered that the seal came with a bonus gift: a small wireless listening device—called a bug in spyspeak. The microphone was impossible to detect when activated by a beam generated from a van parked nearby. It didn't require wires or even batteries—just air to fill the surrounding cavities, supplied by a tiny hole in the eagle's beak. The seal was code-named "The Thing" because no one knew what else to call it.

DOO-DOO TRANSMITTER

CIRCA 1970

When agents and soldiers behind enemy lines needed to hide homing beacons to direct aerial reconnaissance, the Central Intelligence Agency came up with this disgusting disguise. Radio transmitters and "dead-drop" canisters (used to pass secret messages) were camouflaged as convincing chunks of doo-doo, something no enemies would investigate or touch.

TURN THE PAGE FOR MORE GADGETS.

TOOLS OF THE TRADECRAFT CONTINUED

UMBRELLA DART GUN

CIRCA 1978

This umbrella fired a BB-size pellet coated in a deadly poison, which only needed to break the skin to kill. A Bulgarian agent used such an umbrella to assassinate enemy-of-the-state Georgi Markov, who recalled being shot by such a device before falling ill and dying the next day.

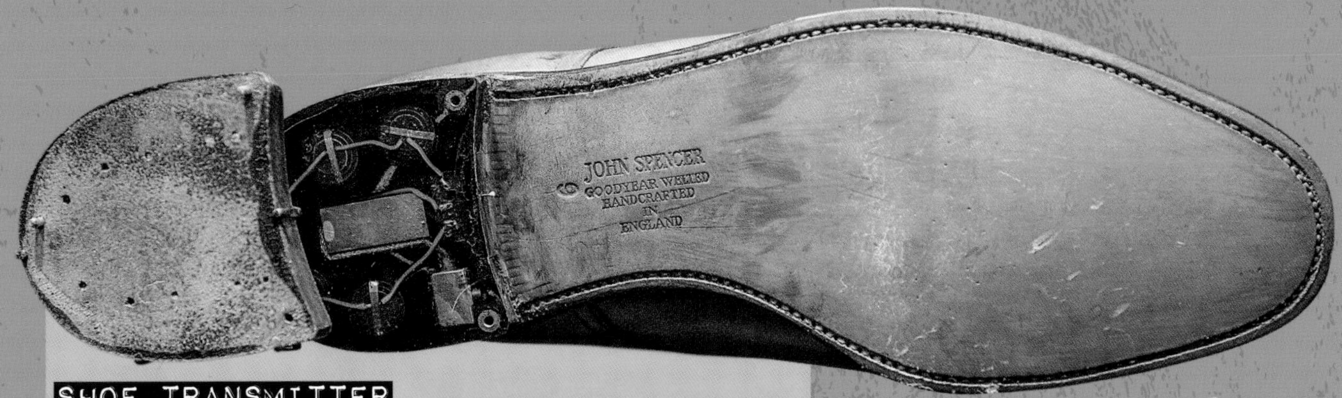

SHOE TRANSMITTER

CIRCA 1960S

A shoe that doubles as a telephone is a famous funny gadget in spy fiction, but the shoe transmitter is more of a sneaky "gift" than a gag. Romanian secret agents installed a microphone and transmitter in the heel of a foreign diplomat's shoes that he ordered though the mail. The diplomat didn't know he was bugged until technicians discovered a radio signal coming from his feet.

TREE TRANSMITTER

CIRCA 1970

CIA agents planted this solar-powered eavesdropping gizmo in the woods near Moscow, where it intercepted radio signals from a nearby Soviet missile system and transmitted the data via satellite to the United States. Despite its clever disguise in a phony tree stump (with a transparent top for the solar panels), the bug was eventually discovered by KGB agents.

POISON-PILL GLASSES

CIRCA 1975

A gadget of last resort, these thick-framed glasses contained a tiny cyanide pill in the arm that desperate agents could swallow if they preferred death to capture. Agents could also chew on the arm of the glasses to eat the poison pill without raising suspicion.

A CLOSER LOOK

No gadget was too wacky or wild for the Research and Development Branch of the Office of Strategic Services (OSS), the U.S. intelligence agency that formed to help the Allies triumph in World War II. Among the lab's more bold ideas were explosives disguised as baking flour and a motorized surfboard. The OSS evolved into the CIA, whose Directorate of Science and Technology still develops top secret spy tech today.

ROBOTS IN DISGUISE

THE CIA'S **"INSECTOTHOPTER"** WAS THE **ULTIMATE BUG**

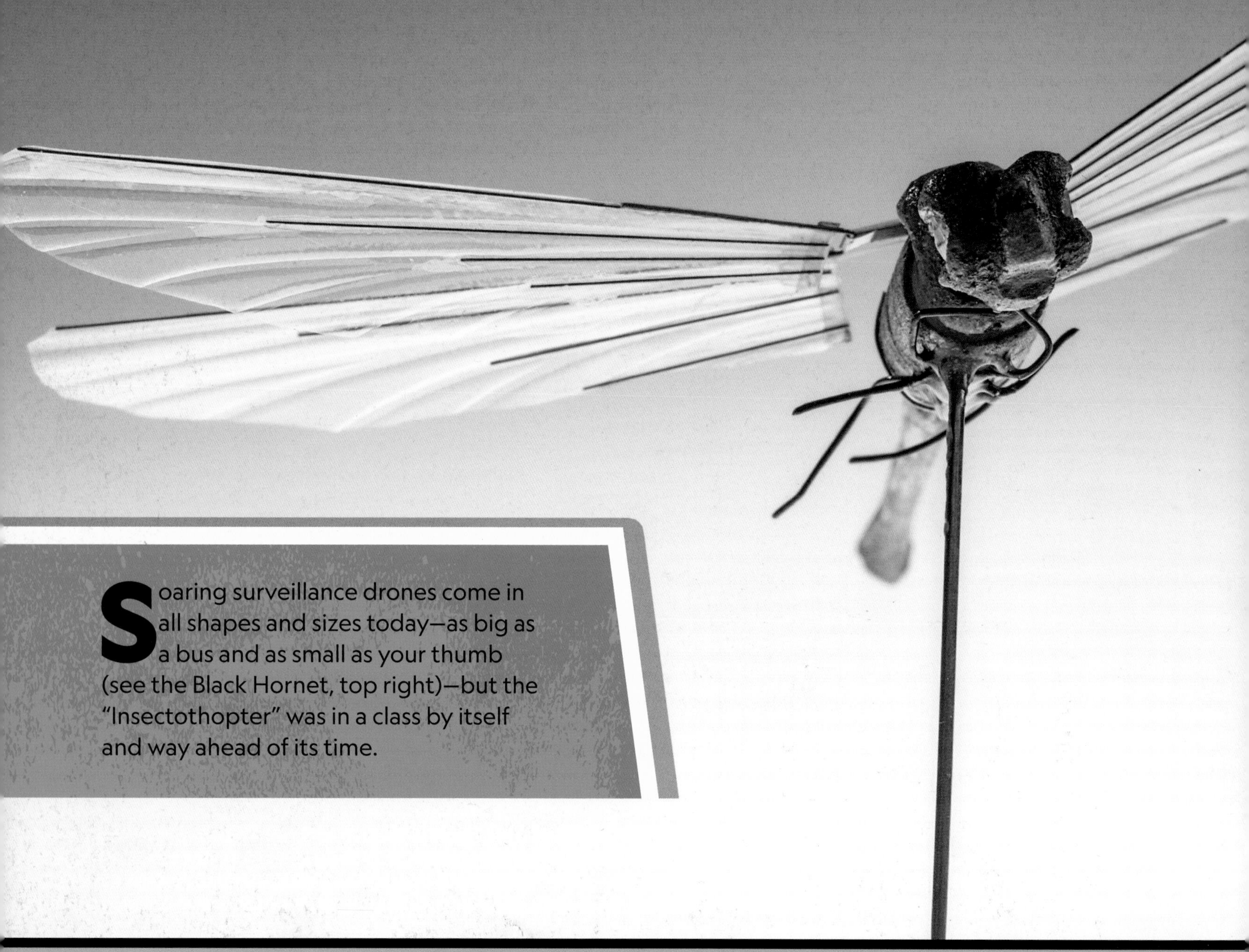

Soaring surveillance drones come in all shapes and sizes today—as big as a bus and as small as your thumb (see the Black Hornet, top right)—but the "Insectothopter" was in a class by itself and way ahead of its time.

The CIA developed this robotic dragonfly back in the 1970s, when such itty-bitty flying machines were unheard of outside science fiction. Insectothopter's mission: fly into foreign embassies and drop listening devices. In other words, it was a bug that laid bugs! In test flights, the laser-guided robot could fly 656 feet (200 m) away for about 60 seconds, just long enough to drop its payload. Unfortunately, Insectothopter had a mortal enemy: any stiff breeze. It buzzed wildly out of control in crosswinds, so the project never really got off the ground.

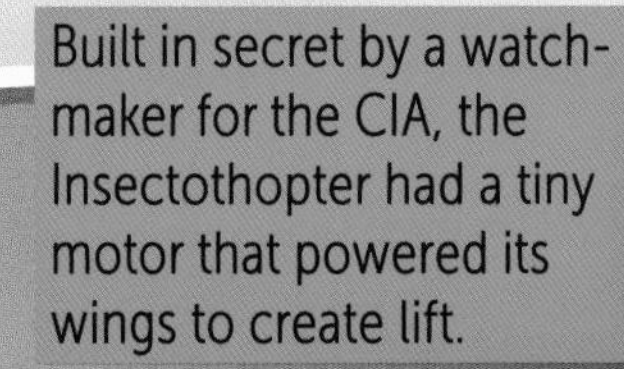

Built in secret by a watchmaker for the CIA, the Insectothopter had a tiny motor that powered its wings to create lift.

INSECTOTHOPTER 2.0

The robobug concept didn't get squashed with the Insectothopter. A company called FLIR has developed a modern version with an insect-inspired code name: the Black Hornet. This "personal reconnaissance vehicle" looks more like a cool toy from a mall kiosk than a state-of-the-art drone, but it can do tricks the Insectothopter's designers never dreamed of. The Black Hornet can fly up to 1.24 miles (2 km) away and broadcast live video back to its smartphone-like controller. And unlike the Insectothopter, the Black Hornet can withstand wind gusts up to 23 miles an hour (37 km/h).

DECLASSIFIED CYBERNETIC SPIES

CHARLIE THE CATFISH

The CIA's sneakiest cybernetic spy didn't walk or fly—it swam. "Charlie" was a fully robotic catfish built by the CIA's Office of Advanced Technologies in the 1990s. It looked like a catfish and swam like a catfish, but it was actually guided by remote control and had a communications system in its plastic hull. Charlie's official mission was to collect "water samples undetected" and test aquatic robotic technology. Any other mission duties remain classified.

CYBER SHARKS

It sounds like a triumph of mad science: the ability to control a shark like a toy submarine. A team of marine biologists in Massachusetts, U.S.A., has figured out the trick. They fitted a small shark with electrodes that stimulated the smell center of its brain. Because sharks always follow their nose, the scientists were able to control their test subject by triggering various odor detectors. Someday, the military might use larger species of remote-control sharks as underwater spies.

SECRET SAUCER

CLIMB ABOARD THE UFO THAT EARTHLINGS BUILT: **THE AVROCAR**

The images you see here, recently declassified and for your eyes only, are definitive proof that flying saucers are real. But this alien-looking craft didn't come from another solar system; it was made in Canada. Code-named the VZ-9 Avrocar, it was a top secret saucer built and flown in the late 1950s. Despite what some conspiracy theorists might claim, the Avrocar wasn't reverse engineered from crashed alien technology. It was the product of a partnership between a Canadian engineering firm and the U.S. military, built by a team of maverick engineers who wanted an aircraft that could zip into the sky like a helicopter but soar as fast as a supersonic fighter jet. In the end, the Avrocar's unique saucer shape proved too unstable for fast flight. Only two prototypes were produced and never flew higher than a few feet. But for a brief time, military officials considered flying saucers to be the aircraft of the future.

CODE NAMES

Throughout its development, the saucer project went by many code names: Spade, Omega, and Project 1794, seen here.

LIFTOFF!

Inside the Avrocar's aluminum hull were three special jet engines that produced downward thrust. The pilot controlled flight by steering a massive metal disc beneath the craft, which directed the thrust downward for takeoffs and in any direction for flight.

The Avrocar had two cockpits but was designed to be flown by a single pilot. The second seat was for an observer along for the ride.

FLYING SO-LOW

The saucer was supposed to reach altitudes of 19 miles (31 km) and zoom four times the speed of sound, fast enough to fly from the East Coast to the West Coast of the United States in an hour. The prototypes never got more than three feet (1 m) off the ground or flew much faster than a family car can drive.

OFFICIALLY GROUNDED

Government officials canceled the saucer project in 1961 after realizing that such craft were dangerous to fly and would never live up to expectations. Fifty-one years later, the project was finally declassified, and the military's UFO became an identified flying object.

TOMORROW'S TECH: DARPA UNCLASSIFIED

FIND OUT ABOUT **FIVE SECRET INVENTIONS** IN PROGRESS

Within the U.S. Department of Defense, one agency is laser-focused on the future. The Defense Advanced Research Projects Agency, or DARPA, was launched in 1958 to help the United States compete in the space race. The secretive group's role has evolved over the years. Today DARPA's job is to chase down the most cutting-edge ideas before other countries think of them. Those ideas have become inventions that have transformed modern warfare and changed the way we live. In 1969, for example, the group launched a network to connect computers. That network was the beginning of the internet. Much of DARPA's work is classified, but we dug up details on five futuristic inventions already in the works. Here's the scoop.

BOT ON THE MOVE

Meet Spot, a creature-like robot with an impressive sense of balance. It can navigate uneven terrain, climb stairs, and pick itself up from a fall. Spot is the latest four-legged bot from Boston Dynamics, but it's not the first. In 2009, with funding from DARPA, the company started developing BigDog, a machine intended to walk alongside soldiers, carrying their equipment. BigDog's engine made the robot too noisy for military missions, so the project was scrapped, but Boston Dynamics continued developing walking robots. Spot is battery-powered, but it won't be trotting into battle. Instead, the robot could be used to inspect construction sites or to help with search-and-rescue efforts.

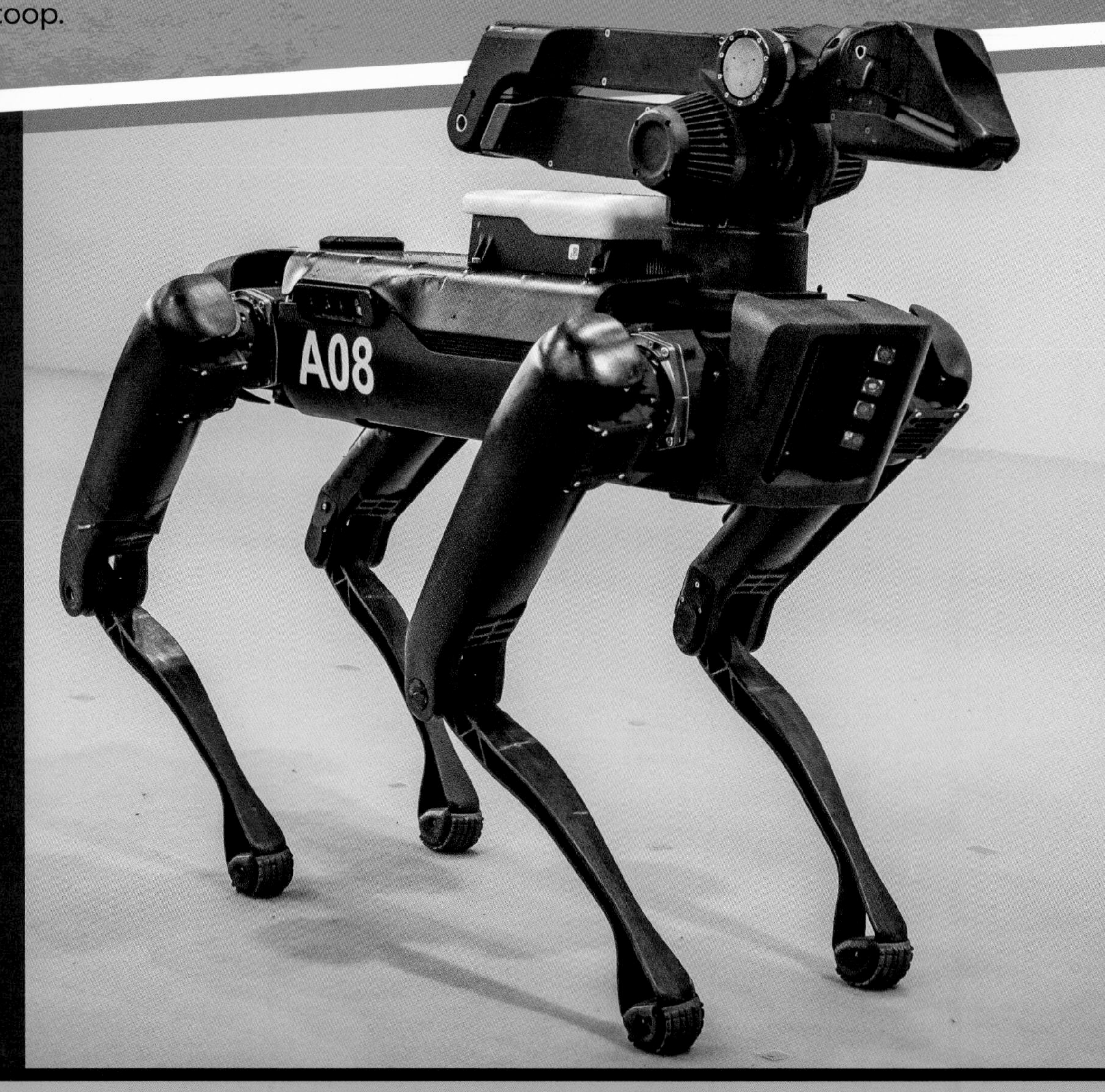

ROBOBUGS

The fly that just buzzed by your ear? It could be the spy of the future. In 2006, DARPA challenged scientists to create their own robobugs. One group of researchers set out to control a bug's flight. They ran wires through a beetle and hooked it up to a mini radio receiver, circuit board, and battery. The scientists were then able to move the bug's wings—and determine which way it flew—by pressing laptop keys. Another team experimented with moths, inserting mechanical implants into the insects at different stages of development. The goal: to determine what moment in a moth's life is the best time to turn it into a robobug.

Will microphone-toting insects someday listen in on conversations? There's no way of knowing since the Defense Department is keeping its creepy-crawly plans under wraps. Either way, you might want to keep an eye out for flies on the wall.

SEA CHANGE

In 2018, the U.S. Navy received a giant gift from DARPA—a 132-foot (40-m)-long ship named *Sea Hunter*. This unique vessel can stay at sea for three months at a time without any people on board. The self-driving ship was built to scout for enemy submarines. In tests, it was able to identify a sub that was more than half a mile (0.8 km) away. *Sea Hunter* is a prototype, and for now, it's the only one of its kind. But the ship might someday have company. DARPA envisions a future fleet of both crewed and self-driving vessels working together at sea.

FREQUENT FLYER

In the past, rockets were typically used one time before they detached from a spacecraft and burned up in the atmosphere or fell into the ocean. Rockets that did blast off more than once had to go through a pricey refurbishing process between voyages. Today multiple developers are racing to change that.

The company SpaceX made headlines in 2017 when it started launching reusable rockets. Now the U.S. military is working with aerospace company Boeing to build a space vehicle that not only flies repeatedly, but also makes back-to-back trips—as many as 10 launches in 10 days. The Space Plane, which is the length of two school buses lined up, is not meant to carry passengers. Instead, its job will be to launch satellites, some of which will be used for spy work. Though the rocket will take off vertically, it will land horizontally like a plane on a runway. Each launch will cost around $5 million. In the world of space transportation, that's a steal.

WEARABLE ROBOTS

Scientists are taking steps to team up human soldiers with machines—by developing exoskeletons that boost the wearer's strength and speed. The latest designs are soft and lightweight. They also adjust to the needs of the wearer in real time, kicking in to help with walking or lifting at just the right moment. The futuristic suits are intended to help not just soldiers but anybody who needs support to walk, run, or lift heavy loads. With exosuits already being tested, it won't be long before we humans are machines on the move.

UNDERCOVER OPERATION

GET IN GEAR

ASK A PARENT OR GUARDIAN'S PERMISSION BEFORE DOING THESE ACTIVITIES!

HOW TO MAKE YOUR VERY OWN **SPY GADGETS**

High-tech spy gear can be pricey. But you don't have to break the bank to have your very own snooping equipment at home! Whether you're a sleuth in training or simply someone in need of a secret safe, we've got you covered with three do-it-yourself spy contraptions.

FINGERPRINT KIT

Every person has a unique set of fingerprints. Crime-solvers have long made use of this identifier to track down criminals. You can, too, with a homemade fingerprint kit.

REQUIRED ITEMS: Ground cinnamon, cornstarch, small bowl, makeup brush or paintbrush, clear tape

DIRECTIONS:

STEP 1. Pour a small amount of ground cinnamon into a bowl. Combine cinnamon with an equal measure of cornstarch. Mix thoroughly.

STEP 2. Find a place where you think a fingerprint may be. Pour a bit of the mixture on the spot. Use the brush to gently brush it off. The dust left behind will stick to the oils in the fingerprint, rendering it visible.

STEP 3. Lift the fingerprint with a small piece of clear tape.

NEED A RIDDLE HINT?

This chapter's code uses a fake language called Eggy-Peggy (read about it on page 9).

If you're still at a loss, turn to page 183 for the answer to this encrypted riddle!

HERE'S ANOTHER HINT. ⇧

Deck of Cards With a SECRET COMPARTMENT

Turn an ordinary deck of cards into a safe. Then store your treasures inside.

REQUIRED ITEMS: Deck of cards with white borders, scissors, duct tape, glue

DIRECTIONS:

STEP 1. Set aside 10 cards.

STEP 2. From the stack that remains, select any card. Fold the card in half so that it is not possible to see the card type. Cut out the inside and discard it, leaving only the white border. Unfold the white border.

STEP 3. Repeat for each card in the stack (but not the 10 cards you set aside in step 1).

STEP 4. Place one uncut card on a table. Stack all the borders on top of it.

STEP 5. Glue the top border to the one directly underneath it and repeat until all of the borders are glued together.

STEP 6. Use duct tape to line the compartment, including the sides of the compartment.

STEP 7. Once the glue has dried, your secret safe is ready! Place money, keys, or jewelry in the compartment. Cover with the cards you set aside. Place the entire stack back into the card box. You can now hide your possessions in plain sight!

REARVIEW SPY GLASSES

A spy always needs to know if he or she is being followed. To keep an eye on what's going on behind you without so much as turning your head, try some sneaky rearview glasses.

REQUIRED ITEMS: Dark sunglasses, two round 1-inch (2.5-cm) mirrors (available at craft stores), craft glue

DIRECTIONS:

STEP 1. Place a small dab of glue on the back of each mirror.

STEP 2. Paste one mirror onto the far-left side of the left lens. Paste the other mirror onto the far-right side of the right lens.

STEP 3. Let the glue dry. Then practice using the mirrors to watch what is happening behind you while appearing to look straight ahead.

Day seven of sailing voyage
through the BERMUDA TRIANGLE.
NO SIGN OF LAND.

SECRET PLACES

No anomalies in sight.
Agreeable weather.
Beautiful sunsets.

"No trespassing!" "Do not enter!" "Authorized personnel only!" "Enter at your own risk!" Always heed such warning signs in real life. But in this chapter, they're more like signposts that you're on the right path. Because you have a full security clearance for a guided tour through secret spaces and classified bases—places that officially don't exist unless you know where to look or whom to ask. You're off to see where the U.S. government supposedly stores its crashed UFOs and how to access the secret chambers of the world's most famous monuments. Turn off your phone's GPS and get ready to get lost. In this chapter, you're wandering off the map.

WAIT, since when is the sunset blue ...?

EXTRA ROOM

THESE HOUSES HAVE **SOMETHING TO HIDE**

Secret rooms are no longer the domain of medieval castle lords and Scooby Doo villains. More and more ordinary homeowners are stashing secret spaces in their houses. They're camouflaging the doors with bookshelves, stairways, wooden paneling, brick walls—all custom-built entrances that open only to those who press the hidden button. Although many of these chambers function as "panic rooms" featuring reinforced walls and heavy locks that keep occupants safe from potential home invaders, just as many are built for the fun of it. Scan these pages to spy secret rooms new and old.

THE SECRET ARCHITECTS
GILBERT, ARIZONA, U.S.A.

When people want a fancy fort in their homes, they call Creative Home Engineering. This Arizona-based firm specializes in designing and installing doorways disguised as everything from simple wall panels to fireplaces that slide aside to reveal hidden hideouts. Activating these surprise portals is half the fun. Move a chess piece to a special spot on the board and—voilà!—the brick wall behind it pops open. One popular option is a book that works as a switch when pulled from a shelf. The company has installed more than a thousand secret doors around the world.

DOGE'S PALACE
VENICE, ITALY

Why settle for a regular tour of this sprawling palace—once home to the rulers (or doges) of Venice—when you can reserve a tour of the Itinerari Segreti, aka the "Secret Itineraries"? You'll get to explore hidden passage-ways, an interrogation room, prisons, and other parts of the palace that are off-limits during regular visits.

WHAT FOLLOWS IS A RIDDLE HIDDEN IN A SECRET CODE. THE ANSWER TO THIS RIDDLE IS A

DEVIOUS DRAWERS

Before banks offered safe-deposit boxes to keep valuables locked away and under guard, the well-to-do stashed their goodies at home in their own furniture. "Secretary cabinets," which reached the height of their popularity and complexity in the 18th century, were marvels of secret drawers and false doors all built into what appeared to be a normal cabinet. The most fantastic of these was the Berlin Secretary Cabinet crafted for King Frederick William II of Prussia in 1779. An engineering marvel of spring-loaded secret drawers, pop-out panels, and clockwork mechanisms, it has been called the most expensive piece of furniture in 18th-century Europe. But such fun furniture isn't a thing of the past. So-called stealth furniture—coffee tables, nightstands, and even couches—with hidden compartments is making a comeback.

KÖRNER'S FOLLY

KERNERSVILLE, NORTH CAROLINA, U.S.A.

Billed as the "strangest house in the world," this rambling mansion features secret underground passages, tiny rooms, trapdoors, and hidden compartments, all built to the eccentric specifications of Jule Gilmer Körner in 1880. Rumor has it an acquaintance told Körner that his house was a folly, or absurd, which tickled Körner so much that he had the name set in a plaque outside. Today, you can tour the house and decide if it was folly or just fun.

CASA DO PENEDO

FAFE MOUNTAINS, PORTUGAL

Not all houses hold their secrets inside. The Casa do Penedo, or "House of Stone," in Portugal's Fafe Mountains was built from four boulders and blends right into the landscape. Despite its Stone Age design, this cozy abode features a fireplace and even a swimming pool!

SINGER CASTLE

DARK ISLAND, NEW YORK, U.S.A.

You'd expect that a castle built on a rock called Dark Island in the middle of the St. Lawrence River would be full of secrets, and you'd be right! Built at the turn of the 20th century by Frederick G. Bourne, the president of the Singer Sewing Machine company, Singer Castle has hidden passages inside its walls and grates through which you can spy on visitors. (Bourne used them to hear what his guests were saying about him.) Tour it today and you might even get to visit its secret dungeon.

KEEP OUT: AREA 51

ENTER THE **RESTRICTED AIRSPACE** OF AMERICA'S MOST TOP SECRET AIR BASE

Put on your spy goggles and inspect the satellite photo to the right. Notice any saucer-shaped ships sticking out of the hangars? Spot any little green men hunkered in the bunkers? This miles-high perspective is the closest you'll get to visiting Area 51, the super-duper top secret Air Force facility located far from prying eyes in the Nevada desert. Established in 1955 near Groom Lake and named after coordinates on a military map, Area 51 is the government's testing ground for classified craft. Conspiracy theorists suspect it's home to something literally out of this world: alien technology. Could they be on to something? The truth is down there.

UFO STORAGE

More than two dozen hangars dot the base. Whatever lies inside is classified, but ufologists have long suspected the government of storing the crashed Roswell UFO (featured in the Secret History chapter on page 42) somewhere in Area 51. The bodies of the alien pilots are supposedly here, too, presumably kept on ice underground.

AREA MAN

Area 51 might have remained forever under the radar of popular culture if not for a man named Robert Lazar. In a series of TV interviews in the 1980s, Lazar claimed he worked as a physicist at Area 51 studying crashed flying saucers and helping the Air Force use the alien technology in top secret aircraft. Skeptics investigated Lazar and discovered he had made up his employment and educational background, although Lazar claimed in turn that the military was merely trying to discredit him to hide the truth.

DESCRIBED ON PAGE 8. PERHAPS THAT IS ENOUGH INFORMATION TO SOLVE THIS RIDDLE,

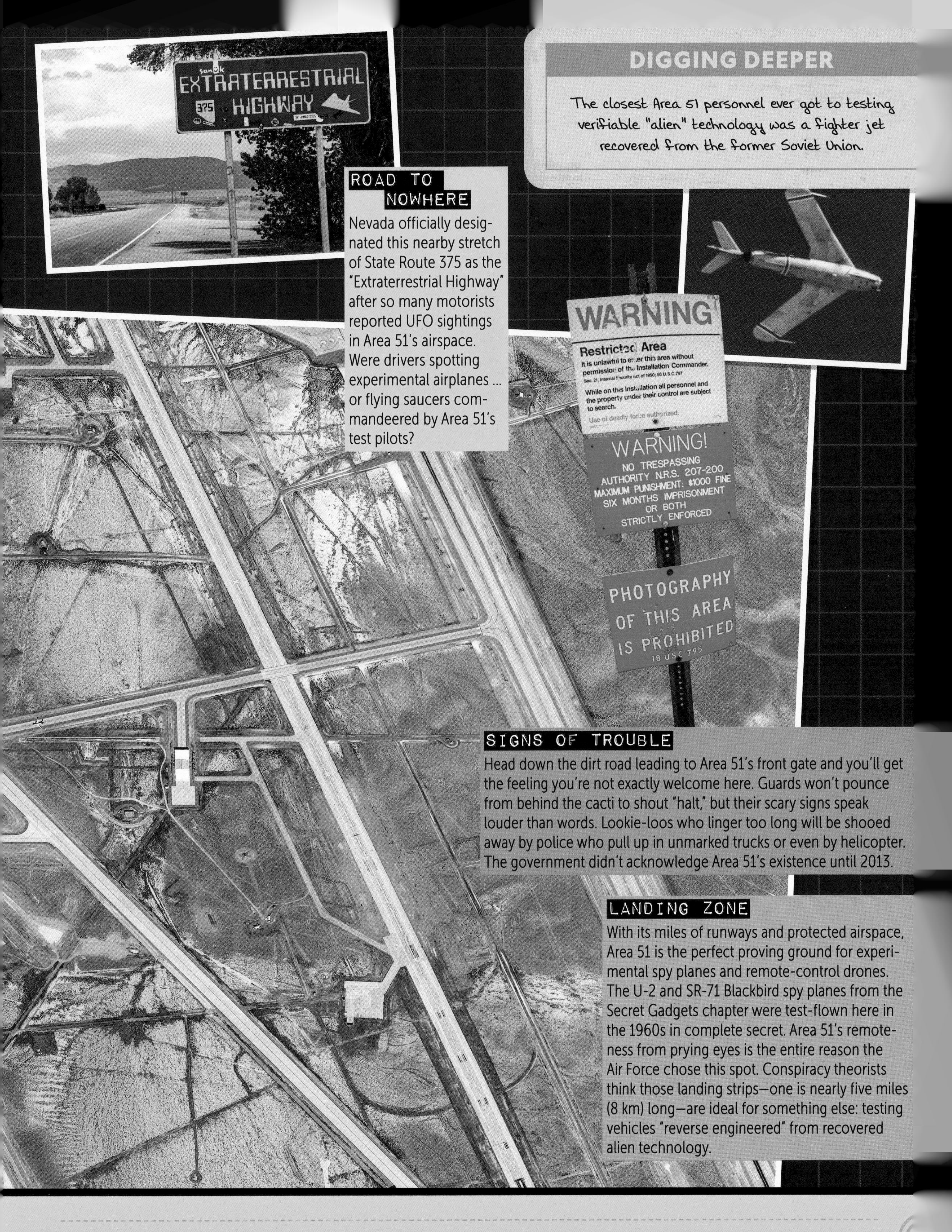

DIGGING DEEPER

The closest Area 51 personnel ever got to testing verifiable "alien" technology was a fighter jet recovered from the former Soviet Union.

ROAD TO NOWHERE

Nevada officially designated this nearby stretch of State Route 375 as the "Extraterrestrial Highway" after so many motorists reported UFO sightings in Area 51's airspace. Were drivers spotting experimental airplanes ... or flying saucers commandeered by Area 51's test pilots?

SIGNS OF TROUBLE

Head down the dirt road leading to Area 51's front gate and you'll get the feeling you're not exactly welcome here. Guards won't pounce from behind the cacti to shout "halt," but their scary signs speak louder than words. Lookie-loos who linger too long will be shooed away by police who pull up in unmarked trucks or even by helicopter. The government didn't acknowledge Area 51's existence until 2013.

LANDING ZONE

With its miles of runways and protected airspace, Area 51 is the perfect proving ground for experimental spy planes and remote-control drones. The U-2 and SR-71 Blackbird spy planes from the Secret Gadgets chapter were test-flown here in the 1960s in complete secret. Area 51's remoteness from prying eyes is the entire reason the Air Force chose this spot. Conspiracy theorists think those landing strips—one is nearly five miles (8 km) long—are ideal for something else: testing vehicles "reverse engineered" from recovered alien technology.

PERHAPS NOT. IF YOU'RE STUMPED, YOU WILL FIND A HINT AND THE CIPHER USED AT THE

MONUMENTAL MYSTERIES

THESE POPULAR LANDMARKS ARE **HIDING SOMETHING**

When you think of places shrouded in mystery, national monuments might not immediately come to mind. After all, these structures are out in the wide open, created for the public to tour and enjoy. But some of the world's most famous landmarks have secret spaces hidden from view. The next time you visit one of these popular destinations, keep an eye out for unmarked doors and hidden passages. You just might stumble upon a long-forgotten chamber, waiting to be discovered!

HIDDEN HISTORY: MOUNT RUSHMORE'S HALL OF RECORDS

SOUTH DAKOTA, U.S.A.

Mount Rushmore is one of the world's most recognizable landmarks. Every year, about three million people visit the colossal stone sculpture featuring the faces of four U.S. presidents: George Washington, Thomas Jefferson, Theodore Roosevelt, and Abraham Lincoln. But few realize that tucked behind Lincoln's head is a hidden chamber, officially known as the Hall of Records. Sculptor Gutzon Borglum, who created Mount Rushmore with the help of 400 workers, came up with the idea for a cavern to house key American documents. But Borglum died in 1941, before the project was completed, and for decades, the room sat empty. Finally, in 1998, a titanium vault was installed in its floor. It contains a box with 16 porcelain panels. Inscribed on the panels is the story of how Mount Rushmore came to be created, why the four presidents depicted on the landmark were selected, and a brief history of the United States. The information is not intended for today's visitors but for people thousands of years in the future.

END OF THIS CHAPTER. NOW GET CRACKING! HERE IS THE ENCODED RIDDLE: QRW DOO ZKR

SECRET STORY: THE 103RD FLOOR OF THE EMPIRE STATE BUILDING

NEW YORK CITY

For a bird's-eye view of New York City and beyond, you can purchase tickets to visit the indoor observatory on the 102nd floor of the Empire State Building. It's called the Top Deck, but that's not exactly accurate. Tickets are not available for the *actual* top deck, a secret terrace on the 103rd floor. The terrace of this world-famous landmark was controversial from the start. In 1929, the group erecting the tower said the 103rd floor would serve as a docking place for airships—large gas-filled planes without any wings. Some people thought the plan was just an excuse to make the skyscraper taller than the Chrysler Building, which was at the time the world-record holder. Either way, airships as a method of transportation never took off, and the 103rd floor has always been closed to the public. From time to time, celebrities, such as Taylor Swift and Ariana Grande, are granted access to the exclusive balcony. The company that owns the Empire State Building hopes the high-profile visits will inspire others to check out the skyscraper. But the experience is not for the faint of heart. Unlike the glass-walled observatory on the 102nd floor, the topmost level has only a small ledge with a low railing separating visitors from the dizzying drop below!

THE PRESIDENT'S HIDEOUT: A SECRET SHELTER AT THE WHITE HOUSE

WASHINGTON, D.C.

A mysterious bunker lies directly beneath the White House. Officially dubbed the Presidential Emergency Operations Center, the underground facility was built during World War II. In recent years, the shelter is thought to have undergone a top secret expansion. Officials were tight-lipped about the details of a $376 million White House construction project completed during the Obama administration. They said it was meant to improve electrical wiring and air conditioning. But one White House staffer told the *New York Times* that the project, which involved digging a cavernous hole in the lawn, was "security-related." Many believe the construction project was more than an update. According to a book by former *Washington Post* reporter Ronald Kessler, a second bunker, at least five stories deep, was added underground. What exactly lies beneath the White House? The public may never know.

OUT OF REACH: THE STATUE OF LIBERTY'S TORCH

NEW YORK HARBOR

The Statue of Liberty might be the United States' best-known sculpture. The copper-covered symbol of freedom was dedicated as a gift from the people of France on October 28, 1886. Millions of people visit the famous landmark every year. And thousands make their way up a 12-story stairway to the statue's crown, where they can peer out the window at New York Harbor. Even better views are found inside the torch. But visitors are not allowed to climb the narrow 40-foot (12-m) ladder that would take them to the famous copper flame. The sky-high observatory has been closed to the public since 1916, when, on July 30, German spies set off a massive explosion nearby. Their motive: to destroy military supplies bound for countries that Germany was fighting in World War I. The blast was so powerful that it shattered windows six miles (10 km) away. The damage to Lady Liberty's torch was repaired, but the highest point of this monument has not welcomed visitors since.

FIN LAND

DO YOU DARE TO DIVE INTO **THE HIDDEN LAIR** OF THE GREAT WHITE SHARK?

ɔ in the Pacific Ocean, halfway between Mexico's Baja Peninsula
che islands of Hawaii, adventurous sailors will find the world's
exclusive cafe. You might be surprised by what's on the menu.
the world's most fantastic fish gather each winter and spring.
recently, no one knew why. Scientists call this remote patch of
acific the "White Shark Cafe."

USIVE JAWS

white sharks are famous for their massive size—up to 20 feet
ong—and powerful jaws containing as many as 3,000 teeth
d in their mouths. But little was once known about these top
predators. They're elusive fish, spending most of their lives
ning thousands of miles in search of food. Scientists used to think
sharks spent their lives cruising along the western coast of North
ca, feeding on the large marine mammals such as sea lions and
whales close to shore. But in recent years, tracking technology
wed marine biologists to keep tabs on great whites. Researchers
gged dozens of white sharks, learning much about their habits,
en giving them names like Eugene and Leona. And like clock-
ch winter and spring, Eugene, Leona, and their fellow great
abandoned the food-rich coastal waters and headed for their
air in the middle of the Pacific.

BUFFET

s had long thought this spot,
e size of Colorado, U.S.A., was
ep-ocean desert. Satellites
no signs of life. So why would
ites turn up here in droves?
mate? Give birth to baby great
ocialize in schools? It turns out
e here to stuff their bellies!
vessels sent to study the area
yer of life deeper than satellites
t. Tiny creatures serve as the base
ood chain that included squid and tuna
great white sharks. Once known as
Shark Lair, the region was renamed
Shark Cafe, the hottest new eatery
an.

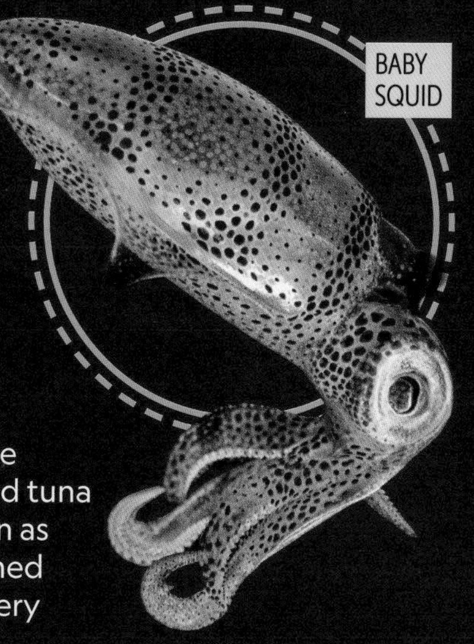

BABY SQUID

TRAPDOOR SPIDER

DEEP TROUBLE

Beware the Lairs of These Top Predators

TRAPDOOR SPIDER: This group of medium-size spiders—which includes roughly 120 species spread across the world—is famous for its horrible hospitality. Each trapdoor spider digs an underground burrow (although some prefer to live in trees) complete with a small door made of leaves, algae, and dirt, which blends in with the surrounding soil. It even has a tiny hinge fashioned from a squirt of spider silk. Outside the hatch, the spider weaves its "welcome mat": a network of silk strands that all lead back to the burrow. Once construction is done, the spider "locks" its door by holding it shut with barbed fangs. The spider waits for tasty bugs to creep closer and closer until they're right outside the door. Then—*whoosh!* In the blink of an eye, the trapdoor spider opens the hatch and pulls in its unfortunate guest.

CANTOR'S GIANT SOFTSHELL TURTLE: Slow and steady might win the race for turtles on land, but this river turtle takes a different approach to survival: slow and deadly! The Cantor's turtle buries its shell—which is mushy and flexible instead of hard—in the mucky bottom of rivers and streams in Asia, leaving only its eyes and mouth exposed above the mud and sand. It sits like this more than 90 percent of the time, only surfacing twice a day to breathe, waiting patiently for a clueless fish to wander too close. That would be like you sitting at the dinner table for 23 hours each day just waiting for food to appear. When a fish does wander too close—chomp!—the turtle snaps it up faster than the eye can follow—the only moment in this turtle's life when it's speedy.

SECRETS OF THE SEA

FOUR MYSTERIES OF THE DEEP ... **SOLVED!**

If alien explorers warped past Earth in their flying saucer without bothering to make a pit stop, they might mistake our world for an ocean planet. After all, more than 70 percent of Earth's surface is covered with water. And scientists know more about the surface of the moon than the depths of the ocean. So it only makes sense that much of our planet has been a source of mystery for most of history. Thanks to extensive exploration by Earthling explorers and modern technology, we can shed light on the ocean's deepest, darkest secrets.

THE BERMUDA TRIANGLE

An area located off the southeastern Atlantic coast of the United States, the Bermuda Triangle is notorious for swallowing planes, boats, and ships. Craft go missing without leaving behind a speck of debris—not a life preserver or even a rivet. According to one reckoning, 75 planes and hundreds of yachts have gone missing in the Devil's Triangle in the last century. Navigators going back to the days of Christopher Columbus reported confusing compass readings here. Pilots have complained of an eerie electrical fog that interferes with their instruments. Why is this stretch of turquoise sea such a hot spot for vanishings? Some believe the Bermuda Triangle is actually a giant doorway to ... somewhere else—possibly the lost city of Atlantis. A more scientifically acceptable theory is that methane gas locked in the Bermuda Triangle's sediment might belch loose in a bubble barrage capable of sinking ships and disrupting a plane's instruments.

WHAT'S REALLY GOING ON? The truth here is not stranger than fiction. The Bermuda Triangle lies in a region prone to tropical storms. Shipwrecking reefs lie just under the surface in some places; the seafloor dips into abyssal trenches five miles (8 km) deep in others. The Bermuda Triangle has been a superhighway for sea traffic since the early days of exploration, so it makes sense that the region would see more accidents than less traveled areas. Wreckage not set adrift by the strong currents could sink into the region's trenches, never to be seen again.

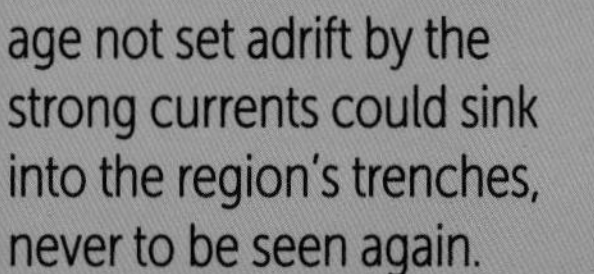

UNIDENTIFIED SUNKEN OBJECT

While scanning the bottom of the Baltic Sea for sunken ships in 2011, a Swedish deep-sea salvage team known as Ocean X found something else entirely: An odd circular structure roughly 200 feet (60 m) across at a depth of 300 feet (90 m). It was sitting at the end of a long gouge in the silt, as if it had skidded to a halt. Had the object crash-landed here? Ocean X's team members were intrigued. They publicized their fuzzy sonar image of the object, which came to be known as the Baltic Sea Anomaly. Observers across the internet noticed its uncanny resemblance to the Millennium Falcon from the Star Wars films. Some speculated that it was a crashed flying saucer, or perhaps an old anti-submarine installation, or maybe even an underwater gateway to another world. Ocean X's members thought the Anomaly could be the undersea equivalent of England's mysterious Stonehenge rock circle.

MILLENNIUM FALCON

BALTIC SEA ANOMALY

WHAT'S REALLY GOING ON? Despite mysterious equipment failures, Ocean X's divers and robotic submarines managed to gather samples of the sunken structure. Scientific analysis of those samples, however, didn't reveal anything out of this world. Instead of exotic alien metals or human-made materials, the Anomaly appears to be made of ordinary rocks, likely deposited ages ago when glaciers crept across what is now the Baltic Sea's bottom. The Anomaly is just a pile of stone that happens to resemble the Millennium Falcon on sonar.

THE BLOOP

The ocean is a noisy place. Whales sing, volcanoes spew, currents surge, icebergs crumble, and glaciers tumble into the sea. Ships and submarines add their background buzz. Using arrays of sensitive underwater microphones called hydrophones, scientists monitor this aquatic racket. They can usually file deep-sea sounds into one of three categories: boat traffic, geological activity, or marine life. In the summer of 1997, researchers recorded a noise they'd never heard before ... and it was *loud*. The signal was detected by Pacific Ocean hydrophones nearly 3,000 miles (4,800 km) apart, making it louder than any known animal noise. Scientists named it Bloop. At least one scientist suspected it came from some type of animal. But *which* animal? Bloop is so overpowering, it could drown out the song of the blue whale, the loudest and largest animal in the ocean.

WHAT'S REALLY GOING ON? As they continued listening, scientists eventually pinpointed the source of Bloop—and it wasn't a sea monster after all. It was caused by a particularly large icequake, or an iceberg breaking away from a glacier in the Antarctic and doing the iceberg equivalent of a belly flop—a splash heard round the world.

THE CHILEAN BLOB

Scientists were stumped when a 12-ton (10.9-t) glob of pink-and-gray goo—nearly half the size of a tennis court—washed up on the southern coast of Chile in 2003. Was it rotting flesh of the fabled giant octopus? A castaway kraken? Some sea creature new to science?

WHAT'S REALLY GOING ON? The Chilean Blob was just the latest in a long line of "globsters"—mysterious masses of boneless tissue that occasionally reach the beach. Most globsters turn out to be the bodies of basking sharks, but some are too decomposed to identify. Analyses of the Chilean Blob revealed it as the remains of a sperm whale, dashing scientists' hopes that they'd finally gotten the fabled giant octopus by the tentacle.

CLASSIFIED CASE

AMERICA'S FORTRESS

TOUR THE WORLD'S MOST **SECURE BUNKER**

"Welcome to Cheyenne Mountain Complex" reads the sign painted in neat lettering on a building buried more than 2,000 feet (610 m) below the summit of a granite mountain near Colorado Springs, Colorado, U.S.A. Despite the warm greeting, it's obvious that no one is welcome here except personnel with top secret clearance. That much is clear from the two 23-ton (21-t) blast doors that seal this vast underground complex, the mile-long (1.6-km) tunnel to reach its entrance, the two security checkpoints just outside, and the scary warning signs bearing messages like "Restricted Area" that line the winding road leading here. Cheyenne Mountain Air Force Station is the most secure and secret bunker in the world. The roughly 350 people who work here (at least half live here) have a nickname for it: America's Fortress.

BUTTONED UP

Engineers blasted away millions of tons of granite to carve out the bunker's tunnels in the mid-1960s, at the height of the Cold War, as a haven for the military's top commanders should the unthinkable happen. Its blast doors and granite walls keep out more than just snoops or enemy soldiers. When sealed—or "buttoned up," as its residents call it—America's Fortress can withstand nuclear bombs, poison-gas attacks, diseases spread by biological warfare, electromagnetic pulses that fry electronics, and solar storms. The buildings inside its interconnected tunnels rest on giant springs that absorb the jolts of earthquakes and bomb blasts. An underground lake and spring provide unlimited fresh water. Generators, backup batteries, and tanks of fuel would keep all the systems running for weeks.

MOUNTAIN FOLK

Top secret safeguards are required for Cheyenne Mountain's primary tenant: NORAD, or North American Aerospace Defense Command. You might hear of this organization every December 25 when it famously tracks the course of a certain jolly old sled pilot (aka Santa Claus), but its primary mission is much more serious: NORAD scans the skies of the United States and Canada for any intruding missiles or aircraft. It's the eyes and ears of North America's military branches in the event of a war, guiding any retaliatory attacks, which is why its bunker is built to withstand any attack. NORAD staff work in a command center that looks to be right out of a movie, with massive monitors displaying maps and the status of the airspace around the continent.

HIDDEN LUXURY

The Cheyenne Mountain Complex might sound like a dark, damp, cold, and depressing place to live and work, but it's more like a subterranean city than a tomb. Its tunnels are home to a store, subway, gymnasium complete with exercise classes, chapel, hospital, dentist office, and cafeteria. Its deep underground lake even has a rowboat so engineers can check for structural cracks or staff can just row off some steam. The bunker needs all the comforts of home because that's exactly what it would become, for weeks or months, if the personnel here ever needed to button up and seal themselves from the outside world.

DIGGING DEEPER

NORAD personnel make up only about 30 percent of Cheyenne Mountain's residents. The other 70 percent work for secret agencies on projects that are strictly classified. It's likely some of these agencies are in charge of America's deepest secrets. The complex isn't just bombproof. It's hackproof. Any information stored on hard drives within its granite walls can't be scrambled by electromagnetic warfare or stolen by hackers from afar. The mountain itself, all 2,000 feet (610 m) of granite, is the ultimate firewall.

SPOILER ALERT

Secret Subterranean Spaces

LASCAUX CAVE: Crammed with more masterpieces than any art museum, this cave complex in the French countryside offers a window into the wild world of our Stone Age ancestors. The cavern walls are awash with stunning etchings of horses, bison, birds, humans, and bulls—one of which is 17 feet (5 m) long—painted more than 20,000 years ago. Opened to the public in 1948, the cavern became a destination, toured by up to 1,200 visitors a day. But all the breath, body heat, and humidity from this tourist crush began damaging the paintings. The cavern was closed to the public in 1963 and is for authorized archaeologists only.

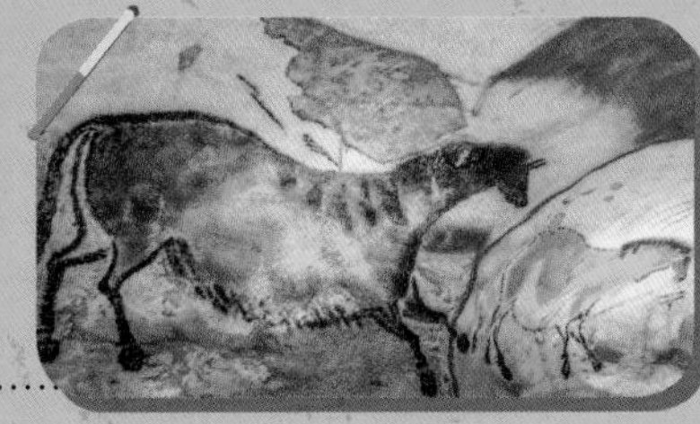

CAMP CENTURY: In 1960, the U.S. military built a nuclear-powered base under the Greenland ice 800 miles (1,300 km) south of the North Pole. Called Camp Century, it was composed of 21 tunnels connecting living quarters to a theater, library, barbershop, laboratories, and more. The military claimed Camp Century was just a research base for studying the Arctic ice, but the project was actually a test run for a secret missile-launching facility. Those plans were scrapped after shifting glacial ice slowly crushed the base. It was abandoned for good in 1967.

HIDDEN WONDER

ONE OF THE **LARGEST CAVES** ON THE PLANET WAS ONLY **RECENTLY DISCOVERED**

C*olossal. Massive. Enormous.* These are the words often used to describe Vietnam's Son Doong Cave, but they always seem to fall short. Traveling from one end of the cavern to the other takes days. Inside are giant rock formations, a rushing river, and even a jungle. The cave ranks among the largest in the world. And yet, not so long ago, no one knew it existed. In the early 1990s, Ho Khanh, a local farmer from a nearby village, was looking for shelter during a storm in the jungle. He followed the sound of rushing water and found a large hole in the limestone. He had discovered the cave's opening. But the entrance was such a steep drop that he turned around and went home. In 2009, he returned with a team of British cave experts. Together they explored an extraordinary subterranean world that had been hidden from view for all of human history. The takeaway is just as tantalizing: If something this immense was just found, imagine what other wonders could be out there, waiting to be discovered.

WATCH OUT FOR DINOSAURS SINKHOLE

During the day, sunlight pours into the cave through giant sinkholes that formed long ago when the roof collapsed. Sunlight means that plants can grow. And grow they do. The cavers who discovered this lush section of the cave thought it looked like a scene from prehistoric times. "Watch out for dinosaurs!" someone joked. And the name stuck.

CAVE ENTRANCE

After two days of intense treks through the jungle, you will reach the entrance to Son Doong Cave. If you want to explore the cavern, the only way to go is down. The cave's entrance is a rocky descent into darkness. Rope and harnesses are required.

HAND OF DOG STALAGMITE

What does this giant rock formation look like to you? An alien? A creature's paw? Cavers named it the Hand of Dog. The limestone formation, called a stalagmite, formed over millions of years as water containing dissolved minerals dripped from the cave's ceiling and collected below.

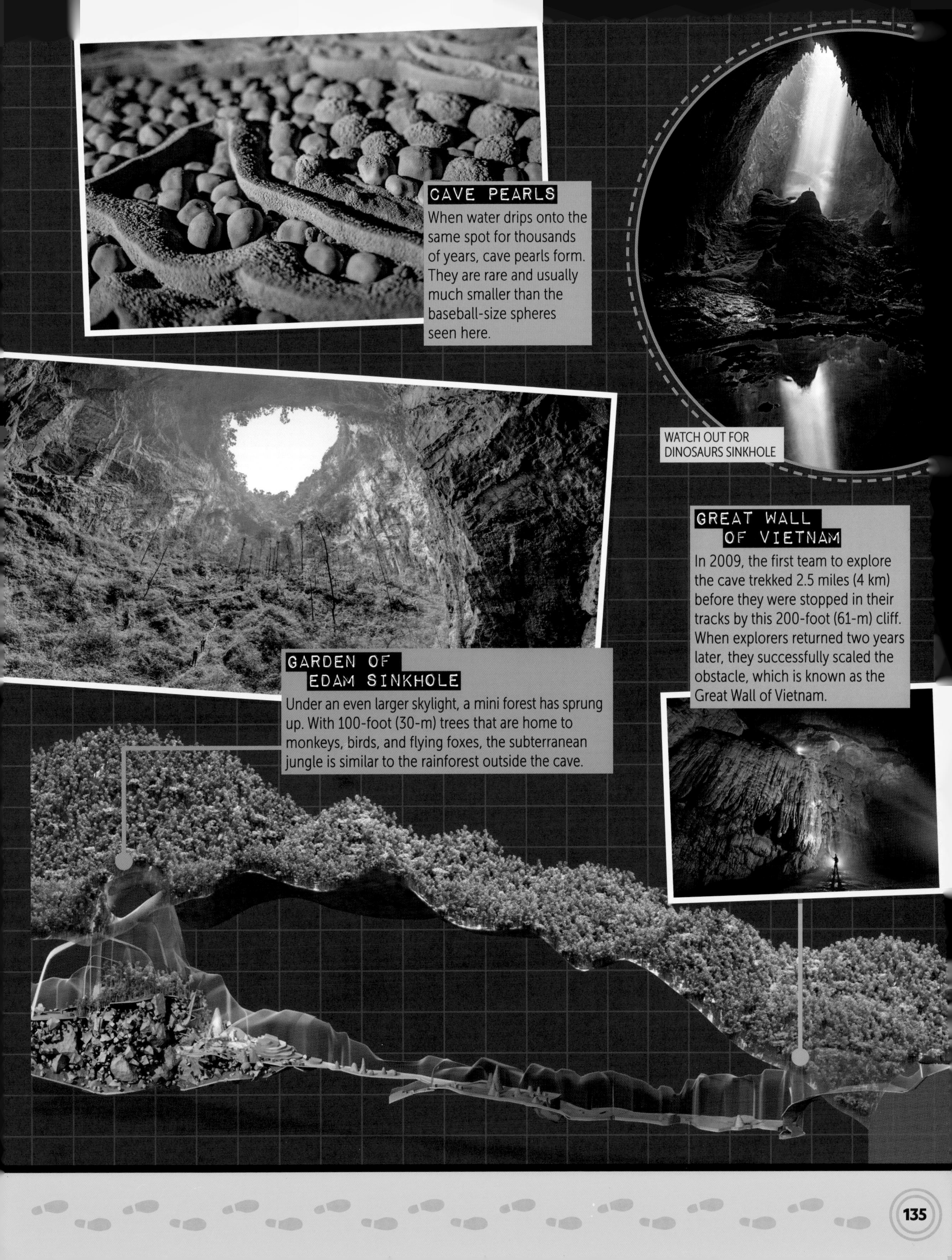

CAVE PEARLS

When water drips onto the same spot for thousands of years, cave pearls form. They are rare and usually much smaller than the baseball-size spheres seen here.

WATCH OUT FOR DINOSAURS SINKHOLE

GREAT WALL OF VIETNAM

In 2009, the first team to explore the cave trekked 2.5 miles (4 km) before they were stopped in their tracks by this 200-foot (61-m) cliff. When explorers returned two years later, they successfully scaled the obstacle, which is known as the Great Wall of Vietnam.

GARDEN OF EDAM SINKHOLE

Under an even larger skylight, a mini forest has sprung up. With 100-foot (30-m) trees that are home to monkeys, birds, and flying foxes, the subterranean jungle is similar to the rainforest outside the cave.

SECRET DESTINATIONS

TAKE A STEALTHY SPIN TO THESE **MYSTERY SPOTS**

ABANDONED SUBWAY STOPS

NEW YORK CITY

One of the world's oldest subway systems, New York City's sprawling network of underground tracks contains more than 15 decommissioned stops that sit like ghost stations under the busy streets. Some have been preserved for tours (such as the stunning, cathedral-like City Hall stop on the 6 train) while others can only be glimpsed by riders who know when and where to look out the window on their daily commute.

PASSETTO DI BORGO

ROME, ITALY

Built over several centuries beginning in the 1200s, this 30-foot (9-m) wall contains a hidden passage that connects the Vatican to Sant'Angelo Castle, about 350 yards (320 m) away. Two popes have used the tunnel to escape sieges at various times in Vatican history. Today, visitors to Rome can tour the Passetto, which means "small passage" despite its length of more than three football fields.

GREENBRIER BUNKER

WHITE SULFUR SPRINGS, WEST VIRGINIA, U.S.A.

Until 1992, no one without the proper security clearance knew about a bomb-proof basement beneath the Greenbrier luxury resort in West Virginia. Given the code name Project Greek Island and stocked with enough food to last 30 years, it was a top secret underground refuge for members of Congress in the event of World War III. Now declassified and open for tours, the bunker stands as a fascinating monument to the Cold War.

INTERNATIONAL UFO MUSEUM AND RESEARCH CENTER

ROSWELL, NEW MEXICO, U.S.A.

The U.S. government denies that an alien spaceship crashed here in 1947. Investigate the incident for yourself at the International UFO Museum, where you'll find firsthand accounts and declassified documents related to the Roswell incident as well as supposed evidence of UFO sightings—and landings—around the world.

INTERNATIONAL SPY MUSEUM

WASHINGTON, D.C.

Learn the art of espionage and inspect high-tech spy gizmos—including the lipstick pistol, buttonhole camera, and invisible ink—at this museum dedicated to clandestine operations. The Operation Spy adventure has you decrypting secret transmissions, infiltrating and escaping a secure facility, and interrogating an enemy agent, all in less than an hour.

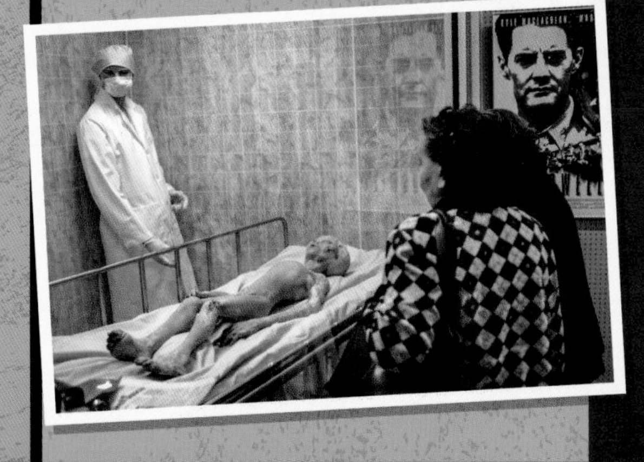

NINJA MUSEUM

IGA, JAPAN

Located in a village that was once a center of ninja training, this museum showcases the tools and tactics of history's sneakiest warriors. Watch trained ninja wield swords, throwing stars, and their own lethal hands and feet, and then tour a ninja residence filled with trapdoors, fake hallways, and hidden rooms to confound intruders.

SPOILER ALERT

Upside Downhills

THE CLAIM: The old adage "What goes up must come down" doesn't apply on "gravity hills," topsy-turvy outdoor tourist attractions found in more than a dozen U.S. states and all over the world. Also known as mystery hills and magnetic hills, gravity hills look like any stretch of hilly forest covered with rustic cabins, except balls roll uphill, chairs sit on walls, and people look taller or shorter depending on where they stand.

THE TRUTH: Gravity hill owners claim their physics-bending attractions are caused by paranormal phenomena, such as crashed UFOs or magnetic meteorites. The truth is more down to Earth. All such hills and houses are actually optical illusions caused when background terrain makes a gentle downhill slope look as if it's actually leaning uphill. Balls that appear to roll uphill are actually going downhill, for instance, or structures are built in such a way as to play with our sense of perspective. The laws of gravity remain unbroken.

INSIDE FORT KNOX

DISCOVER THE SECRETS OF THE **WORLD-FAMOUS SUPERVAULT**

As secure as Fort Knox. This comparison has become a catchphrase to indicate that something is safeguarded to an extraordinary degree. The expression refers to the vault known as Fort Knox—housed in the United States Bullion Depository building—which is said to be the most heavily guarded place on Earth. Built in Fort Knox, Kentucky, U.S.A., in the 1930s to protect the country's enormous trove of gold, the facility still holds a vast fortune in bullion, or gold bars. Though many details of the building's security systems remain as hidden as its gold, some features of this storied, impenetrable vault have been revealed.

LOCATION, LOCATION, LOCATION

The building's valuable contents are no secret, as the street names surrounding this famous depository—Bullion Boulevard and Gold Vault Road—offer more than just a hint of what's inside. In the 1930s, U.S. leaders were worried about the threat of an invading army, so they picked an area far from the country's coastlines. They also recognized the value in the next-door neighbors: Fort Knox Army base and its tens of thousands of soldiers, who could step in at a moment's notice if it was ever necessary.

ON GUARD

A guard box stands at each corner of the building. The boxes are staffed around the clock by heavily armed U.S. Mint police officers. Guards are stationed at the entrance gate, too.

DO NOT ENTER

The facility is ringed with fences topped with razor-sharp wire. Even the lawn is said to be laden with explosives.

THE ULTIMATE SAFE

The vault itself is a box of steel and concrete that sits in the center of the building, surrounded by a ring of offices and storerooms. Inside the vault are 13 compartments stacked from floor to ceiling with gold bars. Displayed on the door of each inner room is a blue sign that specifies the amount of gold inside.

HARD SHELL

The two-story building that houses the vault is made of granite, concrete, and steel. The roof is said to be bomb-proof.

OPEN SESAME

The vault has only one entrance. Its superthick door weighs about 20 tons (18 t)—more than a city bus—and is blast-, drill-, and torchproof. No one person is entrusted with all the information needed to unlock it, so getting in is a team effort. Various officials must dial separate combinations known only to each of them.

DIGGING DEEPER

The vault contains a whopping 367,500 gold bars worth more than $210 billion, as of mid-2019. They are similar in size to regular building bricks, but much heavier. A single bar of gold weighs about 27.5 pounds (12 kg)—as much as a two-year-old child. Through the years, the vault has guarded other valuables as well. The depository provided protection for priceless artifacts from around the world during World War II, including the Declaration of Independence, the U.S. Constitution, the Holy Crown of Hungary, and Great Britain's Magna Carta.

UNDERCOVER OPERATION

SNEAK & SEEK

HOW TO SET UP A **SCAVENGER HUNT!**

Sometimes the best hidden treasures aren't really treasures at all. They might be pictures or tasks or trinkets that have significance only to you and your buddies. This sort of secret stuff makes the perfect subject of a scavenger hunt, a type of game in which teams compete to see who can complete a list of objectives for points or to see who can complete them all first. It's also the perfect contest to show off your sleuthing skills! Here's your guide to a successful scavenger-hunting adventure.

STEP 1. Pick a safe place to host your hunt. Your backyard, a public park, or a nature walk—anyplace with room to roam will do. You can theme your hunt around your chosen location, or choose the location based on your theme.

STEP 2. Come up with a prize for the winners of the hunt. It can be anything from a bag of candy to plain old bragging rights to a trophy you design yourself!

STEP 3. Create the list of "treasures" for your hunters to scavenge. Keep it simple at first: a Hula-Hoop, a pair of socks, a Lego block, and so on. Feel free to assign points to the objectives based on their difficulty.

NEED A RIDDLE HINT?

This chapter's code uses a Caesar cipher shifted three spaces right (read about it on page 8).

If you're still at a loss, turn to page 183 for the answer to this encrypted riddle!

HERE'S ANOTHER HINT. ⇧

STEP 4. Invite some friends to play the game. Divide them into teams. Each team should have no more than four people. The more players you have, the more teams you need.

STEP 5. Play a few simple games until you get the hang of things. The winner is the team that completes their list first (or wins the most points if you scored the objectives based on difficulty).

STEP 6. Get creative! Why make your contestants find a Hula-Hoop when you can make them use the hoop for five minutes in the front yard? Why send them after a single Lego block when you can make them build a robot with it? (The best robot gets bonus points.) Here are some other silly ideas for inspiration:

- Sing a pop song at a bus stop. Record the performance on a digital camera or phone.
- Snap photos of a bird in a tree, another bird in flight, and a third bird on the ground.
- Strike a pose with a statue for a photo.
- Speak a made-up language or communicate only in gestures.

STEP 7. The best part about inventing a game is play-testing it! Try out your silliest objectives on your closest friends, and then revamp the hunt list until your scavenger hunts become the social event of the neighborhood. Most important of all, have fun!

DIGGING DEEPER

You think the sample scavenger-hunt objectives suggested here are silly? Students at the University of Chicago in Chicago, Illinois, U.S.A., throw a hunt that never fails to make the papers. Each annual event takes months of planning and consists of hundreds of objectives, such as building a bridge over a campus pond (worth 60 points) and setting up a meeting with the mayor of Chicago (worth just 25 points).

Close to CRACKING
secret code of enemy
SPY ORGANIZATION.

SECRET CODES

Code-cracking software on laptop.

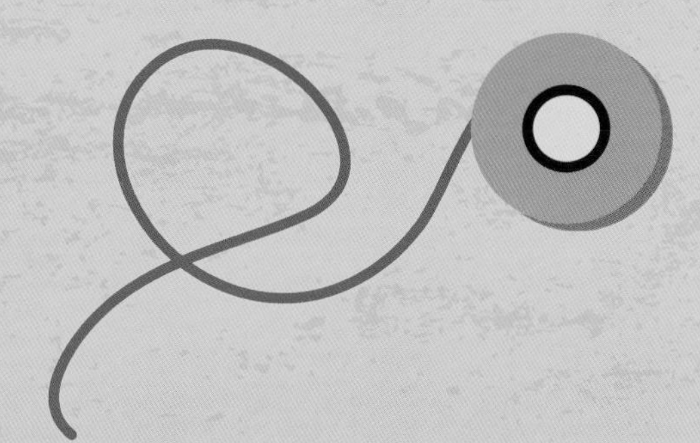

Laptop password is "PASSWORD."

Secret messages aren't just for spies and baseball pitchers. Encryption, or the practice of protecting information from prying eyes by converting it into secret codes, is used on everything from old photos on your thumb drive to emails you get from your wacky Uncle Josh (your computer does all this data encryption for you). Encryption is part of a larger field called cryptography, which is the science of secret messages. For professional spies, cryptography is like a second language used to share information with a select few. In this chapter, that few will include you, as you learn about codes as old as the written word and as new as the internet!

READERS BLOCKED

A TIMELINE OF SECRET CODES

600 B.C.: ATBASH SOUP

One of the first and simplest code systems made its debut in the Old Testament of the Bible. It was called Atbash, which comes from the first, last, second, and second-to-last letters in the Hebrew alphabet. Turn to page 9 to learn how to send messages with the Atbash code.

2000 B.C.: WORDS TO THE WISE

The written languages of both the ancient Egyptians and Chinese cultures used symbols that represented words and phrases. (You can read about Egyptian hieroglyphs in chapter 2 on page 39.) Such systems were incredibly complex—imagine having to learn hundreds or thousands of symbols instead of 26 letters!—and understood by a select few, such as nobles and scribes. It was a type of code for the society's elite, who used it to instill a sense of mystery and importance.

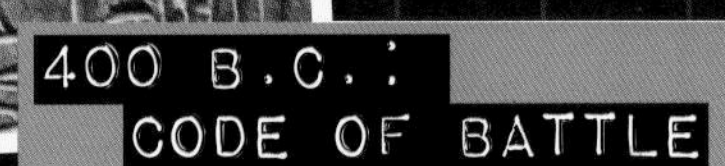

400 B.C.: CODE OF BATTLE

The soldiers of Sparta in ancient Greece were among the most feared warriors in history. Every man in this city-state (a city that's like its own country) was trained for battle since birth and joined the army at age 20 to defend Sparta for life. They considered themselves descendants of Hercules, the buff hero of Greek mythology, and yet they wielded their brains as well as their brawn on the battlefield. To transmit coded messages, the Spartans used an ingeniously simple device called the scytale (rhymes with Italy). It was a rod built to specific dimensions, around which the message writer wound a thin parchment. He or she wrote the message on this parchment, and then unwound it and sent it to the recipient, who carried a rod of the same thickness. By wrapping the parchment around this corresponding rod, the recipient could read the secret messages. It's one of the first examples of cunning codes used for war.

WHAT FOLLOWS IS A RIDDLE HIDDEN IN A SECRET CODE. THE ANSWER TO THIS RIDDLE IS A

1800: CRYPTOLOGY'S FOUNDING FATHER

Author of the Declaration of Independence and third president of the United States, Thomas Jefferson is in every school textbook as one of America's Founding Fathers. But few recognize his other title: the father of American cryptology. Jefferson was obsessed with languages, learning French, Latin, and Greek by the age of nine. By the time he was 20, he was well versed in math and physics. All these interests combined to create a powerhouse codemaking personality. Jefferson wrote letters about his secret crushes to friends. Twenty years later, while serving as George Washington's secretary of state, he invented a wheel cipher—a device made of 36 wooden wheels that spun to create secret messages. The U.S. Army used a similar device more than a century later. As president in the early 1800s, Jefferson relied on a coding system to communicate with the Lewis and Clark expedition to scout America west of the Mississippi River. If the expedition found gold or other treasures, Jefferson didn't want every treasure hunter in the young country to follow.

TODAY: DATA ENCRYPTION

Cryptography has entered the digital age. Technology companies compete to come up with uncrackable encoding systems to protect your emails, online-shopping transactions, and even your phone calls. Encryption schemes use many of the same techniques discussed on these pages, except they harness the computational power of computers to encode your data.

A.D. 500 | 1800 | 1900 | TODAY

1942: WAR!

Millennia of cryptology techniques culminated in World War II, a war of information as well as of nations. Some historians claim the six-year-long war—which sprawled across North Africa, Europe, and the South Pacific—would have lasted at least two years longer if the victorious Allied nations hadn't cracked the codes of the opposing Axis powers. You can read all about the heroes of this information war by turning the page.

TODAY: CYBERWAR

The code-cracking battles of World War II are now waged on a grand scale. Nations employ armies of hackers to swipe information, divert cash, shut down services, and wreak electronic havoc with enemy nations. Such "cyberwarfare" can cripple an enemy country without firing a shot. In 2009, the Pentagon established the U.S. Cyber Command to defend the country from cyberattacks from foreign powers and initiate such attacks against foes.

PERSON, PLACE, OR THING DESCRIBED IN THIS CHAPTER. THE CODE IS BASED ON A CIPHER

CODEMAKER

THE "UNBREAKABLE" SECRET MESSAGES OF THE NAZIS' ENIGMA MACHINE

Communication is crucial in any battle. Commanders must issue orders to soldiers, sailors, and pilots, who in turn need to provide a big picture of the battle at hand. Lack of communication creates the dreaded "fog of war," a perilous situation in which confusion reigns on the battlefield and troops can't tell allies from enemies. But communication is worthless—even dangerous—if it gets intercepted by the other side. It's hard to plan a sneak attack when your foes tune in to every radio transmission.

The Enigma was considered uncrackable by the Germans. They were wrong.

ANTIQUE TELEGRAPH MACHINE

To throw off eavesdroppers, countries embroiled in war developed encryption machines that converted crucial messages into secret codes, which were then deciphered by recipients with the same machine. The most famous encryption machine in history was called the Enigma, which looked like a typewriter and was originally developed by the Germans to encode business communications. When Nazi Germany started the conflict that would become World War II in 1939, German technicians adapted the Enigma to encode secret commands.

DESCRIBED ON PAGE 8. PERHAPS THAT IS ENOUGH INFORMATION TO SOLVE THIS RIDDLE,

MYSTERY MACHINE

The Enigma contained a series of spinning electric rotors that scrambled each keystroke several times, and then printed out the coded message, which would then be sent via Morse code to German officials who had their own Enigma to decode the message. The rotor positions were changed each day, meaning a daily settings key also needed to be sent separately so decoders could set their Enigma rotors properly. Only by having the code, the key, and the Enigma machine could recipients decode the code.

The device was so sophisticated that many thought it would be impossible to crack. Its rotors and various settings allowed for messages to be coded in more than 150 trillion different ways. The Nazis were so confident in the machine's uncrackable abilities that they issued thousands of them to command headquarters, air bases, submarines, and spies across the theater of battle.

Only the vast power of a computer could decode the Enigma's messages, and computers didn't exist yet. So the Allies invented one. Polish engineers reverse engineered the Enigma to create the Bomba, an early computer designed solely to crack the Enigma's messages. But the machine was worthless without ingenious humans to wield it. You'll meet the people who undid the Nazis' Enigma on the next page.

BOMBA MACHINE

A CLOSER LOOK

The Bomba was one of the earliest electronic computers—and with its 11 miles (18 km) of wiring, it looked it. This mighty machine would scan intercepted Enigma messages and compare them against its own series of spinning electric rotors to discover the decoding key.

FAMOUS ENCRYPTION CONTRAPTIONS

PURPLE: Despite warnings from their German allies, the Japanese in World War II refused to believe the United States had deciphered the cipher for their "Purple" encryption machine. The U.S. military's name for their code-cracking project: Magic.

U.S. ARMY M-209: This lunch-box-size encryption system was light and portable—perfect for sending coded messages from the battlefield. The Germans had deciphered its coding system, but the U.S. military knew this and relied more on its code talkers (see page 149) and their indecipherable language.

ONE-TIME PADS: A low-tech way to encode secret messages in the 1930s and 1940s, one-time pads were issued to agents in matching sets of two—one for the sender and one for the receiver. Each set was used to send one message and destroyed after use, making it virtually unbreakable.

CODED COMPACT: By tilting this makeup compact at just the right angle, female agents could read the code imprinted on the mirror and use it to decode secret messages.

PERHAPS NOT. IF YOU'RE STUMPED, YOU WILL FIND A HINT AND THE CIPHER USED AT THE

CLASSIFIED CASE

CODE-BREAKER

MEET THE **WOMAN** WHO **CRACKED** THE NAZIS' **UNTRACEABLE CODE**

When she was just 19 years old, English college student Mavis Batey decoded a mysterious message intercepted from Italy, part of the enemy Axis that—along with Germany and Japan—was England's foe in World War II. The message, sent via the Nazis' Enigma machine (see previous page) read "Today's the day minus three." It was an obvious threat. The Italian Navy was planning an attack on England in three days. If Batey didn't find out where the attack would happen, British soldiers would perish.

MIGHTY MIND

A hero of World War II, Batey didn't fight on the front lines. Her battle raged deep in the English countryside, at an estate called Bletchley Park, one of England's best-kept secrets until three decades after the war. There, more than 10,000 people—most of them women—fought a battle of human versus machine. They were mathematicians, linguists, and puzzle experts, tasked with cracking the Enigma codes intercepted from England's enemies. No less than the fate of the world was at stake.

VITAL STATS	
NAME	Mavis Batey
ACTIVE DATES	1940–1945
BEST KNOWN FOR	Decoding an Enigma message and thwarting an attack on England during World War II

Batey was a college student studying German when World War II broke out. She volunteered to be a nurse, but the British army recognized her knack for finding hidden messages in German newspapers. They dispatched her to Bletchley to join the thousands of code-cracking experts tasked with deciphering Enigma messages intercepted from Axis radio messages. Bletchley's staff used their own ingenuity and the computational power of a primitive computer called the Bombe (not to be confused with the Bomba mentioned on page 147) to unscramble the Enigma's codes and get the jump on their enemy's plans.

UNSUNG HEROINE

Working around the clock for nearly three days, Batey and her colleagues finally cracked the message that told where and when the Italian Navy was planning its attack against the British forces. Using this information, the British Navy attacked first and crippled the Italian fleet. In this battle of woman versus machine, Batey won. Historians estimate that, without the heroic work of Batey and her fellow codebreakers, the war might have lasted up to two years longer. Yet it wasn't until the 1970s that Batey's deeds—and the work done at Bletchley Park—became known to the world.

BLETCHLEY PARK

TOP SECRET

How "Code Talkers" Wielded Words to Win a War

As you've just learned, encryption systems—even the most complex ones—could be cracked given enough time and resources. But the U.S. military found a foolproof secret language not from a machine, but from America's original residents.

Native Americans speak complex languages that are virtually unknown outside their tribes. Since World War I, they've used their unique linguistic abilities in the U.S. military's signal corps as code talkers, translating sensitive communications into their language and transmitting them much faster than any machine. Even if enemies learned to decode Cherokee, Comanche, Navajo, Choctaw, or any of the other code-talker languages, they would still need to figure out the secret terms for words that didn't exist in those languages. The Navajo word for "iron fish," for instance, was used to describe submarines. A tank became "turtle" in Comanche. Their term for Adolf Hitler: "Crazy White Man."

The Navajo code talkers' mission was so top secret they weren't even allowed to share details with their loved ones. Their existence was finally declassified in 1968 (23 years after the end of the war), but it would take several decades before any of the Native American tribes were recognized for their crucial role in winning World War II.

THE SECRET LANGUAGE OF ONLINE GAMERS

1f y0u c4n r34d 7h15, YOU MIGHT ALREADY **KNOW IT**

When it was announced that the Merriam-Webster dictionary's 2007 Word of the Year was "w00t," plenty of people were confused. Some wondered if it should count as a word at all. An official announcement explained that w00t, written with double zeros instead of o's, is "an expression of joy." But online gamers did not need an explanation. They had been using the word for years.

END OF THIS CHAPTER. NOW GET CRACKING! HERE IS THE ENCODED RIDDLE: OM YJR NSYY;R

The word w00t is part of an internet-born code in which numbers and symbols can take the place of letters. The unusual spelling system, called leetspeak or just leet, began as a way for hackers to guard their online conversations. Over time, gamers started using the code in their messages, too.

Since the number 3 looks like a backward letter *E*, leet is also spelled l33t. But some prefer the all-numbers version—1337. If you think that 1337 is hard to read, you are not alone. But that is just the point. Unlike texting shortcuts such as *gr8*, leet is not meant to save time. Instead, the code is supposed to be creative, unpredictable, and even confusing. The word leet comes from *elite*. Top gamers used the language to set themselves apart.

THE RULES OF THE GAME

In leet, a letter can be replaced by any similar-looking number or symbol. Take the letter *s*, for example. Either a 5 or a $ can stand in for it. Another approach: swapping in letters that make the same sound. The combo *ph* can replace *f*. Phun!

There is no one way to spell out any word, and when it comes to capitalization, anything goes. But rules are still in play. Within a message, for example, using different replacements for the same letter is frowned upon. In other words, go ahead and use 4 instead of A. Or use @. Just don't do both in the same message.

NOW YOU KNOW YOUR @, 8, ('S

When it comes to typing in leet, subbing in numbers and symbols is just the beginning. There are abbreviations, special words, and grammar changes that are specific to the code. Often, typos are intentionally added into messages. It's common to mistakenly type *p* instead of *o*, so leetspeakers make a point of switching up those letters. The word *owned* becomes *pwned*. (It's pronounced *poned*.)

Though a handful of words have made their way from the keyboard to conversation, leet is mostly for typing. That could be why the code's use has fizzled in recent years. Not so long ago, online gamers had to type to communicate. Now game systems come with headsets, allowing players to speak to each other. By the time w00t was named Word of the Year, leet was on the decline. As its expressions moved into the mainstream, the language lost some of its luster. After all, there is no secret code without the secret.

GUIDE TO GAMER SPEAK

These Leet Terms Might Be Here to Stay

WORD	LEET SPELLING	MEANING IN LEET
Leet	l33t, 1337	elite, as in the top gamers
Newb	n00b	newcomer or new player (an insult)
Owned	Pwned	when an opponent has been defeated, as in "You've been owned"
Hacker	haxor, h4x0r	someone with a lot of computer knowledge

Want to communicate with just the members of your crew? You're going to need a secret code. Check out three examples from different parts of the world.

THIEVES' CANT: From the 16th to the 19th centuries, thieves in England communicated in their own secret language, known as "thieves' cant." (A *cant* is a private language.) Thieves' cant dictionaries were printed to help people avoid falling prey to sneaky scams.

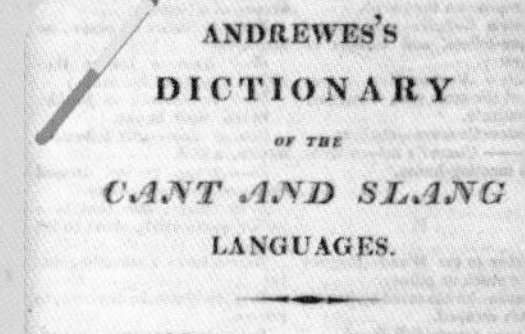
ANDREWES'S
DICTIONARY
OF THE
CANT AND SLANG
LANGUAGES.

BOONTLING: At the end of the 19th century, the residents of a California, U.S.A., town called Boonville started speaking their own secret language. Locals used the slang, called Boontling, to confuse outsiders.

NUSHU: Long ago, in a remote part of southern China, the women in one community developed their own script for writing the local lingo. When scholars learned about the code, they named it Nushu, which means "female writing."

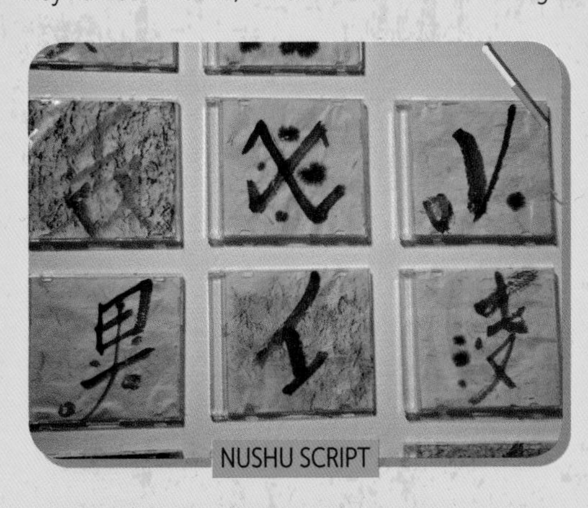
NUSHU SCRIPT

CRACKING THE KRYPTOS SCULPTURE

WILL THIS SECRET CODE **EVER BE CRACKED?**

The CIA is an organization known for keeping secrets. But even the art that adorns its headquarters in Langley, Virginia, U.S.A., is cloaked in mystery. Sitting in the courtyard, not far from the cafeteria, is a sculpture inscribed with a secret message. This work of art—and intrigue—is aptly named Kryptos, the Greek word for "hidden." Ever since the sculpture went up in 1990, codebreakers have been trying to make sense of the letters and symbols etched in its giant copper wave. In 1992, professional codebreakers figured out that the message has four passages, and they managed to decipher three of them. But they kept their triumph quiet, giving others a chance to crack the code. By 1999, two more Kryptos devotees had unlocked the same three passages. The results were shared around the world. A solution to the puzzle seemed within reach. But the final passage remains a mystery. Its 97 characters have defied the efforts of amateurs and professionals alike. The solution is known to at least one person—the sculpture's creator, Jim Sanborn. But Sanborn has said the answer will remain under wraps. Here is a guide to what's been found hiding—in plain sight—on the CIA's lawn.

K1

K2

K3

K4

THE CODE: The Kryptos sculpture is a wave of copper held up by a column of petrified wood. The engraved message has been called the Everest of codes. Why? Cracking Kryptos may be as challenging as climbing Mount Everest, the world's highest mountain! The sculpture's copper wave is engraved with more than 1,700 letters and symbols. The text on the left is a secret code.

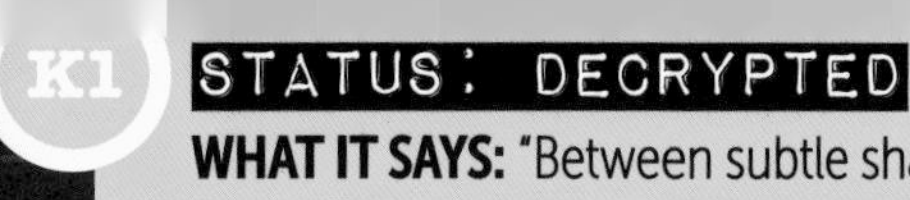

THE MESSAGE: The message has four passages of different lengths: K1, K2, K3, and K4.

THE KEY: On the right is a key to help unlock the code.

K1 STATUS: DECRYPTED

WHAT IT SAYS: "Between subtle shading and the absence of light lies the nuance of iqlusion."

DECODING THE CODE: To encrypt this passage, Sanborn borrowed a method invented by French code expert Blaise de Vigenère in the 16th century. The technique involves using a grid to match up letters with their substitutes. Sanborn says spelling errors, such as *iqlusion* for illusion, are deliberate. They're meant to stump codebreakers.

K2 STATUS: DECRYPTED

WHAT IT SAYS: "It was totally invisible. How's that possible? They used the Earth's magnetic field. x The information was gathered and transmitted undergruund to an unknown location. x Does Langley know about this? They should: it's buried out there somewhere. x Who knows the exact location? Only WW. This was his last message. x Thirty eight degrees fifty seven minutes six point five seconds north, seventy seven degrees eight minutes forty four seconds west. x Layer two."

DECODING THE CODE: Sanborn used the same encryption method for K2 as for K1. But this section is a bit trickier. An X has been inserted between some sentences, making it harder to decipher the message. The initials WW refer to William Webster, a former CIA chief. The geographic coordinates suggest a location near the sculpture on the CIA campus. Could something be buried there?

K3 STATUS: DECRYPTED

WHAT IT SAYS: "Slowly, desparatly slowly, the remains of passage debris that encumbered the lower part of the doorway was removed. With trembling hands I made a tiny breach in the upper left hand corner and then, widening the hole a little, I inserted the candle and peered in. The hot air escaping from the chamber caused the flame to flicker, but presently details of the room within emerged from the mist. x Can you see anything q?"

DECODING THE CODE: This text was taken from a book by archaeologist Howard Carter. In it, Carter describes opening King Tut's legendary tomb. To encrypt the message, Sanborn used a technique called transposition, which involves rearranging the letters.

K4 STATUS: UNSOLVED

WHAT IT SAYS: To be determined

DECODING THE CODE: Here is a hint from Sanborn: The 64th to 74th characters, which read NYPVTTMZFPK, say BERLIN CLOCK when decoded. The clock, which is named for its location—Berlin, Germany—has lights instead of numbers. Could the unusual timepiece hold the key to the secret message?

A CLOSER LOOK

Kryptos sleuths have long analyzed the shape of the sculpture. It is said to resemble the letter s, a flag, and a sheet of paper coming out of a printer. By the entrance of the CIA campus, Sanborn laid out slabs of stone engraved with messages in Morse code. One spells out SOS, a well-known distress symbol. Nearby is an engraved compass rose. Some believe these objects carry special meaning tied to the Kryptos code. Two other people might hold the key to cracking Kryptos. Edward M. Scheidt, a retired CIA code expert, taught Sanborn how to conceal his messages. And at the sculpture's dedication, former CIA chief William Webster was given an envelope that was said to hold the answer to the puzzle. However, Sanborn insists that only he knows the entire solution.

UNBREAKABLE: CODES WE MAY NEVER CRACK

THESE ARE THE WORLD'S **MOST STUBBORN CODES**

n 1799, a Frenchman named Pierre Bouchard discovered a stone with a message inscribed in hieroglyphs and two other types of writing. This find, known as the Rosetta Stone, was the key to unlocking the ancient Egyptian text. But the work of codebreakers is far from finished. Other ysterious types of writing, recorded by people of the past, lay waiting to be deciphered. Perhaps ıe day these codes will be broken. Until then, their messages will remain a mystery.

THE VOYNICH MANUSCRIPT

The Voynich manuscript is no ordinary book. But if you were to flip through its 234 parchment pages, you might not immediately notice what makes it so special. You would find colorful illustrations and pretty, handwritten text. You might even wonder: What's all the fuss about? Upon closer inspection, though, you would see that the book's contents are not quite as they seem. The drawings are peculiar. For example, the first half of the book is filled with pictures of strange plants that don't match up with any real plants on Earth. And the writing is the most bizarre feature of all. It is made up of completely invented letters. Some of the world's top code experts have spent years trying to unlock the meaning of the text, and yet little progress has been made.

The manuscript was created in the Middle Ages. It is named for Wilfred M. Voynich, the Polish bookseller who purchased it in 1912. Voynich hoped it could be deciphered and resold for a hefty price, but instead, years after Voynich's death, the manuscript was donated to the rare books library at Yale University. The curator there frequently receives emails from amateur sleuths claiming to have cracked the code. So far, none of the proposed solutions has panned out.

THE DORABELLA CIPHER

Edward Elgar was an accomplished composer and a covert code-maker. In 1897, he created one that has remained impenetrable to this day. The code appeared in a note that he sent to a friend he affectionately called Dorabella. (Her real name was Dora Penny.) Although Dorabella could not decipher the code, she kept the message for many years. Eventually she published it, and codebreakers have been trying to untangle its meaning ever since.

The Dorabella cipher, as it has come to be called, has 87 symbols spread out over three lines. The symbols are made up of one, two, or three semicircles, and each appears to be turned in a specific direction. There is also a small dot on the third line.

Some people believe the symbols match up to letters. Others think they stand for musical notes. A 2007 competition to break the code didn't yield a single winner. Afterward, the chair of the judging panel concluded that the cipher was not even close to being unlocked. "It will no doubt continue to exercise many minds for years to come," he wrote.

EDWARD ELGAR

SIR ARTHUR EVANS

LINEAR A

The mystery began in the early 20th century. British archaeologist Sir Arthur Evans was digging around an ancient palace on the Greek island of Crete when he found clay tablets imprinted with strange writing. Not all of the writing looked the same. Evans identified two sets of symbols, and he named them Linear A and Linear B.

For decades, scholars struggled to decipher the codes. Some were convinced the ancient messages would never be revealed. But in 1952, British architect Michael Ventris announced on the radio that he had begun to decipher Linear B. With the help of another scholar, Ventris proved that Linear B spelled out an early form of Greek that was spoken by the Mycenaeans, a warlike group that thrived in ancient Greece for hundreds of years. Once the Linear B tablets were translated, it became clear that the Mycenaeans had used them for record-keeping at the palace. One half of the puzzle had been solved.

Linear A, however, is still far from understood. Experts believe the writing was inscribed by the Minoans—an advanced civilization that controlled the island of Crete before the Mycenaeans took over. But nobody knows the language that the Minoans spoke, which makes Linear A tougher to crack. For now, the answer is locked away in the symbols the Minoans left behind.

THE PHAISTOS DISC

In 1908, Italian archaeologist Luigi Pernier was exploring ancient ruins on the Greek island of Crete when he stumbled upon the discovery of a lifetime. In the basement of a building that had been buried in an earthquake was a small clay disc covered in symbols. Scholars have struggled to make sense of the relic ever since.

Named for the site where it was found, the Phaistos Disc is no larger than a bread plate. More than 240 stamps spiral around the disc's two faces. From these, 45 distinct symbols have been identified. But since nobody knows how the symbols work, the message's meaning remains a mystery. So does the purpose of the disc.

Some archaeologists have questioned the artifact's authenticity. They wonder if Pernier's amazing find was too good to be true. Others are holding out hope that another relic with the same symbols will be uncovered. They say such a discovery could help unlock the secrets of the Phaistos Disc.

DECEIT

THE **CRYPTIC QUEST** THAT PUT **HACKERS** TO THE **TEST**

The message was short and simple, embedded in an image of glowing text against a dark background in an online message forum. "Hello," it began. "We are looking for highly intelligent individuals. To find them, we have devised a test. There is a message hidden in this image. Find it, and it will lead you on the road to finding us ... Good luck." And so began the internet's most cryptic quest, a sequence of puzzles that lured thousands of web wonks to the net's nether reaches and even into the real world. Instead of a name, the message was signed with a number: 3301.

THE QUEST BEGINS

Hackers, amateur code crackers, and other intrepid internet explorers took up the challenge, working alone or together in private forums. Within hours of the message's appearance on January 5, 2012, many had decoded a Caesar cipher (see page 8) hidden within the image, which led to more puzzles and clues. Each test required a different expertise: mathematics, music, Maya numbers, literature, programming. Solving a puzzle incorrectly could lead to false clues that threw the unworthy off the trail. Eventually, the tests led to a Texas, U.S.A., phone number and an answering machine, which in turn led to a website with a countdown clock and a large picture of a cicada. The cicada had become the symbol of the quest now known as Cicada 3301, so participants knew they were getting close. The clock ticked down. Cicada seekers buzzed with anticipation.

Symbol of quest success: the cicada

INTO THE DARKNET

When the clock reached zero on January 9, the site revealed 14 coordinates on three continents. Questers fanned out to inspect the spots, which turned out to be lampposts bearing secret codes pointing to a murky region of the web known as the darknet. Uncharted by search engines, the darknet is the internet's seedy underbelly, home to gigabytes of unsavory data and secret networks that want to stay that way. No one knows how many Cicada 3301 participants managed to navigate the darknet to take the prize. A final message—supposedly from the mysterious plotters of the puzzle—surfaced in February 2012. "We have now found the individuals we sought," it read. "Thus our month-long journey ends." In the end, the prize in this scavenger hunt wasn't money or gadgets or even bragging rights. It was the savvy few who could solve the riddle of Cicada 3301.

DARK DOMAIN

More Internet Mysteries

SPIES WANTED: If the CIA really is behind Cicada 3301, it wouldn't be the first time an intelligence agency created a recruitment test. The U.S. Cyber Command hid a code in one of its logos in 2010 and challenged the public to crack it. Perhaps the makers of the logo underestimated the decoding powers of John Q. Hacker, because it took little more than three hours for the public to decipher the code, which spelled out the agency's mission.

NUMBERS GAME: Thousands of people have tried to crack one of the most maddening codes on the internet, first posted in 2011 on the social-media site Reddit by a user with the catchy name "A858DE45F56D9BC9" (or just A858 for short). Since then, A858 has kept up a steady habit of posting long coded strings. Reddit users have created programs to decipher the code, but they've yet to make any significant progress.

TUBE TEST: From alien transmissions to secret messages from Cold War spies, armchair decoders had no shortage of theories for the meaning of odd videos posted to YouTube from September 2013 to April 2014. The 11-second videos, posted on a channel called Webdriver, featured red and blue rectangles that floated around the screen in seemingly purposeful patterns. But late in 2014, the mystery was solved: YouTube owner Google admitted the videos were a testing utility—called Webdriver Torso—for their website.

CYBER SUSPECTS

Who's Behind 3301?

THE CIA? Did America's spy agency set up Cicada as a recruitment tool?

A GAME COMPANY? Video game companies have created elaborate "alternate-reality games" to promote their releases in the past.

ANONYMOUS? Perhaps Cicada was an initiation for this secretive collective of hacker activists.

UNDERCOVER OPERATION

THE MISSING INK

HOW TO MIX **INVISIBLE INK** FOR SECRET MESSAGES

Emails might be left open. Nosy siblings read text messages over your shoulder. Your personal life is an open book if you're not careful. The only surefire way to keep your communications secret is to write with old-fashioned invisible ink. A good spy never repeats his or her tactics, so we've supplied three ink recipes that will keep enemy agents—and gossipy classmates—guessing.

Recipe #1: LEMON AID

REQUIRED ITEMS: Lemon juice, cotton swabs, and a heat source such as a lightbulb (halogen won't work)

DIRECTIONS:

STEP 1. Squeeze a lemon into a bowl and add a little water, or use store-bought lemon juice instead.

STEP 2. Dip the head of a cotton swab into the lemon juice.

STEP 3. Use the swab like a pen to mark your message on a white piece of paper. Apply more juice to the swab if it dries out, but don't soak it or your paper will become a soggy mess.

STEP 4. Allow the paper to dry, and then pass it to the person you want to communicate with secretly.

STEP 5. To reveal the message, carefully hold the paper in front of a heat source such as a lightbulb or even the sun. Never place the paper on the bulb or it might catch on fire. Your hidden message will reveal itself in brown letters.

NEED A RIDDLE HINT?

This chapter's code uses a keyboard cipher shifted one space right (read about it on page 8).

If you're still at a loss, turn to page 183 for the answer to this encrypted riddle!

HERE'S ANOTHER HINT. ⇧

Recipe #2: JUICY SECRET

REQUIRED ITEMS: Baking soda, grape juice (from concentrate is fine), cotton swab, sponge or paintbrush

DIRECTIONS:

STEP 1. Mix equal amounts of baking soda and water in a small cup.

STEP 2. Dip your swab in the solution, and then use it to write your message on a white piece of paper.

STEP 3. Allow the paper to dry, and then pass it to the person you want to communicate with secretly.

STEP 4. To reveal the message, use a sponge or paintbrush to paint the paper with purple grape juice. The slight acidity of the grape juice reacts with the baking soda to reveal your message on the page.

Recipe #3: WHITE NOISE

REQUIRED ITEMS: White crayon, highlighter marker

DIRECTIONS:

STEP 1. Write your message with a white crayon on a white piece of paper. Make sure to press firmly with the crayon.

STEP 2. Pass the paper to the person you want to communicate with secretly.

STEP 3. To reveal the message, go over the page with a highlighter marker until your crayon code stands out.

MESSAGING TIPS

SECRET SPOT: The safest way to deliver your message to an agent is to choose a "dead drop." This is an out-of-the-way spot—such as under a large rock or within the pages of a particular book—where you and your agents agree to leave messages for each other.

SEALED AND DELIVERED: If your dead drop is outside, make sure your message is protected from the elements. Stick it in a plastic bag or an Easter egg shell to keep it dry and undiscovered.

COVER STORY: Passing a blank piece of paper to your agents might arouse suspicion, so write a harmless note in regular ink on the same paper to give your secret message a little extra cover.

Followed subject
[CODE NAME: SNUFFLES]
to the drop zone.

SECRETS ALL AROUND YOU

Subject proceeded to
drink from TOILET.

You don't need top secret clearance to access info that none of your friends know. Secrets are everywhere, hiding in plain sight, sometimes inches in front of your nose. You can find them if you just open your eyes, and this chapter tells you where to look! You'll uncover secrets in advertising, at amusement parks, in video games, at the ballpark, in your favorite restaurants, and even in your couch cushions. You'll learn about the hidden life of your cat and the secrets of your cash. By the time you finish this chapter, you'll see the world in a whole new way—for your eyes only.

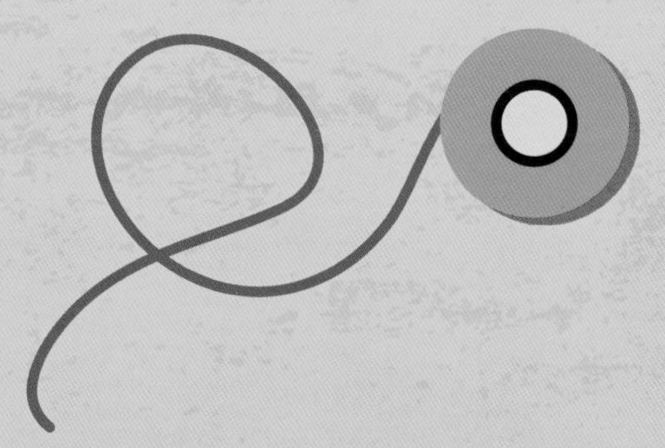

NOTE TO SELF:
Make sure toilet is always flushed.

SOMETHING EXTRA

HOW **EASTER EGGS** CHANGE THE WAY WE PLAY

The 1979 Atari 2600 video game Adventure might not look totally awesome by today's standards—its hero, a tiny featureless square, required imagination to envision as a dashing warrior—but it had all the elements of a modern interactive masterpiece: a kingdom and castles to explore, dragons to slay, puzzles to solve, and a legendary treasure waiting at the end. It also had a secret message buried deep within the game. Only the most worthy players would discover this secret. And when they did, it caused a sensation and spawned a term: the "Easter egg."

KEY TO SUCCESS

Today, Easter eggs—secret messages, inside jokes, hidden characters, and other funny references—are common in video games. Players *expect* to find them. But in the early days of home video games in the late 1970s, they were virtually unheard of. Game company Atari maintained its iron grip on the industry by forbidding its programmers from advertising their talents in end-game credits and thus getting hired away by the competition. Programmer Warren Robinett didn't think this policy was fair. He took matters into his own hands by hiding his name in his game Adventure. Players who found a secret key could unlock a room with a message: "Created by Warren Robinett."

WHAT FOLLOWS IS A RIDDLE HIDDEN IN A SECRET CODE. THE ANSWER TO THIS RIDDLE IS A

A 1990 Batman Atari arcade video game

The Atari 2600 home video game console is popular among retro video gamers.

POWER UP

Robinett's bosses at Atari weren't happy when they learned of his secret room. They even considered removing it from all future copies of Adventure. But then they noticed an interesting phenomenon: Players loved the challenge of finding Robinett's secret. It had become a game within the game. In the days before the internet, word of Adventure's secret spread on playgrounds and around the table in school cafeterias. It was adding extra life to the game.

Instead of removing the secret, Atari's executives made it a requirement that all of their games contain such hidden features in the future. One executive coined the term "Easter egg" to describe these secrets, because finding them was similar to the search for eggs on the Easter holiday. Robinett's quest for credit helped create a new way to play games. And as you'll see on this page, his big idea spilled over into movies and other media, as well.

EASTER EGGS EVERYWHERE

Easter eggs aren't restricted to video games. Hidden characters and secret messages appear in movies, comics, and even classic art. Find these for yourself:

MERMAID AND THE MOUSE: Watch King Triton's entrance scene in *The Little Mermaid* for a famous example. Blink and you'll miss Mickey Mouse and friends in the crowd.

ALIEN FROM ANOTHER GALAXY: The Imperial Senate scene in *Star Wars: The Phantom Menace* features guest stars from a galaxy far, far away. Director George Lucas hid a trio of aliens from the movie *E.T. the Extra-Terrestrial* as a fun little nod to that film's director, Steven Spielberg.

DA VINCI'S CODE: Although the Easter egg term is new, the idea behind it is not. Italian researchers probing the peepers of the "Mona Lisa," Leonardo da Vinci's famous painting, noticed the letters "LV" in her right eye (perhaps the artist's initials) and some indecipherable symbols in her left. It's not just the Mona Lisa's smile that's mysterious!

PERSON, PLACE, OR THING DESCRIBED IN THIS CHAPTER. THE CODE IS BASED ON A CIPHER

QUIET ON THE SET

FILMMAKERS WILL DO **WHATEVER IT TAKES** TO KEEP THEIR PROJECTS **UNDER WRAPS**

To ensure that fans would not meet Ewoks before *Return of the Jedi*'s release, filmmakers used the title *Blue Harvest* as a decoy.

DESCRIBED ON PAGE 9. PERHAPS THAT IS ENOUGH INFORMATION TO SOLVE THIS RIDDLE,

Any Star Wars fan can tell you that the third installment of the series' original trilogy is called *Return of the Jedi*. But during filming in the early 1980s, the movie went by a completely different name: *Blue Harvest*. The title had nothing to do with the actual film, and that was the point. Star Wars producers wanted to keep all aspects of their movie top secret. The best way to do that was to pretend that they were filming something else. While shooting the movie in various locations, producers duped residents into believing they were making a horror film. The title *Blue Harvest* was printed on crew members' T-shirts along with the dramatic tagline "Horror beyond imagination."

A SEQUEL'S SECRETS

The precautions went beyond mere T-shirt tricks. Cast and crew members were not allowed to bring visitors to the set. Actors had code names. Workers who were brought in to help on the set were told as little as possible. A toy company was permitted to make movie-related action figures, but the toys could not be featured in its catalog.

The filmmakers had their reasons for insisting on secrecy. The first two Star Wars movies were megahits that broke box office records. If fans knew where the sequel was being filmed, it would be impossible to keep them away from the set. Plus, producers did not want plot leaks to spoil the film for moviegoers.

Their secret remained as strong as the Force. After more than two years of filming under wraps, *Return of the Jedi* opened in theaters. *Blue Harvest* had just been a Jedi mind trick. Let's take a look at five other famous blockbusters that began with a bogus backstory.

SAFEGUARDING SCREENPLAYS

Studios today have good reason to be extra secretive. With the touch of a button, an entire script can be shared online, long before a movie hits theaters. To prevent that from happening, filmmakers give scripts to as few people as possible. And typically, each actor gets a distinct version of the script. That way, a leaked copy can easily be traced back to its source.

Take, for example, the screenplays to the Hunger Games movies. Every copy had a few different words changed. If a script had shown up online, filmmakers would have known in an instant whose copy it was. Nobody played any games this time: The actors made sure to safeguard their scripts.

MOVIE CODE NAMES

PLANET ICE

In preparation for filming *Titanic*, director James Cameron hired a Russian submarine to take him to the famous shipwreck. He claimed he was doing research for a movie called *Planet Ice*.

GROUP HUG

While filming *The Avengers*, filmmakers threw off fans with the particularly improbable code name *Group Hug*.

A BOY'S LIFE

In 1981, director Steven Spielberg started filming his science-fiction blockbuster *E.T.* under the unassuming title *A Boy's Life*.

CORPORATE HEADQUARTERS

Even the boring code name *Corporate Headquarters* could not keep fans away from the set of the *Star Trek* movie. What tipped them off? Filmmakers had put out a call for extras willing to shave their eyebrows "to portray a Vulcan-type ... shape."

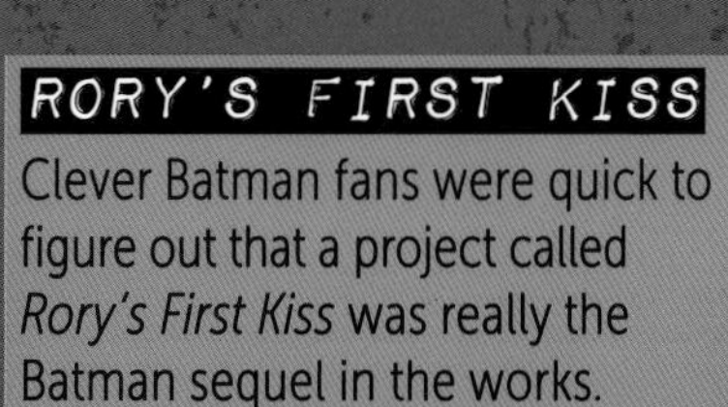

RORY'S FIRST KISS

Clever Batman fans were quick to figure out that a project called *Rory's First Kiss* was really the Batman sequel in the works.

PERHAPS NOT. IF YOU'RE STUMPED, YOU WILL FIND A HINT AND THE CIPHER USED AT THE

WILD THINGS

THE SECRET **SUPERPOWERS** OF ANIMALS

We humans get by fine with our five senses, four limbs, ordinary strength, limited life span, and inability to summon a thunderclap, but some animals need a little extra perception and a superpower or two to survive and thrive in the wild. Take a look at the secret superheroes of the wild kingdom.

TARDIGRADE

SECRET SUPERPOWER: Indestructibility!

Studied for their toughness, tardigrades are eight-legged animals that have been subjected to the most extreme conditions imaginable—including the vacuum of space! They ride out droughts and deep freezes by shutting down their bodies and rolling into balls that look like boogers. While in this switched-off state, a tardigrade is virtually indestructible. Found in soggy environments—perhaps even your own backyard—this extreme survivor would make the perfect creature in a horror flick if not for one fact: A tardigrade is a smidge smaller than the period at the end of this sentence.

END OF THIS CHAPTER. NOW GET CRACKING! HERE IS THE ENCODED RIDDLE: RCDQ HDRRHK

JELLYFISH

SECRET SUPERPOWER: Immortality!

Ah, to be forever young—just like the *Turritopsis nutricula*, aka the immortal jellyfish. Although it's not really a jellyfish (technically, it's a blobby creature called a hydrozoa), this bell-shaped ball of jelly really is capable of living forever. When the going gets tough, the creature reverts to its earliest stage of development and begins the aging process from scratch, hitting the reset button on its life. That would be like you transforming into a baby whenever you wanted! Of course, its life will still come to an end if it winds up in the belly of a sea turtle or other predator. As any wise young *Turritopsis nutricula* will tell you, it's still a dangerous world!

SHARKS AND PLATYPUSES

SECRET SUPERPOWER: Electroreception!

The head of sharks (and rays) and the bill of the oddball platypus are covered with special pores that detect the electrical signals given off by all living things. That means sharks can monitor your heartbeat, muscle movements, and even your brain activity!

AXOLOTL

SECRET SUPERPOWER: Super healing!

Conchs can regrow their eyes, sea stars can sprout new limbs, and zebrafish can mend their muscles, but no animal matches the amazing regenerative abilities of the axolotl, a friendly-faced salamander that lurks in lakes near Mexico City. Lopped-off leg? Walk it off! The axolotl sprouts a new one in a matter of months. Broken heart? Damaged brain? No worries! They'll grow back good as new.

PISTOL SHRIMP

SECRET SUPERPOWER: Thunder-punch!

Alpheus heterochaelis, better known as the pistol shrimp, creates a bigger bang than a bolt of lightning. This small crustacean (tinier than your little finger) wields its oversize claw just like Thor wields his hammer, unleashing an onslaught of sound and light that stuns nearby fish. By snapping its claw shut at lightning speed, the shrimp creates a tiny bubble that bursts louder than a thunderclap. Oh, and each busted bubble is accompanied by a flash of light nearly as hot as the sun's surface!

PIT VIPERS

SECRET SUPERPOWER: Infrared vision!

Rattlesnakes, water moccasins, cottonmouths, and other venomous so-called "pit vipers" didn't earn their name because they live in pits; instead, these serpents possess special heat-sensing organs in pits between their nostrils and eyes. The organs detect even the slightest rise in temperature against the background, giving these snakes extra help when hunting at night.

BTX MSEGQ S MTJEC. XLT IDBCR JLR QKK CDI ELIDJB, NTR XLT'HH AKYDJDRKHX CKSP CDI.

OFF THE MENU

TOP SECRET TRICKS OF FOOD PHOTOGRAPHERS

The next time your stomach grumbles when you see a juicy burger or banana split in an advertisement, tell your belly to hush—it's being lied to! Those featured treats aren't for feasting on. They've been carefully prepared and arranged—down to the sesame seeds on the bun—for their close-up.

Food stylists rely on all sorts of secret tricks when photographing food for advertising, cookbooks, and restaurant menus. They're the makeup artists of the food-fashion world! And they do what they do for two reasons: To make the food look more mouthwatering than it ever would in real life, and to make the dishes last all day during long photo shoots. "When food has been styled well, the viewer should not think about it at all," says Lisa Cherkasky, a food stylist for more than two decades. "The food should be gorgeous and look as though it is naturally that way." Here's how Cherkasky and other stylists trick your taste buds.

QLIK IDBCR KUKJ ESHH CDI QRTJJDJB.

BREAKOUT STARS

MILK SUDS: Real milk—even thick whole milk—can look watery and dull in photos, so stylists often substitute it with gleaming kindergarten glue. Dish soap is dabbled on the surface to give that fresh-poured look. Glue is also used instead of milk in photos of cereal so those frosted flakes don't end up soggy.

BOGUS BEEF: In commercials for steaks, burgers, and other meaty roles, the subject spends less than 30 seconds per side on the grill so it doesn't shrink. Food stylists then draw those perfect char lines on the browned beef using burnt matchsticks, eyeliner—even shoe polish! Next, the bun joins the phony fun as the stylist applies sesame seeds one at a time with glue. All the toppings are carefully arranged and pinned using toothpicks to make sure the big burger looms larger than life.

SECRET SAUCE: Saucy foods such as pasta and even stews and soups receive a helping of visual flair from an extra-icky ingredient: wax. Stylists melt bars of wax in the sauce to give it a deeper color and extra thickness.

BATTER UP: To keep breads from drying out, stylists blast them with a waterproofing spray designed to protect car dashboards. "I rarely get hungry for the food I'm styling," says Cherkasky.

FULL STEAM AHEAD: Meals featured in food photography often sit around in the studio for hours growing cold and stale. To duplicate the fresh-from-the-oven look, a stylist will microwave a soggy cotton ball and hide it behind the subject to create steam.

SPRAYING FOR KEEPS: Stylists spritz pancakes with waterproofing spray so they won't get soggy from the syrup ... which is definitely not real maple syrup. Many stylists dribble the pancakes with motor oil instead.

SCREAM CREAM: Real ice cream would melt into gooey soup under a studio's hot lights, so stylists simulate fresh scoops using cake icing and powdered sugar. Sometimes they even use mashed potatoes! Dull strawberries go to the makeup chair for a lipstick touch-up. And if you see what looks like whipped cream in a food ad, it's most likely shaving cream. Your belly still grumbling?

FOUL PLAY

Those steaming roast chickens and turkeys you see in advertising are mostly raw, baked briefly to get their juices flowing. Stylists then spruce up the birds with food coloring to give them a well-cooked look. Instead of traditional stuffing, the poultry is packed with napkins to keep it plump. Stylists seal any rips in the raw meat with quick-setting glue.

CLASSIFIED CASE

RECIPES UNDER WRAPS

THE **SECRET FORMULAS** FOR THESE POPULAR PRODUCTS ARE KEPT **UNDER LOCK AND KEY**

That food on your plate and drink in your hand might be holding a secret or two. And some food and beverage companies want to keep it that way. They go to great lengths to keep their methods mysterious, at times even locking up their recipes in safes. Why all the fuss? To keep culinary copycats from mimicking their products! Plus, staying super secretive might mean more money for the company. Nothing captures people's attention more than a good mystery. It can drum up interest in a brand, leading to better sales. Is that smart or sneaky? You be the judge.

Coca-Cola king Asa Candler and his wife

THE FORMULA FOR COCA-COLA

Soda sleuths have been trying to figure out Coca-Cola's secret recipe for more than 130 years. The story of Coke's mysterious formula begins in the 1880s, when a pharmacist named John Pemberton started making an early version of the bubbly beverage. Pemberton sold his soda recipe to businessman Asa Candler, who later founded the Coca-Cola company. Candler was so paranoid about rivals stealing the secret formula that he insisted nobody write it down. He even removed the labels from containers holding the beverage's ingredients.

Through the years, the company has remained protective of the recipe, stating that only two employees at any given time know how to make the flavoring. And though some people claim to have figured out the formula, Coca-Cola says the copycats have it wrong. Interest in the mysterious soda recipe is not likely to fizzle anytime soon.

THE COLONEL'S ORIGINAL RECIPE

For decades, Kentucky Fried Chicken's fried chicken recipe has been a closely guarded secret. The company's founder, the white-suit-wearing Colonel Harland Sanders, used to appear in TV commercials, describing the process for preparing his famous chicken. He would say the chicken was dipped in a blend of 11 different herbs and spices. But he would never disclose which herbs and spices were used.

To this day, the recipe is kept under lock and key. To ensure its secrecy, part of the seasoning is blended in one place before being sent to a second location, where the remaining herbs and spices are added. The original recipe, handwritten by Sanders in the 1940s, is locked in a safe that is guarded by video cameras and motion detectors.

But if you are set on replicating the recipe at home, don't despair. In 2016, the colonel's nephew, Joe Ledington, showed a reporter from the *Chicago Tribune* a handwritten recipe he had found in an old family scrapbook. The list of ingredients consists of 11 herbs and spices, and it has the measurements for each one. Ledington believes this recipe is the colonel's original; the company says it is not. You can give it a try and taste for yourself. The result just might be finger-lickin' good!

11 spices — mix with 2 cups white flour

- 2/3 tablespoon salt
- 1/2 tablespoon thyme
- 1/2 tablespoon basil
- 1/3 tablespoon oregano
- 1 tablespoon celery salt
- 1 tablespoon black pepper
- 1 tablespoon dried mustard
- 4 tablespoons paprika
- 2 tablespoons garlic salt
- 1 tablespoon ground ginger
- 3 tablespoons white pepper

KRISPY KREME DOUGHNUTS

Dozens of copycat recipes for Krispy Kreme doughnuts are posted online. But are any of them identical to the one used to make the popular glazed doughnuts in shops around the world? We have no way of knowing, since that recipe has been kept top secret for more than 80 years. Vernon Rudolph, the company's founder, got the recipe from his uncle, who had purchased it from a French chef in New Orleans, Louisiana, U.S.A. In 1937, Rudolph opened a doughnut shop in Winston-Salem, North Carolina, U.S.A. He used the recipe to whip up the warm sugary treats for which Krispy Kreme is famous. Today there are more than 1,300 Krispy Kreme stores. As for the original recipe, it's locked in a safe at company headquarters in Winston-Salem, the town where it all began.

A CLOSER LOOK

In the United States, the Food and Drug Administration requires companies to list ingredients on a product's package. But some ingredients can be named collectively, as "flavors," "spices," or "artificial flavoring." The list on a can of Coca-Cola, for example, includes "natural flavors." What are those, exactly? It's anybody's guess.

MIND GAMES

THE **SECRET RITUALS** OF SPORTS STARS

It's no secret that making it in the world of professional sports takes tons of practice and a bit of luck. But is it possible to make your own luck? Plenty of sports stars seem to think so. Professional athletes have been known to eat, dress, and behave in peculiar ways, hoping to influence the outcome of a game or even a season. Here are five pro athletes whose unusual game-time rituals might have helped them go the distance.

FROM HEAD TO TOE

Serena Williams is one of the most skilled tennis players of all time, but a good luck ritual never hurts. The tennis star reportedly wears the same pair of socks throughout a tournament and won't wash them as long as she keeps winning. She also ties her shoes the same way before each match. When she plays, Williams sometimes sings, too. In her head, that is. She told *Vogue* magazine that her song of choice is "Flashdance ... What a Feeling." "If I stop singing it, I usually start losing," she said.

WINNER, WINNER, CHICKEN DINNER

Baseball Hall of Famer Wade Boggs started eating chicken at least once a day in 1982, the same year he made his major league baseball debut. The self-proclaimed chicketarian even published *Fowl Tips,* his own collection of chicken recipes. His meal of choice served him well on more than one plate, it seems, for after eating his favorite dish of lemon chicken, Boggs got the most hits in a double-header in his career.

BE POSITIVE

Intense training? Check. Balanced nutrition? Check. *Seabiscuit*? Check? The night before a triathlon, four-time Ironman World Champion Chrissie Wellington would get ready to race by vegging out. Her screentime favorite? *Seabiscuit*, the heartwarming movie about a down-on-his-luck racehorse that becomes a national hero. For race-time inspiration, Wellington needed only to look at her bike—named after the champion thoroughbred—and her water bottle, on which Rudyard Kipling's inspirational poem "If" was written.

LUCKY PAJAMAS

NBA player Jason Terry would start prepping for the next day's game at bedtime—by pulling on a pair of shorts from the opposing team. This shorts switch started when he was in college. The night before his championship game, he and his roommate were so excited that sleep seemed impossible. So they got their game on a little early, trading plain old pj's for their uniforms. Their team ended up winning, and the habit stuck. Eventually, Terry began wearing a pair of his opponent's shorts. The logic? Maybe by stepping into the other team's uniform, he could get into their mindset, too!

GAME FACE

Tennis pro Rafael Nadal follows a detailed regimen to get ready for every match. His 45-minute locker-room ritual includes taking a freezing-cold shower, putting the grips on his rackets, and jumping and sprinting to music. Once Nadal is courtside, he carefully arranges two water bottles on the ground so that the labels diagonally face the court. Finally, he looks up to find his family in the crowd. "I don't let them intrude on my thoughts during a match," he writes in his autobiography, "but knowing they are there ... gives me the peace of mind on which my success as a player rests."

A CLOSER LOOK

Believing that a particular pair of socks or a specific snack could help you win a game may seem ridiculous. But rituals may be more rational than they appear. In one experiment, students tried to get 36 little balls into 36 little holes by tilting a box. Some students were told to simply play the game. Others heard the researcher say, "I'll cross my fingers for you," before starting. Guess what? The second group did better. The good luck ritual increased their confidence—and their results.

PAW PATRO

THE SECRET LIVES OF **HOUSE CATS**

Your cat might look cute and lazy when she's purring on your lap, but let her out the door and she becomes a different animal. That's what researchers discovered when they strapped tiny National Geographic cameras to the collars of 60 house cats and unleashed the beasts in the suburbs of Athens, Georgia, U.S.A. The cat's-eye footage revealed the secret lives of friendly felines.

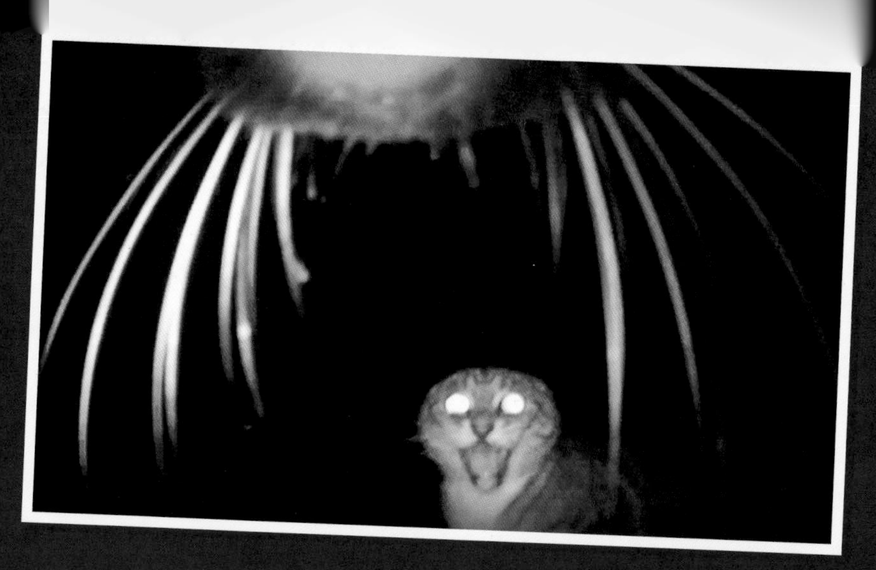

POWER PROWLERS

When Mr. Whiskers' whiskers stink, it's probably from lizard breath! House cats share the same ancestor as lions, leopards, and other fearsome felines. They're like tiny tigers! And like tigers, kitties have killer instincts that never turn off. Nearly half of the cats in the camera-collar experiment stalked animals outdoors to supplement their bowl of Friskies back home. Lizards and small snakes topped the menu, followed by chipmunks and birds—so many birds, in fact, that experts fear our feathered friends might be in danger of extinction in residential areas.

CRAWL SPACE INVADERS

Consider this the next time you let your tabby catnap on your pillow: He may have just crawled from the sewer! Cats are more flexible than dogs, able to squeeze through itty-bitty openings—a talent they use to pursue prey into storm drains, onto rooftops, and deep into spider-infested crawl spaces under houses. It's true that house cats are famously fastidious, but remember: That tongue they use to groom does double duty as sandpaper to lick the fur from captured rodents.

GROSS ENCOUNTERS

House cats in the kitty-cam study kept strange company, carousing with rats, stray dogs, and even possums—all potentially aggressive animals and carriers of deadly rabies. A quarter of the cats also drank from puddles and other dirty sources of water. Your neat freak of a kitty might not be so clean after all.

HOUSE HUNTERS

And now for the ultimate betrayal: At least one cat in the study lived a double life, splitting his time between two families who each thought they were the cat's true owners. The two-timing tabby would scratch at one house's door, nuzzle the owners, tuck into dinner, and then scamper to the other house for a double dose of food and affection. So remember this the next time Fluffy purrs in your lap: You might not be the only human in her life!

RUFF STUFF

The Secret Life of Spot

COUNTER ENCOUNTERS: All good dogs know that kitchen counters are off-limits—when you're home. You better believe they're scouring every surface for missed morsels as soon as you step out.

RANCID ROLLING: It's bad enough when your dog digs up the yard, but ... sniff, sniff? What's that foul smell? Fido's been frolicking in filth again! Some experts believe dogs instinctively roll in poop or dead critters to share these foul finds with pack members. Unfortunately in this case, you're part of your dog's pack!

POOP SNOOPING: Some pooches might have a diet lacking certain vitamins and digestion-aiding enzymes—enzymes they can get from poop.

MICROWAVE REVVED

Your leftovers will cook faster and more evenly in the microwave if you leave an open space in the middle of your plate and arrange the food around it in a circle.

SECRETS OF SUCCESS

TRY THESE **HIDDEN HACKS** TO SIMPLIFY YOUR LIFE

Algebra homework, stinky siblings, social commitments—life is tricky enough without the little things bogging you down. And when the going gets tough, the tough invent "life hacks," or ingenious solutions to common gripes. Here we've assembled some of the least known hacks for dealing with every-day annoyances.

CORD CARRIER

If you have an army of LEGO Minifigures just loafing around, put them to work organizing your audio cords and cables. Their little plastic hands are just the right size and strength to grip USB cables, speaker cables, and other skinny cords.

USB UPS AND DOWNS

It's the most annoying "game" you play on your PC—the guessing game when you plug in a USB cable or thumb drive. You might think you always have a 50-50 chance of plugging it in correctly, but here's a secret tip to help you make heads from tails on the little plug: Look for the logo! USB plugs almost always have a USB logo on the side that should face up when you insert the plug into a USB port (or face forward if you're plugging into a vertical port on the side of a monitor or hub). If your cable or thumb drive is missing the logo, look for the seam in the metal of the plug instead. The seam will show you which way is down. So if you remember that the logo goes up and the seam faces down, you'll never have to play the USB guessing game again!

SUPER CHARGED

If your phone's nearly dead and you need to charge it in a jiffy, put it in "airplane mode" and it will recharge much faster.

EARBUD ID

If you have a hard time telling your right earbud from your left, tie a knot in the cord just below the right one. That way you'll always recognize it.

PLATTER UP

Have you ordered takeout but forgot the plates? Don't panic! Takeout Chinese food actually comes with its own set: each takeout box unfolds into its own plate.

VOLTAGE DROPPED

You can test whether your batteries have any juice by dropping them a few inches bottom-first onto a table. The more charged the battery, the less it will bounce. Fully charged barely bounces, less charge bounces around.

MONKEY SEE, MONKEY DO

There's more than one way to peel a banana. Most people peel from the stem, but it's actually easier if you start at the other end. Squeeze the tip at the bottom of the banana to create a small gap, and then pull the peel away. Easy, right? This secret banana-stripping technique has been dubbed the "monkey peel" because it's supposedly how monkeys open bananas in the wild. In truth, scientists haven't observed monkeys peeling bananas in any set ways. Some peel them from the stem, some from the tip, some from the side; sometimes the monkeys just eat the bananas peel and all!

CUP OF JAM

Can't hear a song playing on your phone? The easiest way to boost the volume is to put the phone into an empty cup.

HUSH MONEY

TOP SECRET FEATURES THAT **PROTECT CASH** FROM COUNTER-FEITERS

No sooner was money invented than clever criminals began trying to copy—or counterfeit—it. In ancient Greece, counterfeiters would clip the edges off gold and silver coins and melt the shavings around worthless metal cores to create passable copies. Modern-day counterfeiters use high-tech copiers and high-resolution printers to create phony bills. So to combat these crooks, the U.S. Mint has riddled its bills with secret security touches that are nearly impossible to copy. All denominations have these features, but you'll find the most on the $100 bill: the highest denomination of U.S. currency. Here's an unclassified guide to your cash.

SECRET THREAD

Visible on both sides of the $100 bill (and all other bills except the $1 and $2 bills), this skinny thread is implanted vertically and imprinted with the tiny words "USA 100." It also glows pink under ultraviolet light.

DETAILS, DETAILS

Individual strands in Benjamin Franklin's hair, filaments on the golden feather, tiny patches of text—itty-bitty details are everywhere on the $100 bill. In fact, all bills, regardless of denomination, bear similar tiny features that even high-definition printers cannot replicate accurately.

FUNNY FEEL

Currency is printed on a special type of paper—actually more like a fabric—made of cotton and linen, which is why your bills don't decompose into mush when they're accidentally run through the wash. That unique paper (combined with the intense pressure of the printing presses) gives genuine money a thin, crisp, distinct feel that's nearly impossible to replicate.

NEW MONEY

The U.S. Mint began redesigning currency with new security features—starting with the $100 bill—in 1996. Any cash still in circulation from before that year is much easier to copy.

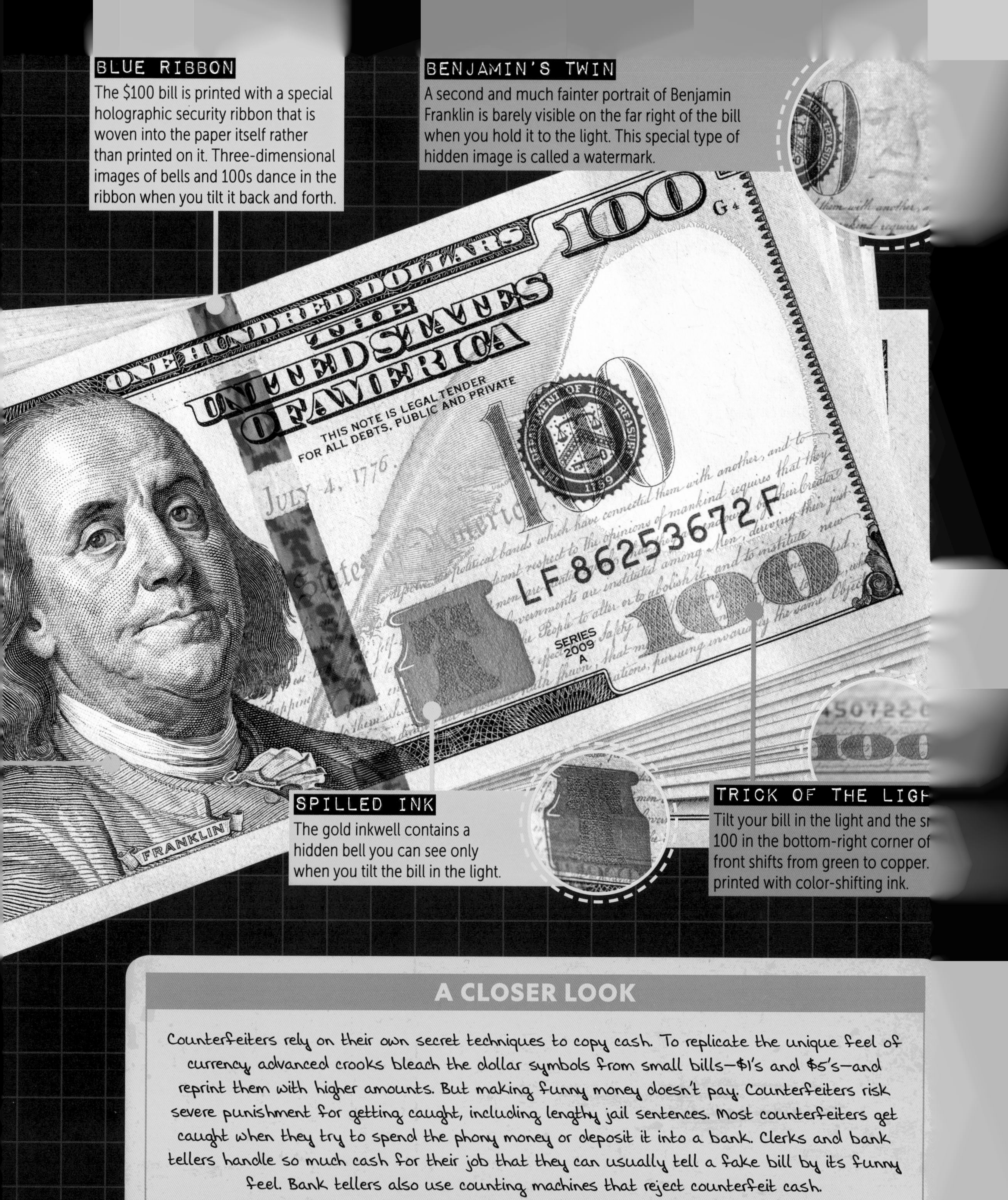

A CLOSER LOOK

Counterfeiters rely on their own secret techniques to copy cash. To replicate the unique feel of currency advanced crooks bleach the dollar symbols from small bills—$1's and $5's—and reprint them with higher amounts. But making funny money doesn't pay. Counterfeiters risk severe punishment for getting caught, including lengthy jail sentences. Most counterfeiters get caught when they try to spend the phony money or deposit it into a bank. Clerks and bank tellers handle so much cash for their job that they can usually tell a fake bill by its funny feel. Bank tellers also use counting machines that reject counterfeit cash.

UNDERCOVER OPERATION

SEEING THINGS

CAN YOU SPOT THE **SUBLIMINAL MESSAGES** IN THESE PRODUCT LOGOS?

Researcher James Vicary popularized the concept of "subliminal advertising"—supposed hidden messages that only the subconscious can detect—in 1957, when he inserted the words "drink Coca-Cola" and "eat popcorn" into a movie called *Picnic*. The words flashed on the screen for just a fraction of a second—too fast for the eye to detect—but Vicary proclaimed that sales of popcorn and Coke jumped among viewers. His results were later debunked, and more recent studies show that subliminal messaging doesn't work, but that hasn't stopped advertisers from hiding words and images for your mind's eye. (Try to) see for yourself.

FLAVOR SAVER

Baskin-Robbins' logo serves two purposes: It showcases the name of the ice cream and advertises its 31 flavors. Can you spot the number?

WINNING GRIN

The smile in the Amazon logo is obvious, but look again and you'll see that it hypes the online store's large selection: everything from A to Z.

NEED A RIDDLE HINT?

This chapter's code uses a keyword cipher with the keyword "sneaky." (Read about it on page 9.)

If you're still at a loss, turn to page 183 for the answer to this encrypted riddle!

HERE'S ANOTHER HINT. ⇧

ANIMAL HOUSE

The logo for the Pittsburgh Zoo is a real jungle. How many creatures do you see hidden in the tree?

MITT WIT

The Milwaukee Brewers' initials are built right into the team's old logo.

DOUBLE DIPPERS

Scrutinize the Tostitos logo to spot two people splitting a chip over a bowl of salsa.

RIDDLE RESULTS

CHAPTER 1

Charging ahead through darkness or light, this creature cannot be stopped. Bullets bounce off its thick skin. Its mission is to protect rather than attack.

THE BEAST, THE PRESIDENT'S INDESTRUCTIBLE CAR

CHAPTER 2

It was once home to the greatest show on Earth. Thousands gathered to watch professional warriors battle to the end for the glory of the empire.

ROME'S COLOSSEUM, SITE OF THE GLADIATOR GAMES

CHAPTER 3

He may have treated Harry like a jerk but this grouchy greasy professor of potions was making sure the Boy Who Lived actually lived.

SEVERUS SNAPE, A DOUBLE AGENT WORKING FOR BOTH DUMBLEDORE AND VOLDEMORT IN THE HARRY POTTER BOOKS

CHAPTER 4

Abandon all hope of escape, ye who enter this fortress in the bay. It is a rock surrounded by shark-infested waters. Nobody gets out alive until the sentence ends.

ALCATRAZ FEDERAL PENITENTIARY, AKA THE ROCK

CHAPTER 5

There is something fishy about this catfish.

CHARLIE, THE CIA'S ROBOT CATFISH

CHAPTER 6

Not all who wander here are lost, and yet sailors and pilots who come in don't always make it out.

THE BERMUDA TRIANGLE, SITE OF MYSTERIOUS SHIP AND PLANE DISAPPEARANCES

CHAPTER 7

In the battle of human versus machine this machine lost and it helped the Allies win a world war.

THE ENIGMA, THE GERMANS' WORLD WAR II CODING MACHINE

CHAPTER 8

This little guy packs a punch. You might not see him coming, but you'll definitely hear him. Some might even call him stunning.

THE PISTOL SHRIMP, WIELDER OF THE MOST FEARSOME CLAW IN THE SEA

PHOTO CREDITS

Cover (goggles), CreativeHQ/Shutterstock; (drone), FLIR Systems, Inc.; (Area 51 sign), Fer Gregory/Adobe Stock; (cipher), Victor Moussa/Shutterstock; (retina scan), Thananit/Moment RF/Getty Images; (four-legged robot), Laura Chiesa/Pacific Press/Alamy Live News; (pyramid symbol), Paulpaladin/Dreamstime; (binary code), Fotomay/Shutterstock; back cover, Vladimir Gjorgiev/Shutterstock; (binary code), Fotomay/Shutterstock;throughout (cork-board background), piotr_pabijan/Shutterstock; throughout (binary code), Fotomay/Shutterstock; 4 (UP), Reklamer/Shutterstock; 4 (LO), Maigi/Dreamstime; 5 (LE), enzozo/Shutterstock; 5 (RT), Bettmann/Getty Images; 7, Vladimir Gjorgiev/Shutterstock; 8, rangizzz/Shutterstock; 9 (plates), SnappixPro/Shutterstock; 9 (paper fastener), Andre Bonn/Shutterstock

CHAPTER 1: 11 (UP), Mikadun/Shutterstock; 11 (CTR LE), Petras Malukas/Getty Images; 11 (CTR RT man), Dean Drobot/Shutterstock; 11 (CTR RT barrel), vchal/Shutterstock; 11 (LO), cubart/Shutterstock; 12 (LE), Chinese School/Getty Images; 12 (RT), Visions of America, LLC/Alamy Stock Photo; 13 (UP LE), Mary Evans Library/Adobe Stock; 13 (UP RT), alesinya7/Adobe Stock; 13 (LO), North Wind Picture Archives/Alamy Stock Photo; 14, skynesher/Getty Images; 15 (UP LE), Mauricio Graiki/Shutterstock; 15 (UP RT), Alivepix/Shutterstock; 15 (CIA logo), cubart/Shutterstock; 15 (Chinese flag), Mikrobiuz/Adobe Stock; 15 (Mossad logo), Al/Adobe Stock; 15 (KGB logo), mishaabesadze/Adobe Stock; 15 (Mexican flag), Mikrobiuz/Adobe Stock; 15 (Kenyan flag), Maksym Kapliuk/Adobe Stock; 15 (MI6 logo), Al/Adobe Stock; 15 (GRU logo), Militarist/Shutterstock; 16 (UP), Creatista/Shutterstock; 16 (LO), Job Garcia/Dreamstime; 17 (UP LE), Jeffrey Markowitz/Getty Images; 17 (UP RT), Mikadun/Shutterstock; 17 (CTR), Andrus Ciprian/Shutterstock; 17 (LO LE), Fresnel/Shutterstock; 17 (LO RT), Chronicle/Alamy Stock Photo; 18, Bernard Hoffman/Getty Images; 19 (UP), Fernando Gregory/Dreamstime; 19 (CTR), Science Photo Library/Getty Images; 19 (LO), Klubovy/Getty Images; 20, Altrendo/Getty Images; 21 (UP LE man), Dean Drobot/Shutterstock; 21 (UP LE barrel), vchal/Shutterstock; 21 (UP RT), Lucian Coman/Shutterstock; 21 (LO RT), CRM/Shutterstock; 21 (LO LE), yousang/Shutterstock; 22 (UP), David Howells/Getty Images; 22 (CTR), David Howells/Getty Images; 22 (LO), Everett Collection, Inc./Alamy Stock Photo; 23, Rawpixel.com/Shutterstock; 24, jiawangkun/Shutterstock; 24-25, Saul Loeb/Getty Images; 25 (UP), Digital Media Pro/Shutterstock; 25 (LO), Pool/Getty Images; 25 (Donald Trump), Library of Congress Prints and Photographs Division; 25 (Barack Obama), Library of Congress Prints and Photographs Division; 25 (George W. Bush), The U.S. National Archives and Records Administration; 25 (Bill Clinton), Everett Collection/Shutterstock; 25 (George H. W. Bush), Bachrach/Getty Images; 25 (Ronald Reagan), Universal History Archive/UIG/Shutterstock; 26, Gerckens-Photo-Hamburg; 26-27, Speculator27/Dreamstime; 28 (UP), John Rogers/Getty Images; 28 (LO), ZUMA Press Inc/Alamy Stock Photo; 29 (UP LE), Catherine Ledner/Getty Images; 29 (UP RT), CreativeHQ/Shutterstock; 29 (CTR RT), Nadezda Murmakova/Dreamstime; 29 (CTR), Greg Mathieson/Mai/Getty Images; 29 (CTR LE), Alexis Rosenfeld/Getty Images; 29 (LO LE), Adam Henderson/U.S. Navy; 29 (LO RT), Petras Malukas/Getty Images; 30 (UP), Vitaly Titov/Shutterstock; 30 (CTR), Pressmaster/Shutterstock; 30 (LO), Speculator27/Dreamstime; 31 (UP LE), mubus7/Shutterstock; 31 (UP RT), bonga1965/Shutterstock; 31 (LO), MultifacetedGirl/Shutterstock

CHAPTER 2: 33 (UP), Swisshippo/Adobe Stock Photo; 33 (LO), Tatiana Popova/Shutterstock; 33 (CTR LE), adike/Shutterstock; 33 (CTR RT), Paul Paladin/Dreamstime; 34 (UP), Sevenkingdom/Dreamstime; 34 (INSET), Brian Bumby; 34 (LO), agsaz/Shutterstock; 35 (UP LE), Visharo/Shutterstock; 35 (UP RT), Attila JANDI/Shutterstock; 35 (CTR LE), Srdjan Pletikapa/Dreamstime; 35 (CTR), Print Collector/Getty Images; 35 (CTR RT), Colbalt88/Dreamstime; 35 (LO), Photo 12/Getty Images; 36 (UP), Morphart Creation/Shutterstock; 36 (LO), Noppasin Wongchum/Dreamstime; 36-37, Wesley Roberts/Alamy Stock Photo; 37 (LE), Lanmas/Alamy Stock Photo; 37 (RT), delcarmat/Shutterstock; 38 (UP), Reklamer/Shutterstock; 38 (LO), Historic Images/Alamy

Stock Photo; 39 (UP), Evgeniy Fesenko/Dreamstime; 39 (CTR), Print Collector/Getty Images; 39 (LO), The Picture Art Collection/Alamy Stock Photo; 40 (LE), David Cole/Alamy Stock Photo; 40 (CTR), Charles Walker Collection/Alamy Stock Photo; 40 (RT), Historia/Shutterstock; 41 (UP LE), ktsdesign/Shutterstock; 41 (UP RT), Chronicle/Alamy Stock Photo; 41 (LO), Johsua Roberts/Getty Images; 42 (UP), fergregory/Adobe Stock; 42 (LO), David Zaitz/Getty Images; 43 (UP), Science History Images/Alamy Stock Photo; 43 (LO), Eden Manus/Dreamstime; 44, Kalifer/Adobe Stock; 45 (UP), Daniel Lolo/Dreamstime; 45 (CTR), mmzgombic/Shutterstock; 45 (LO LE), Elena Schweitzer/Shutterstock; 45 (LO RT), The Advertising Archives/Alamy Stock Photo; 46 (UP), Juliet Butler/Alamy Stock Photo; 46 (LO LE), Konstantin Yolshin/Shutterstock; 46 (LO RT), Harris Brisbane Dick Fund, 1949/Metropolitan Museum of Art; 47 (UP LE), Bible Land Pictures/Alamy Stock Photo; 47 (UP RT), Erik S Lesser/EPA/Shutterstock; 47 (LO LE), Bruce Dale; 47 (LO CTR), Bill Curtsinger; 47 (LO RT), Robert Clark; 48, NASA; 49 (UP), U.S. Army Center of Military History; 49 (LO), U.S. Army Center of Military History; 49 (CTR LE), NASA; 49 (CTR RT), U.S. Army Center of Military History; 50 (UP), Paulpaladin/Dreamstime; 50 (LO), Florence Haywood/Shutterstock; 51 (UP), Dinodia Photos/Alamy Stock Photo; 51 (LO LE), Bridgeman Images; 51 (CTR), Christie's Images/Bridgeman Images; 51 (LO RT), MelissaMN/Adobe Stock; 52 (UP), Francisco Javier Espuny/Dreamstime; 52 (LO), Bildagentur-online/Getty Images

CHAPTER 3: 55 (UP), Zysko Sergii/Shutterstock; 55 (CTR LE), CIA; 55 (CTR RT), FBI; 55 (LO), Lebrecht Music & Arts/Alamy Stock Photo; 56 (UP), Fotokvadrat/Shutterstock; 56 (LO), KPG_Payless/Shutterstock; 57 (UP RT), Ijansempoi/Dreamstime; 57 (UP LE), The Picture Art Collection/Alamy Stock Photo; 57 (LO RT), Zysko Sergii/Shutterstock; 57 (LO LE), Werner Forman/Getty Images; 58-59, Bridgeman Images; 58, Oleg Voronische/Shutterstock; 59 (UP), Album/Alamy Stock Photo; 59 (CTR), Peter Newark American Pictures/Bridgeman Images; 59 (LO), North News and Pictures; 60, Moviestore Collection/Shutterstock; 60 (INSET), Keystone/Stringer/Getty Images; 61 (UP), Everett Historical/Shutterstock; 61 (CTR), Sunset Boulevard/Getty Images; 61 (LO LE), PictureLux/The Hollywood Archive/Alamy Stock Photo; 61 (LO RT), The Stanley Weston Archive/Getty Images; 62, CIA; 63 (UP), Michael Bradley/AFP/Getty Images63 (LE), CIA; 63 (CTR), CD1/Carrie Devorah/WENN/Newscom; 63 (RT), Archive PL/Alamy Stock Photo; 64, Bernard Radvaner/Getty Images; 65 (mimic octopus UP), Borut Furlan/Getty Images; 65 (feather star), etfoto/Adobe Stock; 65 (mimic octopus CTR), Jurgen Freund/Minden Pictures; 65 (sole fish), anemone/Adobe Stock; 65 (mimic octopus LO), imageBROKER/Alamy Stock Photo; 65 (lionfish), Cigdem Sean Coope/Shutterstock; 65 (fox), Erni/Shutterstock; 65 (walking leaf), Marianne Brouwer/NiS/Minden Pictures; 66 (UP), UtCon Collection/Alamy Stock Photo; 66 (LO), UtCon Collection/Alamy Stock Photo; 67 (UP), Schomburg Center for Research in Black Culture, Manuscripts, Archives and Rare Books Division/The New York Public Library; 67 (CTR), Sputnik/Alamy Stock Photo; 67 (LO LE), Associated Newspapers/Shutterstock; 67 (LO RT), FBI; 68, TCD/Prod.DB/Alamy Stock Photo; 69 (UP LE), Abagnale and Associates; 69 (UP RT), Civic painting, transferred 1972/Bridgeman Images; 69 (CTR), Chronicle/Alamy Stock Photo; 69 (LO), Zhukovsky/Dreamstime; 70, Lebrecht Music & Arts/Alamy Stock Photo; 71 (UP), Jim Altgens/AP Photo; 71 (CTR LE), Aleksandr Ivakin/Dreamstime; 71 (CTR RT), Notto Yeez/Shutterstock; 71 (LO), FBI; 72 (LE), Peter Etchells/Dreamstime; 72 (RT), Peter Tangen; 73 (Nyx), Peter Tangen; 73 (Superbarrio), Sergio Dorantes/Getty Images; 73 (Life), Peter Tangen; 73 (Civitron), Peter Tangen; 73 (DC Guardian), Peter Tangen; 73 (Thanatos), Peter Tangen; 74 (UP), metamorworks/Shutterstock; 74 (CTR), Pavel L Photo and Video/Shutterstock; 74 (LO), Hayk_Shalunts/Shutterstock; 75 (LE), Rawpixel.com/Shutterstock; 75 (RT), ESB Professional/Shutterstock

CHAPTER 4: 77 (UP), Lukas Hlavac/Shutterstock; 77 (CTR LE), Dorling Kindersley ltd/Alamy Stock Photo; 77 (CTR RT), Look and Learn/Bridgeman Images; 77 (LO), happiness time/Shutterstock; 78, Look and Learn/Bridgeman Images; 79 (UP), Uncredited/AP/Shutterstock; 79 (CTR LE), Joe Sohm/Dreamstime; 79 (CTR RT), Ghost Army Legacy Project; 79 (LO), Ghost Army Legacy Project; 80 (UP), Mary Evans/The National Archives, London/The Image Works; 80 (LO), Mary Evans/The National Archives, London/The Image Works; 81 (UP), National Archives; 81 (CTR LE & CTR RT), Mary Evans/The National Archives, London. England/The Image Works; 81 (LO), Bettmann/Getty Images; 82, Ilkin Guliyev/Dreamstime; 82 (INSET), Sovfoto/Universal Images Group/Shutterstock; 83 (UP), Phil Wills/Alamy Stock Photo; 83 (LO LE), Alexey Broslavets/Shutterstock; 83 (LO CTR), ZUMA Press, Inc./Alamy Stock Photo; 83 (LO RT), Sputnik/Alamy Stock Photo; 84 (LE), happiness time/Shutterstock; 84 (RT), Northcliffe Collection/ANL/Shutterstock; 84-85, ullstein bild/Getty Images; 85 (UP), David Cooper/Alamy Stock Photo; 85 (LO), PA Images/Alamy Stock Photo; 86 (UP), Str/EPA/Shutterstock/Shutterstock; 86 (LO), M. Unal Ozmen/Shutterstock; 87 (UP), Alisha Arif/Alamy Stock Photo; 87 (LO), Bennian/Shutterstock; 88, FBI; 88-89, kropic1/Shutterstock; 89 (UP), Dorling Kindersley ltd/Alamy Stock Photo; 89 (CTR), Llewellyn/Alamy Stock Photo; 89 (shark), Sergey Uryadnikov/Dreamstime; 89 (LO), Science History Images/Alamy Stock Photo; 90, Hung Chung Chih/Shutterstock; 90-91, Bule Sky Studio/Shutterstock; 91 (UP), Sarin Images/Granger; 91 (CTR), myLAM/Alamy Stock Photo; 91 (LO LE), Gaby

Fassbender/Alamy Stock Photo; 91 (LO RT), Marcel Clemens/Shutterstock; 92 (UP), Khadi Ganiev/Shutterstock; 92 (LO), twilightproductions/Getty Images; 92 (UP INSET), Chronicle/Alamy Stock Photo; 92 (LO INSET), Bridgeman Images; 93 (UP), Pictorial Parade/Archive Photos/Getty Images; 93 (CTR LE), The Picture Art Collection/Alamy Stock Photo; 93 (CTR), SSPL/NMeM/Glenn Hill/Getty Images; 93 (CTR RT), Hotshotsworld-wide/Dreamstime; 93 (LO), Dale O'Dell/Alamy Stock Photo; 94 (UP), Jason Stitt/Shutterstock; 94 (LO), Photoquest/Dreamstime; 95, Charles Walker Collection/Alamy Stock Photo

CHAPTER 5: 97 (UP), NASA; 97 (CTR LE), Yoshikazu Tsuno/Getty Images; 97 (CTR RT), Boyer/Roger-Viollet/The Image Works; 97 (LO), HANDOUT/KRT/Newscom; 98 (LE), CIA; 98 (RT), urbans/Shutterstock; 99 (UP), Boyer/Roger-Viollet/The Image Works; 99 (CTR LE), CIA; 99 (CTR RT), HANDOUT/KRT/Newscom; 99 (CTR), Courtesy FBI; 99 (LO), Central Intelligence Agency; 100, Sergey Nivens/Shutterstock; 101 (UP LE), imageBROKER/Shutterstock; 101 (UP RT), Bloomberg/Getty Images; 101 (CTR LE), Victor Habbick Visions/Science Source; 101 (CTR RT), Aflo Co. Ltd./Alamy Stock Photo; 101 (LO LE), Caliburger Restaurant; 101 (LO RT), Oleksiy Maksymenko/age fotostock; 102 (UP LE), NRO; 102 (UP RT), NRO; 102 (LO), NRO; 103 (UP LE), Joseph Sohm/Shutterstock; 103 (UP RT), Olga Danylenko/Shutterstock; 103 (LO LE), F.Schmidt/Shutterstock; 103 (LO RT), Central Intelligence Agency; 104, Yoshikazu Tsuno/Getty Images; 105 (UP LE), David A. Litman/Shutterstock; 105 (UP RT), alesinya7/Adobe Stock; 105 (CTR), nimon/Shutterstock; 105 (LO LE), Wladimir Bulgar/Science Photo Library/Getty Images; 105 (LO RT), W. Scott McGill/Shutterstock; 106 (UP), US Air Force; 106 (LO), NASA; 107 (UP LE), US Air Force; 107 (UP RT), Ibl/Shutter-stock; 107 (LO), Phil Sandlin/AP/Shutterstock; 108, Toni L. Sandys/The Washington Post/Getty Images; 109 (UP LE), HANDOUT/KRT/Newscom; 109 (UP RT), Central Intelligence Agency; 109 (CTR), Central Intelligence Agency; 109 (LO LE), John Rooney/AP/Shutterstock; 109 (LO RT), Bill Kotsatos/Polaris/Newscom; 110, Cary Wolinsky; 110 (UP INSET), Cary Wolinsky; 110 (LO INSET), Mark Wilson/Getty Images; 111 (UP), Olivier Douliery/ABACAUSA.COM/Newscom; 111 (CTR), Hyungwon Kang/Reuters; 111 (LO LE), Mike Goldwater/Alamy Stock Photo; 111 (LO CTR), jakkapan/Adobe Stock; 111 (LO RT), Thomas M Perkins/Shutterstock; 112-113, Central Intelligence Agency; 113 (UP RT), Bloomberg/Getty Images; 113 (UP LE), Central Intelligence Agency; 113 (LO RT), Central Intelligence Agency; 113 (LO LE), by wildestanimal/Getty Images; 114, PJF Military Collection/Alamy Stock Photo; 114-115, Fortean/Top-Foto/The Image Works; 116, Pacific Press Agency/Alamy Stock Photo; 117 (UP LE), Kelvin Chng/Newscom; 117 (UP RT), DARPA; 117 (LO LE), DARPA; 117 (LO CTR), Rob Carty/U.S. Army; 117 (LO RT), David McNally/U.S. Army; 118 (UP), Mark Thiessen/NGP Staff; 118 (CTR), Mark Thiessen/NGP Staff; 118 (LO), Central Intelligence Agency; 119 (LE), Bjorn Hovdal/Dreamstime; 119 (RT), Melissa/Adobe Stock

CHAPTER 6: 121 (UP), Urs Zihlmann/Caters News Agency; 121 (CTR LE), Sandra Foyt/Dreamstime; 121 (CTR RT), Christopher Partridge/Alamy Stock Photo; 121 (LO), Chirawan/Adobe Stock; 122 (UP LE), Creative Home Engineering; 122 (UP RT), Creative Home Engineering; 122 (LO LE), Dreamer4787/Dreamstime; 122 (LO RT), Christopher Partridge/Alamy Stock Photo; 123 (UP LE), bpk Bildagentur/Kunstgewerbemuseum/Staatliche Museen/Art Resource, NY; 123 (UP RT), Library of Congress Prints and Photographs Division; 123 (LO LE), StockPhotosArt/Shutter-stock; 123 (LO RT), Cindy Hopkins/Alamy Stock Photo; 124, Fortean/TopFoto/The Image Works; 124-125, DigitalGlobe/ScapeWare3d/Getty Images; 125 (UP LE), Sandra Foyt/Dreams-time; 125 (UP RT), National Security Archive; 125 (LO), Dan Callister/Getty Images; 126, JJM Photography/Shutterstock; 126 (INSET), National Park Service; 127 (UP), Sueddeutsche Zeitung Photo/Alamy Stock Photo; 127 (CTR LE), The U.S. National Archives and Records Administration; 127 (CTR), Andreykr/Dreamstime; 127 (CTR RT), Library of Congress Prints and Photographs Division; 127 (LO), Nestor Noci/Shutterstock; 128, Willyam Bradberry/Shutterstock; 129 (UP LE), Jody Watt/Getty Images; 129 (UP RT), Jkht/Dreamstime; 129 (LO LE), Ribe/Dreamstime; 129 (LO RT), Jeffrey Schwilk/Alamy Stock Photo; 130 (map), WindVector/Shutterstock; 130, Victor Habbick Visions/Getty Images; 130 (INSET), Carlos Villoch/Alamy Stock Photo; 131 (UP), Richair/Dreamstime; 131 (CTR), Hauke Vagt; 131 (LO RT), gameover2012/Getty Images; 131 (LO LE), Konrad Wothe/imageBROKER/Shutterstock; 132 (UP), North American Aerospace Defense Command; 132 (LO), 001 Images/Alamy Stock Photo; 133 (UP), 001 Images/Alamy Stock Photo; 133 (LO), Suse Schulz/Dreamstime; 134, Carsten Peter; 134-135, Bryan Christie/National Geographic Image Collection; 135 (UP LE), Vietnam Stock Images/Shutterstock; 135 (UP RT), Urs Zihlmann/Caters News Agency; 135 (LO LE), Martin Edstrom; 135 (LO RT), Carsten Peter; 136 (UP), Demerzel21/Dreamstime; 136 (LO), RealyEasyStar/Daniele Bellucci/Alamy Stock Photo; 137 (UP LE), Dynamic Photography/Shutterstock; 137 (UP RT), Jim Lo Scalzo/Shutterstock; 137 (CTR LE), Jacquelyn Martin/AP Photo; 137 (CTR), Luc Novovitch/Alamy; 137 (CTR RT), Rudra Narayan Mitra/Dreamstime; 137 (LO), Toshifumi Kitamura/Getty Images; 138 (LE), Chirawan/Adobe Stock; 138 (RT), Graham Wood/ANL/Shutterstock; 138-139, AP/Shutterstock; 139 (UP LE), Shutter-stock; 139 (UP RT), Oleksandr_Delyk/Shutterstock; 139 (LO), Barry Thumma/AP/Shutterstock; 140 (UP), Shnarf/Shutterstock; 140 (LO), Grodfoto/Shutterstock; 141 (UP), kali9/Getty Images;

(CTR LE), Artem Varnitsin/Adobe Stock; 141 (CTR RT), Adwo/
obe Stock; 141 (LO), Rubens Alarcon/Alamy Stock Photo

APTER 7: 143 (UP), Giorgio Rossi/Shutterstock; 143
R LE), Prismatic Pictures/Bridgeman Images; 143 (CTR RT),
ishiapply/Shutterstock; 143 (LO), Gianni Dagli Orti/Shutter-
ck; 144 (UP), The Cloisters Collection, 2018/Metropolitan
seum of Art; 144 (CTR), Fedor Selivanov/Shutterstock; 144
), Fletcher Fund, 1927/Metropolitan Museum of Art; 145
), Burstein Collection/Getty Images; 145 (LO LE), Everett
torical/Shutterstock; 145 (LO RT), Bill Roche/U.S. Army; 146
), Giorgio Rossi/Shutterstock; 146 (LO), cmannphoto/Getty
ages; 147 (UP LE), PJF Military Collection/Alamy Stock Photo;
(UP RT), Central Intelligence Agency; 147 (CTR LE), Pictorial
ss Ltd/Alamy Stock Photo; 147 (CTR RT), Central Intelligence
ency; 147 (LO), Central Intelligence Agency; 148 (UP),
smatic Pictures/Bridgeman Images; 148 (LO), Shutterstock;
(UP), Geoff Robinson Photography/Shutterstock; 149 (LO
Gordon Bell/Shutterstock; 149 (LO RT), Everett Collection
/Alamy Stock Photo; 150, OHishiapply/Shutterstock; 151 (UP
Josh Edelson; 151 (UP RT), British Library; 151 (CTR), Xinhua/
my Stock Photo; 151 (LO), David Wei/Alamy Stock Photo;
-153, MAI Photo News Agency, Inc.; 154, Cesar Manso/Getty
ges; 155 (UP), IanDagnall Computing/Alamy Stock Photo;
(CTR LE), Universal History Archive/UIG/Shutterstock; 155
R RT), Manuel Litran/Getty Images; 155 (LO), Gianni Dagli
i/Shutterstock; 156, Maksim meljov/Adobe Stock; 157 (UP
Morphart Creation/Shutterstock; 157 (UP RT), Central
elligence Agency; 157 (LO LE), cubart/Shutterstock; 157 (LO
, pixarno/Adobe Stock Photo; 158 (UP), New Africa/Shutter-
ck; 158 (CTR), Dorling Kindersley ltd/Alamy; 158 (LO LE),
smatic Pictures/Bridgeman Images; 158 (LO RT), Dave Pixel/
utterstock; 159 (UP LE), Bunphot Phairoh/Shutterstock; 159
RT), Ratt_Anarach/Shutterstock; 159 (LO), Hilary Andrews/
P Staff

APTER 8: 161 (UP), Sebastian Kaulitzki/Shutterstock; 161 CTR
, Leonard Zhukovsky/Shutterstock; 161 (CTR RT), The Print
lector/Alamy Stock Photo; 161 (LO), Dmytro Vietrov/Shutter-
ck; 162 (LE), Svitlana-ua/Shutterstock; 162 (RT), Interfoto/
my; 163 (UP), ArcadeImages/Alamy Stock Photo; 163 (CTR
Pit Stock/Shutterstock; 163 (CTR RT), Universal/courtesy
rett Collection; 163 (LO), The Print Collector/Alamy Stock
oto; 164, Album/Alamy Stock Photo; 165 (UP), Lionsgate/
bal/Shutterstock; 165 (CTR LE), Jon Paul Dominic

Everett Collection; 166, Sebastian Kaulitzki/Shutterstock; 167
(jellyfish), Yiming Chen/Getty Images; 167 (shark), by wildest-
animal/Getty Images; 167 (axolotl), Has Asatryan/Shutterstock;
167 (platypus), Hotshotsworldwide/Dreamstime; 167 (shrimp),
Subphoto/Shutterstock; 167 (snake), Matthijs Kuijpers/Dreams-
time; 168, Chudovska/Shutterstock; 168-169, Renée Comet;
169 (BOTH), Renée Comet; 170 (UP), David Goldman/AP/
Shutterstock; 170 (CTR), Saikorn/Shutterstock; 170 (LO),
Library of Congress Prints and Photographs Division; 171
(UP), AP/Shutterstock; 171 (LO), Library of Congress Prints and
Photographs Division; 172 (LE), Anton Starikov/Dreamstime; 172
(RT), Leonard Zhukovsky/Shutterstock; 173 (UP LE), Reed Saxon/
AP/Shutterstock; 173 (CTR), hlphoto/Shutterstock; 173 (UP RT),
Photosport/Shutterstock; 173 (LO LE), Maxisport/Shutterstock;
173 (LO RT), Pat Sullivan/AP/Shutterstock; 174, Astrid Gast/
Shutterstock; 175 (UP LE), National Geographic Society; 175 (UP
RT), Enya/Shutterstock; 175 (CTR), Martincp/Dreamstime; 175
(LO LE), National Geographic Society; 175 (LO RT), schulzie/
Getty Images; 176 (UP), goffkein.pro/Shutterstock; 176 (LO),
Ekaterina_Minaeva/Shutterstock; 177 (UP LE), maodoltee/
Shutterstock; 177 (UP CTR), Dimarik16/Dreamstime; 177 (UP RT),
Noppadol_l/Shutterstock; 177 (LO LE), J.K2507/Shutterstock;
177 (LO CTR), Mark Thiessen/NGP Staff; 177 (LO RT), rakimm/
Shutterstock; 178-179, Dmytro Vietrov/Shutterstock; 178-179
(ALL INSETS), Lori Epstein/NGP Staff; 180 (UP), Jatuporn
Chainiramitkul/Shutterstock; 180 (CTR), Andrei Gabriel
Stanescu/Dreamstime; 180 (LO), Fotokostic/Shutterstock; 181
(UP LE), Dylan Buell/Stringer/Getty Images; 181 (UP RT), Keith
Srakocic/AP/Shutterstock; 181 (LO), SV_Digital_Press/Shutter-
stock; 182 (UP LE), Speculator27/Dreamstime; 182 (UP RT), ESB
Professional/Shutterstock; 182 (LO LE), RGR Collection/Alamy
Stock Photo; 182 (LO RT), f11photo/Shutterstock; 183 (UP LE),
Central Intelligence Agency; 183 (UP RT), Photo Junction/
Shutterstock; 183 (LO LE), Giorgio Rossi/Shutterstock; 183 (LO
RT), Fred Bavendam/Minden Pictures

Flip to the dedication at the end of this book for one final code to crack!

Boldface indicates illustrations.

A

B

C

DEDICATED TO ALL **NZHGVI HKRVH DSL XIZXP GSRH XLWV**

Since 1888, the National Geographic Society has funded more than 12,000 research, exploration, and preservation projects around the world. The Society receives funds from National Geographic Partners, LLC, funded in part by your purchase. A portion of the proceeds from this book supports this vital work. To learn more, visit natgeo.com/info.

For more information, visit nationalgeographic .com, call 1-877-873-6846, or write to the following address:

National Geographic Partners
1145 17th Street N.W.
Washington, D.C. 20036-4688 U.S.A.

Visit us online at nationalgeographic.com /books

For librarians and teachers: nationalgeographic.com/books/librarians-and -educators

More for kids from National Geographic: natgeokids.com

For rights or permissions inquiries, please contact National Geographic Books Subsidiary Rights: bookrights@natgeo.com

Designed by Sanjida Rashid

Names: Boyer, Crispin, author.
Title: Top secret / Crispin Boyer.
Description: Washington : National Geographic Kids, 2020. | Includes index. | Audience: Ages 8-12 | Audience: Grades 4-6 | Summary: “Information about intelligence gathering and spy agencies for children”-- Provided by publisher.
Identifiers: LCCN 2019034687 | ISBN 9781426339127 (hardcover) | ISBN 9781426339134 (library binding)
Subjects: LCSH: Intelligence service--Juvenile literature. | Espionage--Juvenile literature. | Spies--Juvenile literature.
Classification: LCC JF1525.I6 B68 2020 | DDC 327.12--dc23
LC record available at https://lccn.loc.gov/2019034687

The publisher would like to thank the team that made this book possible: Crispin Boyer and Suzanne Zimbler, writers; Ariane Szu-Tu, editor; Grace Hill Smith, project editor; Lori Epstein, photo director; Danny Meldung, photo editor; Molly Reid, production editor; and Anne LeongSon and Gus Tello, design production assistants.

Printed in Malaysia
20/QRM/1